# LUDENDORFF'S OWN STORY

FIELD-MARSHAL VON HINDENBURG

# LUDENDORFF'S OWN STORY

## August 1914 - November 1918

*The Great War from the Siege of Liege to the Signing of the Armistice as viewed from the Grand Headquarters of the German Army*

By

### ERICH VON LUDENDORFF

Quartermaster-General of the German Army

With Frontispiece
and Many Maps

VOL. II

Harper & Brothers Publishers
New York and London

# CONTENTS

# CONTENTS

## MAPS

# LUDENDORFF'S
# OWN STORY

## THE ENTENTE OFFENSIVE IN THE FIRST HALF OF 1917

The Withdrawal to the Siegfried Line—The Reasons for Defensive Tactics in the West—The Russian Revolution—America's Declaration of War—The Battle of Arras, and the Twin Battles of the Aisne and Champagne—Battles of the Wytschaete Salient and Local German Attacks—Battles in the East—Chancellor von Bethmann and Count Czernin—A Change of Chancellors and the Peace Resolution—Patriotic Instruction and Propaganda—The Questions of Lithuania, Greater Poland, and Alsace-Lorraine.

I

AS far as human judgment could foresee, everything pointed to the Western front as the scene of our chief defensive fighting in 1917, although a severe struggle was also going on in the East. Direct co-operation with the Austro-Hungarian High Command was not so necessary as it had been during the campaign against Rumania, after the command on the Eastern front had been reorganized in a less complicated form. The supreme importance of the Western theater of war now demanded the presence there of the Commander-in-chief. I suggested Spa or Kreuznach as the new headquarters. Spa was rejected; Kreuznach was particularly suitable, as many of the cables to the front passed near the town, and it had suitable hotel and other accommodation. Orders were accordingly given for General Headquarters to be established at Kreuznach, Münster am Stein, and Bingen, and the second fortnight of February was contemplated as the time when the transfer should take place. Meanwhile, the possibility of having to return to Pless had to be kept in view.

The Austro-Hungarian High Command was transferred to Baden, near Vienna.

The submarine-cruiser campaign opened on February 1, 1917, and as soon as it became evident that the troops that had been concentrated on the frontiers of Holland and Denmark to meet a possible attack from these quarters would not be required, these forces and their staffs, which had been held in reserve for this purpose, were liberated for use on the Western front.

In the West a continuation of the British attack on the Somme, perhaps extending to the north, had to be reckoned with. It was possible that this would be accompanied by a French offensive between Roye and Noyon, but the probabilities were that France would choose our Soissons-Rheims-Argonne front for attack, as she had done in the autumn of 1915. The Entente would thus have gained a strategic advantage by pressing on both flanks of the salient we had pushed into French territory. It was impossible to foresee which part of the front the French would select. They might cause a diversion at Roye, and reports also pointed to the possibility of an offensive on the Lorraine front and Sundgau, where we had made very little progress toward the consolidation of our lines. We had always been conscious of a certain weakness in this sector, as local engagements were to be expected here, and it was only with difficulty that we could bring up reinforcements. Verdun was also occasionally mentioned, as the French were always in a position to open an attack at this point. Lastly, an extension of the British offensive toward the north was indicated. Consequently we had to be prepared to offer a stubborn resistance at any point along our whole front. It was impossible to tell what was going to happen.

There was no doubt about the continuation of the struggle on the Isonzo front. Trieste was Italy's goal. Attacks were more than likely in Macedonia and on the Vardar, and certain in Turkey, Palestine, and Bagdad.

In the East I anticipated an attack upon the Austro-Hungarian troops in the southern section of the front. A sudden Russian advance in the direction of Mitau at the end of January alarmed both ourselves and the Commander-in-chief on the Eastern front. It was, however, stemmed by reserves which were rapidly brought up.

It was not yet possible to foresee when the great offensive would take place. On the Eastern front it was scarcely to be expected before April. The big Russian advance in the spring of 1916 began in March and was considerably hampered by the bad weather and the condition of the ground. It was unlikely that the Russians would repeat this attempt so early in the year. It was also possible that the Entente would accordingly postpone its offensive in the West. The situation on the Somme, however, was so tense that we had to be prepared for an earlier attack.

The general situation made it necessary for us to postpone the struggle in the West as long as possible in order to allow the submarine campaign time to produce decisive results. Tactical reasons and a shortage of ammunition provided additional reasons for delay. At the same time it was necessary to shorten our front in order to secure a more favorable grouping of our forces and create larger reserves. In France and Belgium we had 154 divisions facing 190 divisions, some of which were considerably stronger than ours. In view of our extensive front, this was an exceedingly unfavorable balance of forces. Moreover, we had on certain sectors of our line to endeavor to avoid strong enemy attacks as long as possible by preventing our adversaries from concentrating strong forces in front of them. At the same time we secured positions in which weaker divisions, wearied by fighting, could be employed.

These considerations, taken in close connection with the opening of the submarine campaign, led to the decision to straighten our front by withdrawing to the Siegfried line, which was to be in a condition of defense by the beginning of March, and methodically to carry out the work of demolition over an area of fifteen kilometers in breadth in front of our new position.

Under the rubric "Alberich" the group of armies under the Crown Prince Rupprecht had worked out a program for the work of clearance and demolition which was to be spread over five weeks. If an attack on the part of the enemy made it necessary, we could at any moment interrupt this program and begin our retreat. Our first object was to avoid a battle, our second to effect the salvage of all our raw material of war and technical and other equipment that was not actually built into the position, and finally the destruction of all highroads, villages, towns, and wells, so as to prevent the enemy establishing himself in force in the near future in front of our new position. Poisoning of the wells was forbidden.

The decision to retreat was not reached without a painful struggle. It implied a confession of weakness bound to raise the morale of the enemy and lower our own. But as it was necessary for military reasons, we had no choice; it had to be carried out. General von Kuhl and I were in constant communication on the subject. The Field-Marshal and the Kaiser gave their

FIG. 15. "ALBERICH RETREAT," BETWEEN ARRAS AND SOISSONS,
MARCH 1917

consent. On February 4 the order was given to carry
out "Alberich" according to plan. The first Alberich
day was February 9. The retreat was to begin on

March 16, but under enemy pressure might start at any earlier date. This would, however, have involved great loss of material, not to mention the partial abandonment of the work of demolition. At the same time Lieutenant-Colonel Nicolai received instructions to mislead the enemy by furnishing them with special news. He and Colonel von Haeften had so to influence the home and neutral press that no inkling of the intentions above described should be given. I myself personally informed the Chancellor of our scheme.

The Alberich program was carried out according to plan. It was successful in every detail. Many treasures of art were removed from the zone we were evacuating, and in accordance with the terms of the Hague Convention stored in places of safety in the occupied territory. The fact that much property belonging to the inhabitants was destroyed was to be deplored, but it could not be helped. The bulk of the population was driven eastward, only a small proportion being collected in certain places, such as Noyon, Ham, and Nesle, and provided with rations for several days and left behind. On the one hand it was desirable not to make a present to the enemy of too much fresh strength in the form of recruits and laborers, and on the other we wanted to foist upon him as many mouths to feed as possible.

On the Somme front, fighting with the British had never quite come to a standstill. At the beginning of March, signs were not wanting that the battle north of the Somme might break out afresh. South of Roye, too, French preparations for attack became ever more conspicuous. Whether the attitude of both armies was the outcome of the measures we had taken, it is impossible to say. It was a severe strain on the nerves of the local commanders to keep, in spite of everything, to the date originally fixed upon for the retreat to begin. In the event this did not prove entirely practicable, as in the north from about the 11th, and in the south from about the 13th, minor modifications of the line were effected in order to evade the attack which seemed every day more and more imminent.

The great retreat began on March 16, according to plan, and was carried through without a break in a few stages of moderate length. The object of General Headquarters was in general to avoid battle and to allow the troops time to prepare the Siegfried line before the enemy reached it in superior force. Some of the divisions in reserve at the time were ordered to the new position. In other places divisions had to remain at their places in the front line.

Only south of St.-Quentin was the enemy to be attacked after crossing the Somme and the Crozat Canal; this was done, but the attack was not carried out with sufficient energy. Its success was not conspicuous. The group of armies under the Crown Prince Rupprecht and we at General Headquarters had weighed the possibility of a general counter-attack along the whole of the Siegfried line, for we should have liked to wipe out our confession of weakness by a great tactical success. The condition and numbers of our troops, however, were such that it was impossible for us to throw in sufficient forces to guarantee a real victory on a battle-field rendered impassable, and General Headquarters had, therefore, for better or worse, to give up the idea of a great counter-attack.

The Entente armies followed closely on the heels of our retiring forces and tried to make out that our retreat was a great success for themselves. But the press had been so cleverly and effectively manipulated that they did not succeed. As a matter of fact, they had not gained any military triumph. Thanks also to the false intelligence we had circulated, they had not even interfered with our work of demolition and clearance. The whole movement was a brilliant achievement on the part of both commanders and troops, and is evidence of the careful foresight and work of the German General Staff.

We were now more compactly and firmly established than we had been along our previous extended line. The tactical measures of the enemy had been frustrated. He was no longer able to attack in the same directions as before. The country we had traversed was devastated, and in order to carry on war there a certain amount of restoration was essential. Before an attack could be launched over it an infinite amount of road and bridge building would have to be done. The enemy, therefore, established himself in relatively slight strength in front of our new line. We, for our part, could now thin out our forces by taking away whole divisions.

We had completely achieved the object of the Alberich program, which was to reach and occupy the Siegfried line. It stood us in good stead for some considerable time. The retreat had been well worth while. Indeed, all our commanders wished that the German Army had possessed many another Siegfried line, with its concrete dugouts, for the conduct of the war during 1918 would then have been easier. The labor required for their construction, however, was not available. Moreover, the best lines ultimately gave way before the tanks, which were able to overcome the greatest obstacles.

We had to put up with the fact that the Entente nations turned our exceedingly thorough demolition of the territory and dispersal of the population to account, in order once more to call us Huns and to play the organ of their propaganda with all the stops pulled out. One cannot blame them. Nevertheless, we had acted in accordance with the laws of warfare and had not

even gone so far as the belligerents in the American
Civil War.

During our retreat in Poland in 1914 we had spared
the country as far as possible, for there, on account of
the vast distances, I had set all my hopes on the
destruction of the railways.  But in the present case
the area evacuated was so small that the country
had to be more severely handled.  In Poland we were
able to leave the inhabitants of enemy territory alone;
here both humanity and prudence demanded that we
should drive them out.  Ought we to have left them
to perish in the devastated districts?  In all the
measures we took, the exigencies of war alone proved
the decisive factor.  Otherwise the dictates of humanity
were obeyed as far as possible.  We were too powerful
to wish to increase the suffering of others by unjustifiable harshness and spite.  This was the case not only
here, but everywhere.  We acted with severity only
where military security demanded it—in the matters
of contre-espionnage.

II

In summing up the strategic value of our retreat I
counted on the British offensive developing to the north
at the end of March.  It was impossible to foretell
with certainty where it would take place.  An attack
near Arras seemed likely.

In the middle of February 1917, in order to improve
its position, the Third Army had undertaken a local
operation on the Champagne battle-fields of September
1915.  This operation was successful.  Among the captured material there was found an order of the 2d French
Infantry Division, dated January 29, clearly pointing
to a great French offensive on the Aisne for April.
This gave us an extremely important clue.  Little

attention was now paid to news of attacks in Lorraine and Sundgau.

Thanks to their ample labor-supply, the Entente armies had been in a position to furnish, not only the Verdun sector, but also a large portion of their front, with all the means of communication and munitions necessary for an attack. It was, therefore, possible for them in the shortest space of time and at various parts of the front to develop an offensive without betraying their plans by their preparations. The photographs of the enemy's field defenses and works, and the continual checking and verification by new photographs secured by our aviators, could give only general indications of his intended movements.

The French front between Vailly on the Aisne and the Argonne was particularly well constructed, so that special preparations for attack were not necessary. The works that were actually built south of the Chemin des Dames we saw when we advanced in 1918. Their construction seems to have dated from 1915–16. It is possible that the French had intended to make an offensive here in 1916, but were prevented by the German onslaught on Verdun.

Conditions on the Western front had become more secure, but the depression due to the battles on the Somme and at Verdun still weighed down the minds of our people and increased the nerve-racking tension inseparable from being on the defensive. The distribution of the Higher Command had been improved. Crown Prince Rupprecht's command included the Fourth, Sixth, First, and Second Armies, between the canal and La Fère. Next to this was the German Crown Prince's command, with the Seventh, Third, and Fifth Armies, which extended almost as far as the Orne, east of Verdun. Then came the command of Field-Marshal Duke Albrecht of Württemberg, who had

handed over the Fourth Army to Gen. Sixt von Arnim
(army groups C, A, B), whose Chief of Staff was Gen.
Kraft von Dellmensingen.   Owing to the formation
of this group of armies, conditions on the Alsace-
Lorraine front were very considerably improved.

The shortening of the line between Arras and Laon
made it possible to remove the command of the First
Army from this district.   It was transferred to the
group of armies under the German Crown Prince, on
either side of Rheims, between the Seventh and Third
Armies.   Such a transfer and readjustment of an army
command is a troublesome undertaking, on account of
the changes it entails in the lines of communication.
It cannot be done in a day if serious friction is to be
avoided.

I hoped that the army command would be settled,
with headquarters in Rethel, before the French attack
upon the group of armies under the German Crown
Prince was opened.   The troops had had two extra
months for rest and training, as a result of the successful carrying out of the Alberich program.   They
had certainly gained considerably in strength, but in
the group of armies under the Crown Prince Rupprecht
there were still some divisions that required rest.

Training was suspended.   Some of the new formations were already being employed in quiet sectors of
the line; others had only just come into use as reinforcements.   Divisions from Rumania had arrived in Belgium.   General Headquarters had also exchanged divisions unfit for the Western front for good fighting forces
from the East, although this necessarily involved a
weakening of our defenses there.   The consolidation of
the front was pushed on.   The labor which had been
liberated by the occupation of the Siegfried line was
employed behind those sectors where attack was anticipated, and the completion of the support and rear-

ward trenches had to be accelerated. The supply of munitions had improved, the increase being due to the diminished consumption during several months. A reserve had been created which gave a certain security as long as the battles east and west did not last too long. The Hindenburg program gradually became practicable, and the further supply of munitions was insured.

On the Italian front all was quiet. In Macedonia local attacks by the Entente in February and March at Monastir and Cernabogen were repulsed with heavy loss. In the war zone in Asiatic Turkey fighting had begun again with the fine weather. The British had finished their preparations and opened an offensive. In Palestine the British attacks on Gaza failed, thanks to the efforts of Colonel von Kreuz. In Mesopotamia it soon became evident that the Turkish Army in the Irak area had lost all power of resistance. Kut-el-Amara fell on February 25, and by March 11 Bagdad was occupied by the British—a severe blow for Turkey, who was thereby forced to evacuate the Persian borderland. In consequence of these events Enver approached General Headquarters with the request that the command of a German group of armies with an auxiliary corps might be put at his disposal for the recapture of Bagdad. This undertaking involved months of preparation. The organization of the lines of communication had to be complete before the troops arrived. The completion of the Amanus tunnel for standard-gage traffic in January 1917, and that of the narrow-gage way through the Taurus tunnel, to be opened in the autumn, improved communications in Asia Minor. Enver's projected enterprise seemed practicable. There was a likelihood of bringing strong Turkish forces into action again, supported by a few German battalions, which would compel the British to increase their effectives in Irak.

General Headquarters agreed to Enver's request, though not exactly with enthusiasm, and at his desire General von Falkenhayn was given command of the group of armies. The Ministry of War began the equipment of the weak corps in Asia. In the East vast changes had taken place. In March the Tsar was overthrown by the Revolution, which was favored by the Entente. A Government of pronounced Socialist leanings came into power. The Entente nations' reasons for backing the Revolution are not clear. They may have imagined they were confronted by a national movement which they could not ignore, and with which they consequently threw in their lot, or they may have thought that the Tsar had become inclined for peace, owing to fear of an internal collapse, and were therefore in favor of getting rid of him. Possibly there were other reasons. At all events, it is certain that the Entente countries expected the Revolution to bring them some advantage in the war. They wished at least to save anything that could be saved, and consequently did not hesitate to act. The Tsar, who had begun the war in order to please the Entente, had to be removed. This line of conduct revealed an inexhaustible willpower, which would stick at nothing in order to win the war. The same thing would have happened if Stürmer had really favored peace in 1916.

The outbreak of the Revolution threw a strong sidelight on conditions in Russia. The army and nation were rotten to the core or it would never have taken place. In Russia, as with us, the army was part of the nation; there, too, nation and army were one. How often had I not hoped for a revolution in order to lighten our military burden! But my desire had been merely a castle in the air. Now it had come as a surprise. I felt as though a weight had been removed from my chest. At that time I never contemplated the possibility that it might later on undermine our strength also.

It was impossible to tell to what extent efforts in the East would be relaxed, and for the moment attacks had to be expected. Nevertheless, the Revolution was a serious blow for the Entente, as it inevitably entailed a diminution of Russia's fighting capacity and brought considerable relief to us in the extremely difficult position in which we were placed. For General Headquarters this consisted first of all in the saving of troops and munitions in the East; and the exchange of worn-out divisions from the West for fresh troops from the East was undertaken on a large scale.

Orders were given for propaganda to be set on foot at once to encourage a strong movement for peace in the Russian Army.

The outbreak of the Russian Revolution was a factor in the war upon which no general could dare to count with certainty. Now at last it was no longer a hope, but a reality with which I could deal as a soldier. Our general position had considerably improved, and I could look forward with confidence to the battles in the West. The results of the submarine campaign were distinctly favorable and far exceeded the expectations of the navy. The loss of tonnage and material sunk was bound to tell. *The Economist* of September 7, 1918, calls the spring of 1917 the most critical and perilous period through which England had passed since the outbreak of war. The Entente found itself forced to employ for naval warfare men and material hitherto destined for the conflict on land, and this continued in an ever-increasing degree.

The United States declared war upon us on April 5. The collapse of Russia, the success of our submarine campaign, and the desire to use their forces to combat the U-boats must have been factors in the decision.

On February 3 America had broken off diplomatic relations with us, and I doubt whether it would have been possible to come to terms with her in the mean time without disturbing the basis upon which the submarine campaign was being conducted.  The attempt on the part of our Foreign Office to establish military relations with Mexico strengthened public opinion against us in the United States.  In spite of my warnings, the Foreign Office had used an antiquated and easily decipherable secret code.

Soon after America's declaration of war, the whole world was ranged against us, only a few states, including the Argentine and Chile, preserving their neutrality in face of enemy pressure.  The American declaration of war included all the states of the Quadruple Alliance, with the exception of Bulgaria, where the American representative continued to hold his post at Sofia.  The German Government failed to secure his recall through the Bulgarian Government, although I requested several times that it be done.  This failure brought heavy retribution upon us later on.

It was not a matter of surprise to me that the United States joined the ranks of our enemies.  I had reckoned upon her doing so, provided the balance of war continued in our favor, even if the unrestricted submarine campaign had never been opened.  As far back as the spring of 1915 an American correspondent on the Eastern front had expressed views to this effect, and they certainly did not reflect his own personal opinion alone. America had never known Germany in time of peace, and she now viewed us and all the events taking place in Europe through the glasses of Entente propaganda, strengthened by her ties of blood with England.  The German-American population had little influence.  To appeal to their loyalty for the country of their birth, as against the country of their adoption, as we did for a time, was clumsy and bound to produce an unfavorable effect. I have not been able to get a clear account of the attitude of the Irish section of the population. The oppression of this unfortunate country left the United States cold.

Wilson's reply to the Kaiser's letter of the autumn of 1914, in which the latter appealed to America's sense of justice with regard to the Belgian atrocities, gave food for thought. America was led by economic interests ever more and more to the side of the Entente, for England had surrendered to her the position she had hitherto enjoyed as the first capitalistic Power in the world. The Entente nations were deeply in America's debt, and their defeat would have involved her in heavy loss.

The attitude of the United States in regard to the question of the supply of munitions left no doubt about her one-sided conception of neutrality. England's monstrous violations of international law at sea were possible only as long as America connived at them. In a conversation at the Foreign Office several years before the war I was assured that America would never agree to such tactics. We reckoned with certainty on unlimited imports through Holland.

As a matter of fact, the American Government did actually raise objections to the arbitrary methods of English naval warfare. The American note of protest of March 30, 1915, was couched in serious language. It asserted in unequivocal terms that the so-called British blockade was "an almost unqualified denial of the sovereign rights of the nations now at peace," and continued with the warning that to tolerate England's procedure in this respect would be to assume "an attitude of unneutrality to the present enemies of Great Britain which would be obviously inconsistent with the solemn obligations of this [the U. S.] Government in the present circumstances." This declaration was perfectly plain. A second American note of November 5, 1915, emphasized the fact that the so-called blockade of March 11 of the same year must be considered ineffective and therefore illegal. Both protests were bluntly rejected by England. The United States Government accepted the rebuff. According to its own verdict, its attitude to Germany for nearly two years was unneutral.

The opinion of the German ambassador, Count Bernstorff, on these proceedings is contained in a memorandum to the Government and people of the United States, published in *The Times* of April 13, 1915. It runs as follows: "If the American people desire to observe true neutrality, they will find the means to stop the exclusive export of arms to one side, or, at least, use this export trade as a means to uphold legitimate trade with Germany, especially trade in foodstuffs."

From one-sided favoritism to open partizanship was but a small step. I will mention only two instances: Mr. Choate, the late American ambassador in London, wrote on April 7, 1917, to Earl Grey: "As you know, I have thought from the beginning that while for the time being we might better serve the cause of the Allies by remaining neutral and supplying all that we could in the way of arms and munitions, and, I am happy to say, some men, as our neutral right was, that nevertheless, when by entering into the war with all our might and with the aid of all our boundless resources, we could help to bring it to an end in the right way by the complete suppression of Prussian militarism and the triumph of civilization, it would be our duty to do so. That time has now come." And on June 3 the American Admiral Sims spoke as follows in London: "In 1910, when our fleet visited England, I made a short but very undiplomatic speech. . . . In that speech I expressed an opinion which is now being translated into action. . . . This is what I said: 'In my opinion, if the time ever comes when the integrity of the British Empire is seriously threatened by a European coalition, you may count on every ship, every dollar, every man, and every drop of blood of your kinsmen across the sea.'"

Very characteristic of the views of American official circles is the following conversation which took place between a certain reliable personage and an American consul-general, and it is in complete harmony with the opinions given above.   Asked whether the *Lusitania* affair had really led to American intervention, the consul-general replied: "No, that was only the match that set fire to the straw, and it has been fully exploited as propaganda.   But for this we should have had to find other convincing reasons for coming into this business! If we had not joined the Allies we should have been nowhere after the war.   Now we expect to be number one—and we shall be number one!"   To the question as to what part America would play as number one, he replied: "Germany was undoubtedly the most industrious country in Europe before the war.   We in America and England saw to what an exalted height Germany was climbing, and realized that in a few decades she could reach the pinnacle of power and be in a position to dictate, not only to Europe, but to the whole world.   She had become a menace and we in America recognized the fact.   For this reason we tackled the problem and thought we understood it. We are convinced that our people will take the lead after the war.   It is we who are going to dictate, not only to Germany, but to the whole of Europe.   The nations will expect great things from us, above all, peace.   And they will get it, but on our conditions and at our price!"

"Will America impose her will upon her Allies?"

"Yes, indeed she will! But they will get better conditions than other countries [the Central Powers], just as we [America] shall get better conditions from them [the Allies]. It is all a matter of business. That is what war has always been!"

The American consul's prediction regarding his country's position after the war was ill founded, though only because the Revolution rendered Germany defenseless and gave world dominance to Great Britain. For America could no longer count upon any opposition to England in Europe. However that may be, the war was certainly no matter of business for Germany. It was forced upon us. Our economic future and independence were bound up in it; to us it was a question of life or death.

I will not discuss how far the above opinions coincided with those of President Wilson and the majority of the American people. All that need be said is that they became supreme. Under the pretext of the submarine campaign America entered the war against us at a period critical for the Entente. Whether, without the excuse afforded by the U-boats, she would have done so in time to prevent our winning the war in 1918 is open to doubt. But it is impossible to say how events on land would have turned out if the submarine campaign had never been opened.

As a matter of fact, on January 9, 1917, no one could have foretold the collapse of Russia and nobody calculated upon it. With the help of our submarines we reckoned on a decision in our favor, at the latest before America, with her new armies, could intervene in the war; without them we calculated that the Quadruple Alliance must be defeated in 1917. As it was, the history of this year took a completely different turn: the Western front held firm, but the submarine campaign brought no decision, and Russia collapsed.

On the Eastern front we were in a condition of neither peace nor war. A solution then became possible of which no one could have dreamed before the autumn of 1917—namely, to aim at a decision of the war on land in the year 1918 by means of an offensive, which must succeed if the submarines had by that time been able at least in so far to reduce enemy tonnage that the quick transport of the new American armies was out of question, or even if a certain proportion of the transports had been sunk. The navy counted upon being able to do this.

### III

General Headquarters began to reckon on the great Entente offensive in France, Macedonia, and on the Isonzo for the middle of April. From Kreuznach, whither we had moved at the end of February, I had often visited the Western front, and had discussed the situation with the command of the groups of armies and the army commanders, as well as with the generals in charge of the most dangerous positions; and we had exchanged views on tactics. The group of armies under the Crown Prince Rupprecht and the German Crown Prince were strengthened with divisions, artillery, and munitions, and were provided with everything necessary for successful defense. Where help was desired I gave it to the best of my ability.

The Sixth Army wanted to make a rectification of its line by means of a local advance at Souchez between Lens and Arras, and prepared to carry it out at the beginning of April. I had no doubt that a great British offensive was imminent at Arras. The operation at Souchez was abandoned. I begged the command of the group of armies to bring up its reserves nearer to the line in the area of the Sixth Army. The last attacks at Verdun in October and December had confirmed the

FIG. 16.   SPRING BATTLE AT ARRAS, 1917

old adage that the right place for reserves is close to the firing-line. The tactics of a defensive battle de-manded that, in many places on the front under attack,

counter-attack divisions should be held in readiness
in the second line to meet and throw back the enemy
if he broke through the first line.

The divisions which constituted the second and third
waves were indeed moved up by the Sixth Army, but
on the 8th were not close enough up. On the 9th,
after a short but extraordinarily intense artillery preparation, our army encountered a powerful attack, led
by tanks, on both sides of the Scarpe. Several of our
advanced divisions were overcome. The neighboring
divisions which stood firm suffered heavy losses. The
enemy succeeded before noon in reaching our battery
positions and seizing heights which dominated the
country far to the east. The counter-attacking divisions were not there to throw the enemy back; only
portions of the troops could be brought up by motor
transport. The situation was extremely critical, and
might have had far-reaching and serious consequences
if the enemy had pushed farther forward. But the
British contented themselves with their great success
and did not continue the attack, at least not on April 9.

On that day I celebrated my birthday at Kreuznach.
I had looked forward to the expected offensive with
confidence, and was now deeply depressed. Was this
destined to be the result of all our care and trouble
during the past half-year? Had our principles of defensive tactics proved false, and if so what was to be
done? I was not at that time able to get a clear view
of all the details of the battle. I sent for officers who
had taken part in the conflict in the front line, and by
means of conversations with them and telephonic communications gained the impression that the principles
laid down by General Headquarters were sound. But
the whole art of leadership lies in applying them correctly. Moreover, a division had failed here which had
previously enjoyed a high reputation. The battle of

Arras on April 9 was a bad beginning for the decisive struggle of this year.

April 10 and the following days were critical. The consequences of a break-through of twelve to fifteen kilometers wide and six or more kilometers deep are not easy to meet. In view of the heavy losses in men, guns, and ammunition resulting from such a break-through, colossal efforts are needed to make good the damage. It was the business of General Headquarters to provide reserves on a large scale. But it was absolutely impossible, with the troops at our disposal and in view of the military situation, to have a second division immediately behind every division that might possibly fall out. A day like April 9 threw all calculations to the winds. Many days had to pass before a new line could really be formed and consolidated. The end of the crisis, even if the troops were available, depended very largely, as it generally does in such cases, on whether the enemy, after his first victory, would attack again, and by further success aggravate the difficulty of forming a new line. Our position having been weakened, such victories were to be won only too easily.

The British attacked again at the same spot from the 10th onward in great strength, but not really on a grand scale. They extended their offensive on both sides, especially to the south as far as Bullecourt. On the 11th they took Monchy, and during the following night we evacuated Vimy Ridge. April 23 and 28 and May 3 were again days of severe fighting, and in the intervals sharp local engagements took place. The battles continued; we launched minor counter-attacks, which were successful, but also suffered slight losses of territory here and there.

The Commander-in-chief of the Sixth Army, General von Falkenhausen, whose Chief of Staff was Colonel von Loszberg, was very energetic in organizing the defense of the new position, and was supported in his efforts by the commands of the groups of armies and by General Headquarters. A further withdrawal to the Wotan position, which was still under construction, though contemplated for a time by the Sixth Army, was not found to be necessary.

The battle of Arras was at its height in the second half of April, and was swallowing up a liberal supply of reserves and material, when, on April 16, the French also opened their formidable offensives on the Aisne and in Champagne. Doubtless exceedingly important strategic objects lay behind the British attack, but I have never been able to discover what they were. I took for granted, in spite of the restricted area of their onslaught, that a great break-through was planned, and not merely a battle of attrition and diversion. But possibly the British Army had not quite recovered from the battle of the Somme and had undertaken a diversion here while the Fremch Army was to gain a decision.

The ultimate strategic object of General Nivelle was to break through the German line between Vailly and Rheims in the first few days. Following on this a push east of Rheims as far as Suippe was to widen the breach and shatter our front for seventy kilometers. The decisive blow was to be struck by the French Army against the group of armies under the German Crown Prince. The pressure from Arras eastward on Douai and the break-through on both sides of Rheims *via* Rethel in the direction of Mézières was to envelop the Siegfried position, the construction of which had been surveyed by hosts of aeroplanes. The Entente intended to make our whole front reel as far as the sea.

The preparations for defense were carried out with extraordinary care by the group of armies under the German Crown Prince and the Seventh and Third

Armies. The Crown Prince and his Chief of Staff, Colonel Count Schulenburg, were indefatigable. The command of the Seventh Army was in the hands of General von Boehn, one of the best generals in the German Army, a Prussian officer of the old school, a good trainer of troops, and a man of untiring energy. His Chief of Staff, Colonel Reinhardt, was a clever man, whose careful work made him a useful complement to his commanding officer. General von Einem, who was in charge of the Third Army, is well known as Minister of War, an able and far-sighted officer who knew the army well and understood the psychology of the troops. His Chief of Staff, Colonel, later General, von Oldershausen, was a man of irrepressible vitality and loved work; he, too, was the right complement to his superior. The headquarters staff of the Third Army afterward withdrew from the conflict. In the first fortnight of April the headquarters staff of the First Army took over the command under Gen. Fritz von Below. He had as his assistant Lieutenant-Colonel von Klüber, who had gained valuable experience in the battle of the Somme, and, like his general, was a particularly sound judge of tactics. He was afterward murdered by Sparticists in the discharge of his duties.

At first the troops would not believe in the possibility of an offensive, as they had seen no preparations for it. But gradually they brought themselves to face the severe fighting that lay before them.

After several days' artillery preparation the French attacked early on April 16 between Vailly and Brimont, to the northwest of Rheims. They broke through at various points on the Chemin des Dames and forced us to withdraw with heavy losses from the Vailly salient to the heights of the Chemin des Dames. Farther to the east the French clung firmly to the ridge that to the north falls sharply into the Ailette valley. Between the

Winterberg and the Aisne the French pressed forward
with tanks to the outskirts of Juvincourt, but were here
held up by a counter-attack division. Due east of the
Aisne our troops held their ground. Toward Brimont
another break-through was made, but was neutralized
by a push on the part of our counter-attack forces.
On April 17 and 18 the enemy renewed the assault, but
was unable to gain any advantage.

Meanwhile offensives in Champagne had also been
opened, and directed against the heights of Moron-
villiers. One division gave way, and we lost the heights
which formed a key position. When the French attempted to descend the northern slope they were exposed to our artillery fire, which mowed them down
and brought them to a standstill. Our counter-attack
divisions, as I subsequently ascertained in personal
conversation with the regimental commanders, were
thrown in too hastily, so that on the 19th we failed to
recapture the heights. The loss of them was a severe
blow, as they afforded a view to the north, right over
the whole country; but we had to make the best of
it. The crisis of the April battle had been survived.
In these battles the French infantry had attacked in
close formation, and its losses had been appalling.
Both on the Aisne and in Champagne General Nivelle
again attempted to score a victory. By this time our
line was once more re-established and consolidated, so
that on both the fields of this great dual battle the new
offensive came to grief with heavy loss.

May 7 saw fierce fighting all along the front, after
which the attack on the Aisne died out, and subsequent
to the 9th it flickered down in Champagne also, though
here it blazed up again on the 20th. The French offensive had collapsed with terrible loss of life, and,
although France was obliged to celebrate it as a victory,
it caused great depression. The Minister of War ad-

EXPLANATION

German line before April 16, 1917.
Direction of French main attack, Apr. 16, 1917.
German line at end of May 1917.

FIG. 17. DOUBLE BATTLE ON THE AISNE IN CHAMPAGNE, SPRING 1917

27

mitted in July that the attack had failed with losses
that must not again be incurred. These losses were
so great that the morale of the army began to suffer and
mutinies broke out, though we heard but little about
them, and that only by degrees. Only later on did we
learn the whole truth.

Changes were also made in the French High Command. General Nivelle was replaced by General Pétain.
Both had made their reputation at Verdun, General Pétain by his defense in the spring and summer of 1916,
General Nivelle by his offensive of October to December. The tactics which had succeeded then were expected to lead the French Army to final victory in the
spring of 1917.

Thanks to the measures we had taken for defense and
the resistance of the group of armies under the German

FIG. 18. DOUBLE BATTLE ON THE AISNE IN CHAMPAGNE, SPRING 1917

Crown Prince, this promised victory was turned into a
defeat. By superhuman efforts we gained a great success and showed ourselves superior to the enemy in
training. Our wastage of men and material was extraordinarily high. It was impossible to foresee what

turn the conflict might take and what claims we might have to meet.

In spite of the seriousness of our position on the Western front, the absence of any Russian attacks in the spring of 1917 prevented a general crisis in our situation such as we had experienced in September 1916. I had never been one to indulge in fruitless speculation, but I could not help considering what our position must inevitably have been had the Russians attacked in April and May and met with even minor successes. We should then, as in the autumn of 1916, have had a desperate struggle. Our supply of munitions had diminished to an alarming extent. If the Russian successes of July had occurred in April and May I do not see, as I look back, how General Headquarters could have mastered the situation. During these two months of 1917, in spite of our Aisne-Champagne victory, it was the Russian Revolution alone that saved us from serious trouble.

The Russian offensive took place later on in July, two months after the Anglo-French attack, and even then it was not a united blow, as in the autumn of 1916. It was a divided push, and operating, as we did, from interior lines, we were able to repel and overcome our isolated opponents one by one.

On the Italian front, too, there was violent fighting in May. The tenth battle of the Isonzo once more closed without victory for the Italian Army. In Macedonia an enemy offensive on a large scale collapsed before the Bulgarian lines. The submarine campaign again achieved good results in April and May and relieved our Western front.

IV

After their great failure in April and May and the collapse of Russia in the interval, England and France

saw themselves faced with a new situation. They decided upon a second great offensive, with the object of
winning the war before the end of 1917. At the same
time they wished to secure guaranties that final victory
might be assured, at any rate by 1918. The chief
weight of the blow was directed against Ypres, with a
view to capturing the German submarine base in
Flanders. The transport of the new American troops
to France in 1918 had to be safeguarded by a war
against our U-boats.

For the moment the French Army remained inactive
in order to recuperate after its recent defeat. Later
on it confined itself only to local engagements, although
these were of considerable intensity. The main forces
of the British and Belgian Armies, supported by French
troops, were held in readiness for the attack in Flanders.
Fresh offensives were also to be opened on the Isonzo,
in Macedonia, and Palestine.

In the summer of 1917 I naturally was not able to
form such a clear idea of the intentions and measures
the enemy were then maturing as I did in July and
August.

A weakening in the French attacks was perceptible
in the second half of May, and the French Army continued to be comparatively inactive. Meanwhile I had
to reckon on a reopening of their offensive, which was
possible at any moment, either here or in any sector of
the line. The British Army continued fighting on the
old battle-field east of Arras in the second half of
May, not, indeed, with the intensity shown in the
Somme battles, but still pursuing its tactics of attrition.

At the beginning of June, increased activity on the
part of the enemy was noticeable in the neighborhood
of our salient at Wytschaete, south of Ypres. The
straightening of this salient really began in the great
Flanders battle in June. As long as it remained in

German hands every British attack at Ypres and to the north of that town was outflanked from the south. The tactical position of the German troops in the Wytschaete salient was by no means favorable. There were some thoughts of evacuating it and withdrawing to the Sehn position. The Army, however, was of opinion that it could be held. Repulsed attacks are always to the advantage of the defending side, owing to the immensely heavy losses they entail for the enemy. The group of armies and General Headquarters therefore agreed that the salient should be held. We should have succeeded in retaining the position but for the exceptionally powerful mines used by the British, which paved the way for their attack, consisting, as usual, of fierce artillery fire supporting a closely massed infantry advance. The result of these successful mining operations was that the enemy broke through on June 7.

The heights of Wytschaete and Messines had been the site of active mine warfare in the early days of the war. For a long time past, however, both sides had ceased to use such tactics; all had been quiet, and no sound of underground work on the part of the enemy could be heard at our listening-posts. The mines must, therefore, have been laid long before. The moral effect of the explosions was simply staggering; at several points our troops fell back before the onslaught of the enemy infantry. Powerful artillery fire penetrating the Wytschaete salient hindered effective intervention by our reserves and the recovery of the position. The Sehn line was then taken up with our consent. I refused to countenance any suggestion of further withdrawals. June 7 cost us dear, and, owing to the success of the enemy attack, the price we paid was very heavy. Here, too, it was many days before the front was again secure. The British Army did not press its advantage;

apparently it intended only to improve its position for the launching of the great Flanders offensive.

It thereupon resumed operations on the old Arras battle-field and also between La Basséc and Lens. The object of the enemy was to wear us down and dis-

EXPLANATION
━━━ German line before June 7, 1917.
•━•━• German line after June 7, 1917.

1:200000

FIG. 19.   BATTLES IN WYTSCHAETE SECTOR, 1917

tract our attention from Ypres.   The command of the Sixth Army had been changed.

General von Falkenhausen had taken the place of the late General von Bissing as Governor-General of Belgium.   He was a particularly striking personality, who, upon taking up his new position, retained our complete confidence.   The Sixth Army had been given to

Gen. Otto von Below, who relinquished the command of the group of armies in Macedonia to General von Scholtz, latterly in command on the Eastern front.

The end of the Aisne-Champagne battle had left the Seventh and First Armies on a very unfavorable line, particularly at many points along the Chemin des Dames. To give up the ridge would have meant a French success and would have had a depressing effect on the troops who had held it so bravely. The group of armies under the German Crown Prince and the Seventh Army wished to secure improved positions by a series of minor engagements, so as to establish a line suitable for a permanent position. This plan coincided with the views of General Headquarters. As the result of various actions, prepared with the greatest care by the commands which took part in them, and skilfully carried out by the forces engaged, a more favorable line was gradually formed here and fresh life was put into the troops.

General von Gallwitz, too, the Commander-in-chief of the Fifth Army, wished for the same reason to undertake a local improvement of position on the west bank of the Meuse, which the group of armies there considered particularly important. The group of armies under the German Crown Prince supported the proposal and General Headquarters gave its consent. The attacks on June 18 and 19 succeeded. But here again we realized, as we had done before, that to attack is easier than to hold what has been won.

In all these engagements, undertaken by the Seventh and Fifth Armies in order to improve their position, the possibility of enemy counter-attacks was reckoned with, and their repulse provided for, in the estimates for men and munitions furnished to General Headquarters. We wished to avoid anything in the way of a wild gamble. Although everything was prepared against these enemy counter-attacks, they succeeded far too often. The Seventh Army had been equal to them. Before Verdun the French deprived us of the greater part of our gains. I was glad when the battles there came to an end, and sorry that I had ever allowed the attacks to be made. I was as little in favor, as when the Commander-in-chief on the Eastern front, of continuous battering tactics, in which the gain does not outweigh the loss.

Near the Fourth Army the British had been established ever since 1914 in a narrow bridge-head close to the coast on the right bank of the Yser. This place had always been the Naval Corps' weak spot. The Fourth Army, which was supported by this corps, received permission to take this bridge-head. The attack took place on July 10 and was successful. The Yser effectively prevented all enemy counter-attacks.

In spite of the severe fighting for the Wytschaete salient in the first half of June and other engagements on the British front, the activity in the West from the middle of May till June was such that some of the troops at least were able to recuperate, and we were in a position to create reserves. The Western Army was well prepared when events in the East reached a sudden crisis.

V

Events turned out as we had expected; the Russian Revolution had weakened the enemy's fighting strength. The wish for peace seemed to be gaining ground in Russia, but the attitudes of the new Russian Government and of the Russian people and army in this matter were not united. The Minister of Foreign Affairs, Miliukow, pressed for the continuation of the war and the recasting of the map of Europe at the expense of the Quadruple Alliance. Other ministers talked about a peace without annexations or indemnities and the right of nations to self-determination. But they were all unanimous in demanding adherence to the alliance with the Entente Powers, and we had to reckon with their deliberate efforts to quell any ground for expecting any relaxation of their desire to annihilate us.

The attitude of the Russian troops was in some places friendly, and we gladly met them half-way. On other parts of the front active fighting continued, but we kept as quiet as we could. In April and May, and right on into June, the general military position was not such as to encourage us to seek greater activity on the Eastern front. The Government was also afraid that an attack on our part might check the disintegration of Russia. At the beginning of April events there were developing very rapidly. Von Linsingen's group of armies carried out a local attack on a bridge-head on the Stochod, northeast of Kowel, which had survived the fighting of 1916. This was in itself an important undertaking, but the number of prisoners we took was so large that even I was astonished. The Imperial Chancellor approached me with the request to make as little as possible of this success, and I did as he asked, though extremely unwillingly. The troops who had carried out the attack did not deserve to be passed over in silence. In the press our reserve about the Stochod battle gave rise to a certain amount of criticism. I understood this, but considered it my duty to accede to the Chancellor's request, in order not to disturb in any way the prospects of peace, which at this moment really were looming into view. General Headquarters forbade any further demonstrations of force.

With Kerensky's bolder activity in May the great danger of the Russian Army being reorganized increased. England, France, and the United States

spared no effort to achieve this object. In view of this
frequent discussions took place at General Headquarters as to whether a rapid attack on the Eastern
front with troops that the Commander-in-chief there
could furnish, strengthened by a few divisions from the
West, would not be better policy than continuing to
play the part of inactive spectators; for now was the
moment to level a blow at the Russian Army, while
it was still in diminished strength. I did not concur
in this idea, although the position in the West had
improved. I was unwilling to do anything, even in
appearance, that might injure a real prospect of peace.
From a military point of view, too, this line of conduct
was justified, because every revolution undermines and
rots the fighting strength of an army. I certainly won-
dered whether in this case it were so, when on July 1
the first Russian attack took place in Galicia. The
time of tedious waiting in the East was over and
General Headquarters no longer had its hands tied,
but was given full freedom of action.

The Russian offensive was planned on a large scale.
The attack was to be made from the Riga bridge-head,
at Dünaburg on Lake Narotch, at Smorgon, and to
the south, and in the whole of Galicia, from the Tarno-
pol-Zborow-Lemberg Railway as far as the Carpathians.
The center of action lay here in the south. The Commander-in-chief in the East was not unaware by the
end of June of the projected offensive. Numerous
deserters had kept him well informed, and he took all
the necessary defensive measures. To carry out the
counter-attack he had planned, he needed reinforcements from the West. It is true that for the moment
things were quieter there, but it had to be assumed
that fighting would continue. Nevertheless, whatever
might happen there, General Headquarters was bound
to exploit the opportunity offered in the East. In or-

FIG. 20.   BATTLES IN EAST GALICIA, SUMMER 1917

der, if it were by any means possible, to come to a
final reckoning with Russia, and so gain a free hand on
one side, six divisions were set free for the East.   More
was not possible at the moment, and it was only very
unwillingly that the officers in command on the Western
front gave up the divisions for the other front.   They
were unable to grasp the magnitude of the undertaking.

The most favorable point of attack on the Eastern
front was near a crossing of the Dvina above Riga, the
Zborow-Sereth-Niederung line in East Galicia.   From
here an attempt might be made to envelop the southern
portion of the Russian Army, and it was the intention
of the Commander-in-chief to put this plan into action
at once.   General Headquarters was able to give its
consent.   How the attack would turn out, and whether
it was to be regarded as a major operation, as I secretly
hoped, or merely as a tactical counter-attack, and how
the Russian and also the Austrian armies would fight,
remained questions whose solution I awaited with the
keenest suspense.

The Russian attack in East Galicia was made in
close formation with a vast expenditure of munitions.
It succeeded against Austrian troops, but not against
German and Turkish.   On July 1 strong Russian forces
broke through the Austro-Hungarian line between
Zborow and Brsheshiny.   Austrian troops were deserting to the enemy in large numbers.   On July 2 the
Commander-in-chief had to throw in substantial reserves to ease the pressure.   Further Russian attacks
collapsed.   The offensive against the Southern Army
began on July 4.   The fierce struggle lasted for several
days and ended with a complete success for the defense
made by General Count von Bothmer's army, which
consisted almost exclusively of German troops.

South of the Dniester the Russian attack against the
Austrian Third Army on July 6 and 7 was completely

successful. The Austrian troops gave way; a German division which had but recently arrived tried to stem the retreat, but was carried along by it. The Russians pressed forward to the Lomnitza and occupied Kalusch. The position was critical for the Commander-in-chief. He had collected his reserves for the intended counter-attack between Zborow and the Sereth, in the direction of Tarnopol, and the Western divisions were being moved to this area. Just as in the spring the Arch-duke Karl's front had to be strengthened before we could march on Rumania, so now the Commander-in-chief had to stiffen the Austrian troops, and especially the Third Army, before he could carry out his preparations for the counter-attack. He was the more to be congratulated inasmuch as, in spite of the retreat south of the Dniester and the violent attacks which now began in the north, he made his push north of Zborow and carried through the operation without a hitch.

At Kalusch luck favored us. The Russian Army had already paid too dearly for its early keenness to attack, and had made no further progress on the Lomnitza. The first German troops to arrive were consequently able, thanks in part to the energetic intervention of Major von dem Busche, of my staff, to hold the position. On July 15 they succeeded in gaining ground, and the crisis was overcome.

The most violent of the Commander-in-chief's attacks on the old front was the one that took place on July 21 south of Smorgon near Krewo; here the Russians broke through a division of the Landwehr occupying a very wide front, though it defended itself with extraordinary courage.

For a few days things looked extremely serious, until our reserves and artillery fire restored the situation. The Russians evacuated our trenches; they were no longer what they had been. Meanwhile the counter-attack forces had finished their march up between Zborow and the Sereth. Unfortunately the attack had to be postponed two or three days, until July 19, on account of extremely bad weather. This was the day on which the peace resolution was debated in the German Reichstag. The attack was a brilliant success; ground was won over an area twenty kilometers in breadth and fifteen kilometers in depth. The whole army was in high spirits. In the Reichstag the victory for German arms was called a "morale-raiser."

The next day the push was continued in the direction of Tarnopol, which fell on July 25, and the Russians began to withdraw from our position south of the Zborow-Tarnopol Railway. The tactical counter-attack developed into an operation on a grand scale. The disorganization of the Russian front extended farther and farther to the south. The Southern Army, the Austrian Third and Seventh Armies, which had a specially strong stiffening of German troops, moved up. The Eastern front was ablaze right into the Bukovina. The Russian Army retired in disorder; the Revolution had destroyed its backbone.

On August 2 and 3 we succeeded by steady fighting in reaching the Zbrutsch, and took Czernowitz and Kimpolung. This was the utmost to which we could effectively develop the counter-attack of July 19. It is true that for a time I hoped that the Austrian Third and Seventh Armies would press forward into Moldavia, but the Austrian powers of attack were not equal to the task, and the Germans alone were not strong enough. Communication with the rear turned out so difficult that the proper provisioning of the armies could not be managed until the railways had been repaired. Large bodies of men were set to work at this, but the destruction was so thorough that weeks elapsed before we could think of extending operations to the south of the Dniester.

The German troops, as in the previous autumn, had done splendidly in this open fighting; they felt relieved from the terrible grip of trench warfare. But the Austrian Army, in spite of all the care lavished upon it, showed a diminution of fighting power which was in the highest degree alarming.

On the Zbrutsch the struggle swayed backward and forward for a few days longer; south of Czernowitz the group of armies under the Archduke Joseph, who had taken over the chief command in Hungary from the Emperor Charles, pressed a little bit farther eastward; but although battles had begun on the Rumanian front, the major operation was over.

Here, in the mountains between Focsani and the frontier, a Russo-Rumanian offensive had opened on July 24 to relieve pressure elsewhere. It chanced to strike a weak spot in our line and won a local success.

Our advance north of the Carpathians, down from the Dniester and through the Bukovina toward Moldavia, suggested the idea of resuming operations against the Rumanian troops and an attack on the lower Sereth, while the Austrian armies retained their advanced position above Czernowitz and to the south. Various considerations led us to send the Alpine Corps to Rumania and still further weaken the Western front. This attack was still under contemplation when the Russo-Rumanian push mentioned above took place. It was arranged that Von Mackensen's group of armies was to make an advance northward on the west bank of the Sereth, and the southern group of armies, under the Archduke Joseph, from the Oitoz Pass toward Otzna. The battles began in the first half of August and lasted into the second half. They scored local successes in both places, and forced the enemy to surrender the ground won on July 31. By means of French co-operation the Rumanian Army had gained so greatly in stability that strategic successes seemed out of the question for us as long as the offensive in Bukovina remained at a standstill. For the present it was impossible to continue it. The attacks of the groups of armies under Von Mackensen and the Archduke Joseph were arrested. The Rumanians, in their turn, now made unsuccessful attacks. Gradually the fighting died down here also.

The great Entente offensive to which we were intended to succumb in the early summer of 1917 had petered out; owing to the Russian Revolution there had been no concerted action. When the Anglo-French-Italian advance was made Russia fell out, and when Russia took the offensive the Western front had weakened. We had held out, though we had suffered heavily, and on the Eastern front we had won a notable success. The military collapse of Russia was patent to the whole world.

Six months of the submarine campaign had gone by. It had accomplished much; according to mere members, more, but in its final result less, than had been anticipated. I still hoped that the expectations of the Navy would be realized in the near future. But I began to wonder whether as many U-boats as possible were really being built. It was imperative that every effort should be made to increase the effect of the submarine campaign. It is true that, in view of the anxious military and economic situation, General Headquarters was not in a position to transfer skilled workmen to any great extent from the army to the navy, or to curtail the Hindenburg program for the sake of the latter.

## VI

Hard work and an unflinching determination, helped by the Russian Revolution, had enabled us to relieve the military situation. But meanwhile, as had already been the case in Austria-Hungary, the breaking up of the united will of the German people, under pressure of this upheaval and of economic privations, combined with the growing influence of enemy propaganda, was to bring about events which steadily lowered the fighting strength of both the allied states and jeopardized our military gains. From this time onward the hope of the Entente for the inner collapse of their enemies was continually fed. Peace would be immeasurably more difficult, and the end of the war was postponed.

Chancellor von Bethmann and Count Czernin were both completely obsessed by the influence of the Russian Revolution. They both feared a similar catastrophe in their own countries, and thought of nothing but possibilities of peace, which had, unfortunately, receded into the dim distance, whereas until peace had been attained they should have taken energetic measures to prosecute the war. They ought to have raised the morale of the nation by creative activity, just as General Headquarters had succeeded in improving the army's fighting strength in a desperate struggle against a powerful adversary. As it was, their policy led to perpetual concessions at home, and they gave up the task of leading the nation. The whole tendency of their ideas made them overlook the unspeakable harm they were doing to the strength of their respective countries, which ought to have shown a united front to the enemy, and they did not realize how they were interfering with the conduct of the war. Neither of these men, whom destiny had placed at the head of their people at this terrible crisis, possessed the strong char-

acter that events demanded. No doubt they had to
face serious internal difficulties. Count Czernin, with
his conglomerate Empire, had an infinitely complex
task. The problems presented to Herr von Bethmann
were probably easier; he had only to act in accordance
with the conclusions that could be drawn with overwhelming force from the nature of the war and from
our position in face of a foe determined to destroy us.
Instead of harping ever more and more on the idea of a
peace of reconciliation, which was always out of the
question, he ought to have knitted the nation together
and pointed out to it the great tasks before it and the
objects to be attained, and then have given us in the
army a free hand. The German people ought to have
been shown again and again what they were fighting
for, and what the enemy in his heart of hearts really
wanted. The majority would then have followed him
as they had done in 1914. There are always some who
can never be taught. Was there really any room for
doubt regarding the ideas and objects of our enemies,
as interpreted in the light of their whole history and
their whole mentality, not to mention their answer to
our peace offer of December 12 and to Wilson's note
of December 18? Could any one fail to realize that the
weakening of the war spirit at home must cripple the
conduct of the war?

How seriously the position was regarded by General
Headquarters the decision for the submarine campaign
and the retreat to the Siegfried line had shown drastically and clearly enough even to the lay mind. It must
have been obvious to the Government that earnest and
thoroughly conscientious effort alone could pull us
through.

At the beginning of April 1917 the Kaiser received
the Emperor Charles at Hamburg. The latter was
accompanied by Count Czernin and General von Arz.

The Chancellor, the Field-Marshal, and I were also summoned. Herr von Bethmann and Count Czernin had already met. On March 27 these gentlemen had come to an agreement, recorded in the "Vienna Document" of that date. It included the minimum conditions of peace, based on the *status quo ante*, and, in case of a favorable outcome of the war, a program of settlement in accordance with the ideas I represented. No mention was made of any renunciation whatever. This important document was first known to the Secretaries of State and General Headquarters on February 5, 1918.

While kings and councilors were discussing affairs at Hamburg, General von Arz, the Field-Marshal, and I held a consultation on the situation. We had occupied the Siegfried line, and were expecting the great April offensives. I considered the British attack imminent. The result of the submarine campaign in March had been good, and the Ministry of the Interior began to build high hopes upon it. The importance of America was given due weight. Our verdict on the situation was grave but confident; we hoped to repulse the Entente attacks in the near future, but for the rest had to await the results of the submarine campaign and the developments of events in Russia.

General von Arz had similar hopes for the Austro-Hungarian front, but added that, in consequence of lack of raw materials and of the heavy demands on man-power, the Austro-Hungarian Army could fight on only until the winter. There was no difference of opinion as to the necessity for prosecuting the war for the present with the utmost energy. It was impossible to foresee how events might have developed by the winter.

About midday there was a consultation between the German Imperial Chancellor, Count Czernin, the

Field-Marshal, General von Arz, and myself. The Chancellor asked me, before the discussion began, whether I thought the time had come to make a move for peace. I could answer only that the Entente was about to make an immense effort, and that I did not think the moment favorable from the military point of view. The question was not further discussed, even in connection with the Russian Revolution. Count Czernin proposed that in order to obtain an early peace we should give Alsace-Lorraine to France. Austria-Hungary was to hand over Galicia to Poland and support the union of Poland and Germany. At this moment our meeting with the two statesmen, which had lasted about ten minutes, was interrupted. The Chancellor and Count Czernin were summoned to the two Emperors. This ended the official part of the Imperial meeting as far as I was concerned. In the afternoon I was received by the Emperor Charles.

After lunch Count Czernin explained his views to me in a private conversation. He based his wish for peace upon the internal condition of the Dual Monarchy. I had no reason to conceal my personal opinion. After all, I was the son of my Fatherland, and had a perfect right to express what I thought. I told Count Czernin that he ought to lead the peoples of the Dual Monarchy more firmly and raise their morale. He replied that this was impossible. I then turned to his proposals. His Polish project seemed to me very dubious. What would Poland's attitude toward it be? What effect would it have upon our eastern provinces? I was all the more astonished at this whole scheme, as Austro-Hungarian policy regarding Warsaw showed no signs of honest concern about German interests. The Polish project was quite indefinite; the surrender of Alsace-Lorraine to France, however, presented a perfectly clear issue, of which, in my opinion, there could be no question as long as we were not beaten. Every nation stands or falls by its honor. All German parties —even the Independent Socialists—were united in regarding Alsace-Lorraine as German, and in considering it a point of honor for us to fight to the utmost in defense of this possession. Any authority, whether civil or military, which failed to recognize this would have been rightly swept away by indignant public opinion. Our situation was certainly serious, but we were still capable of putting up a stiff fight; we needed only the will to do so. The surrender of Alsace-Lorraine would have been an open confession of weakness, and would have been condemned as such even by well-meaning people. At that time there was no need for such a sacrifice. It might confidently be expected that the Entente would see nothing in all these proposals but a trap or a confession of military defeat that would make them raise its demands considerably.

Count Czernin could give no definite answer to my inquiry as to whether the Entente would really be satisfied with the surrender of Alsace-Lorraine. He expressed views of the gravest kind on Germany's internal conditions. He must have been in possession of excellent information. This closed our interview. Count Czernin did not again mention the separation of Galicia from the Austrian Empire, though he continued for some time to urge that Rumania should be included in Austria-Hungary's sphere of influence, and the East, including Poland, in that of Germany. These were broad and clear generalizations with which General Headquarters could only agree. They were recorded in the Kreuznach Agreement of May 17 and 18.

Soon afterward, however, Count Czernin supported the Austro-Polish solution with great energy and skill, and thus revealed the real character of his country. For Austria to renounce Poland would have produced disastrous effects in the monarchy. The prestige of the young Emperor was also at stake. It was obviously Count Czernin's intention to oust us in Poland as well as in Rumania. The Austro-Polish solution entailed grave dangers for Prussia and Germany. The Field-Marshal and I feared that it meant the break-up of the Alliance, and was a direct threat to our eastern provinces. The Poles would always pursue their claims to German territory, and the Prussian Poles would play into their hands. The Vienna Government would find itself forced to become the agent of their wishes. As long as these views were advanced by an isolated Poland, Germany could deal with them, but if a Slav Austria stood behind them the whole thing assumed a different aspect. Germany's vital interests would be seriously threatened, conflict would arise between the two Empires, and would find Germany in an extraordinarily difficult position, both from the military and the political point of view. The province of Silesia would have been encircled and our communications with East Prussia, Lithuania, and Courland threatened. The annexation of these two districts was at that time by no means a fantastic dream. Neither did I see how, from the economic point of view, Germany could reconcile herself to the Austro-Polish solution, which in Poland itself was bound to entail the gravest difficulties and to cut us off from the Russian market. We knew from experience what an obstacle Austria-Hungary presented as a route for our trade to the Balkans. The question was often to be discussed by us in the future, and the verdict passed upon it by the German Government to undergo strange transformations.

Austria-Hungary was constantly discussing the early conclusion of peace. Thus, about the middle of April, the Emperor Charles, in a letter addressed to His Majesty, dealt with the possibility of having to make great sacrifices in order to obtain it. The dangers of an international revolution were described in great detail, and the urgent need for such a peace deduced from it. These and similar letters were handed by His Majesty to the Imperial Chancellor to answer. The Field-Marshal and I had to comment upon them from the military point of view, and the Chief of the Naval Staff from the naval. Of course we said, as in duty bound, what we thought was right; how our comments were made use of was the business of the Imperial Chancellor. In this instance his ideas coincided with ours and with those of the Chief of the Naval Staff

Early in May the Chancellor replied to the effect that, considering the great hopes the Entente had at the moment, both of the success of its offensive and of the re-establishment of Russia, our efforts would be doomed to absolute failure if we made our readiness for peace too obvious. It would merely make the Central Powers appear hopelessly exhausted and thereby make the enemy intensify his efforts. At the moment peace was obtainable only by submitting to the will of our enemies, but that kind of peace the people would neither understand nor permit.

Conditions in Russia had so far developed favorably for us. In that country the demand for peace was becoming more and more insistent. Our difficult task was to follow the process of development and disintegration in Russia with the closest attention, hasten it if we could, and deal with any approaches from that quarter in such a way that actual peace negotiations might follow. Possibly such negotiations might then become the prelude of a general peace.

This constituted the official reply to the Emperor Charles's letter.

On many other occasions Count Czernin pressed for peace. He continued to advocate the surrender of

German territory to France, but he was never able to say whether the Entente was inclined for peace or whether any tangible method of attaining it had presented itself. Count Czernin would surely have told us if he had discovered it.

In his speech of December 11, 1918, he discussed the questions of war and peace at great length, presumably merely in order to show that he had seen disaster coming. That is an unproductive occupation.

Pessimists are always clever people. When the evil day arrives they are gaped at for their wisdom. The mob offers them incense—and to itself at the same time. The mob has always anticipated disaster. If it does not come, then the pessimists and the mob are more satisfied than ever. So they both enjoy themselves, anyhow. Men of action are not so fortunate; they are right only when they are successful. Then the mob cheers them. But if they are not successful or, worse, meet with disaster, the same mob stones them. Pessimists and the mob do not ask what they themselves, or the men of action, have done to avert disaster. The mob lacks judgment and cannot be expected to ask.

But I am surprised to find Count Czernin behaving in the same way. Has he really fairly told himself and the world what he actually did in the situation in which he found himself to avoid losing the war and so save his own and his allies' countries from disaster and shame?

Unfortunately, Count Czernin omitted to inform us earlier of those facts which did not come to my knowledge until I read his speech. He said: "On several occasions our representatives got into touch with those of the Entente, but, unfortunately, these feelers never got to the stage of concrete proposals. We frequently had the impression that we should be able to make a separate peace without Germany, but we were never informed of the definite conditions on which Germany, on her side, might have peace.

"Above all, we were never told that Germany would be allowed to retain the possessions she held before the war. . . . As the Entente never declared its willingness to negotiate with a Germany that had no desire for conquest, but kept reiterating its desire to destroy Germany, we were forced into a defensive war on Germany's behalf and our rôle in Berlin was made amazingly difficult."

These words, if spoken earlier, would have silenced all our talk about a peace of reconciliation and have revived the warlike spirit and so brought blessings to our people.

Count Czernin, however, held his peace, and so took upon himself an enormous responsibility. Or perhaps he informed the Imperial Chancellor and the latter neglected to enlighten the people. The German people have the right to know the truth.

It was not only in Berlin, as Count Czernin thinks, but in Vienna also, that a statesman was lacking who was equal to the demands of this war and could collaborate with the military leaders in securing victory.

The leading statesmen had no faith in victory, failed to find the road to peace, and yet remained in office.

VII

I deeply regretted the events which took place in Germany in the spring and summer of 1917, as I did all other manifestations of weakness. They were bound to react unfavorably on our conduct of the war, and therefore on the subsequent peace. Looking back, I can see that our decline obviously began with the outbreak of the Revolution in Russia. The Government was oppressed on the one hand by the fear that it might spread to Germany, and on the other by the knowledge of its inability to revive the resolution and warlike ardor of the people, waning as they were through the combination of innumerable circumstances. No doubt our precarious military position and, later, the want of success achieved in the submarine war, of which some people had, unfortunately, been too confident, made it more difficult to rouse our energy. It was obvious that it suffered from these causes.

But after all, owing to the collapse of Russia, our position in the summer of 1917 was better than that of the Entente. We were justified in being hopeful. But there were other reasons for our spiritual decline. The Government lacked the resolution to deal energetically with abuses. And behind it there was the Reichstag, with no united will, in part sincerely anxious about our future, in part merely striving for power for selfish reasons.

On April 7 there was published a decree by His Majesty on the franchise. I heard of it only after the publication. Neither the Emperor nor the Imperial Chancellor, Von Bethmann, ever spoke to me about internal affairs. Nor was it my business to originate discussions on these subjects, as internal politics had nothing to do with me.

The connection between the franchise decree and the Russian Revolution was too obvious. That was what made it so ill advised. If a change in the franchise was necessary—as it doubtless was—it should have been made before the war, at the latest in August 1914, with a *grande geste*, as the free gift of a strong government. Worst of all, the Government now made the Crown the center of political discussion, instead of keeping it clear of party strife. Besides, apart from a small section this step pleased only the enemy, who probably grasped the reason for it with gusto. At every step the Government should have considered its probable effect on the enemy, as well as at home.

During the war, home politics should have been dominated and directed by consideration of the effect on the enemy. The greater the prominence given to questions of internal politics the lower the warlike ardor of the nation will sink. Any statesman should know that. The decrees of April 7 and July 11 disclosed our weakness to the enemy and revealed our fear of revolution. The enemy must have said to himself that there is no smoke without fire, and a conflagration is therefore possible. Revolution will come. He must therefore have concluded that he had only to hold out and fan the flame to attain his object—revolution in Germany and her ultimate destruction.

The effect of the April decree at home was very much what it was abroad. The revolutionary elements perceived the Government's anxiety and became more exacting. Their reply was the strikes of the second half of April. They were an echo of the Russian Revolution, and proved how dreadful was the lack of sympathy with the fighting-men at the front. They also showed to what extent the mass of the workers had escaped from the control of their leaders. The decree produced no soothing effect, as the Government had hoped. It was too late for that, and the Government itself was too weak and too incapable of producing anything new from its own resources.

The people were not much affected by the Prussian franchise; only a few politicians and newspapers took a lively interest in it. Unfortunately it proved an instrument to widen the split at home and intensify the secret agitation. No one in the army took any interest in the question. The navy, which was nearer home and not engaged in active operations, is said to have been less apathetic. The thought of elections in time of war only filled me with anxiety. They were bound to reduce our strength still further. I also considered an election to be an injustice toward the soldier at the front, who could, of course, according to the idea prevalent at that time, take no part in it. I was drawn into the party conflict by partizans and opponents of the right to vote, although I never expressed my opinion on the matter in public. I often spoke of this to the ministers.

Personally I had hoped a solution of the franchise difficulty might be found in a professional qualification, such as Bismarck had had in mind. This, perhaps, might have imparted new vigor to our stagnant and sterile public life. At that time we had not yet reached that stage. Now we have a new, vague catch phrase, "Anchoring the workmen's councils in the constitution," which again points to some sort of representation by professions, at any rate in the First Chamber. It is inconceivable that only one class should have constitutional rights and the rest be sent away empty.

Further events announced the waning of our ardor —which had been alluded to with such kindling words in the Reichstag on February 27—before the Russian Revolution. In utter disregard of the destructive intentions of the enemy, the idea of peace by reconciliation made ever greater progress among the German people. It was swallowed most eagerly by those who feared the effects of victory on their political aspirations. During May and June a number of delegates, with facilities from the Government, undertook journeys to Stockholm, Austria-Hungary, and Switzerland. We walked into the traps of the Entente. I was against these journeys, and so was the Commander-in-chief in the marches. The Emperor decided in favor of them, and the deputies of the General Staff in Berlin had to prepare the passports. Count Czernin also sent the Socialist leaders of Austria-Hungary to Stockholm.

From there, supported by the Russian Revolution, the laboring classes of the hostile states were to be called upon to proclaim and carry out the "reconciliation of mankind." These endeavors revealed woeful ignorance of human nature, and certainly took no account of the spirit of the enemy nations, nor of our own; they did, however, in some cases pursue decidedly revolutionary objects. No impression was produced on the enemy, but with us and in Austria the fighting spirit was weakened more and more. Confidence in our own strength was lost. The Government allowed the conduct of affairs to slip more and more from its grasp; and the worst of it was, it abandoned them, not to the people as a whole, but to certain groups which, through their history, had always displayed critical and never constructive faculties.

These assemblies and all the talk of peace by understanding suited the Entente very well. They disclosed our state of mind. But, with a clear idea of national feeling, they allowed no Socialist leaders to go to the meetings and declined to be bound in any way. They pursued quite different aims.

In the summer of 1917 the French Premier, Ribot, expressed so clearly his country's intention of destroying Germany that no misunderstanding was possible without deliberate self-deception. No one with the slightest sense of reality could doubt that for the Entente all the beautiful catchwords were mere window-dressing, intended to deceive the multitude and to give might the appearance of right. The Government, the Reichstag, and most of the people took it all for gospel. In the Reichstag, for the first time in the war, Socialist representatives openly threatened revolution. The "helots' peace" (of which the Imperial Chancellor spoke to General Headquarters about this time), which would come if we gave in before the enemy felt any inclination to peace, was on its way.

The High Command observed the great spiritual decline with increasing anxiety, and in view of the uncompromising attitude of the enemy governments felt bound to draw attention to the harm that was being done to the people and the army, especially in Berlin. More than once the Field-Marshal reported to His Majesty how greatly General Headquarters missed the support of the Imperial Chancellor. We had urged the latter far more frequently to strengthen the war spirit of the nation.

On June 19, 1917, Field-Marshal von Hindenburg wrote to him as follows, to warn him against the view that the war would be over that autumn at the latest:

"These dangers" [of the submarine warfare] "are undoubtedly recognized by clear-thinking people among our enemies. If in spite of this they advocate continuation of the war, it is because they expect the collapse of Germany and her allies to take place before their own. It may be that they hope to bring about this collapse by a victory on land, but they rely far more on economic and political causes, such as food difficulties, shortage of raw materials, disunion, discontent, and the supremacy of the German Radical Social Democracy. They base this expectation on the waning of our power of resistance at home, the growth of international sentiments, the state of our food-supply, and the longing for peace to which we unfortunately give expression so often.

"A revival of our internal strength would be the most potent means of persuading our enemies of the futility of prolonging the war until their own means of existence are in danger of destruction. On the other hand, every complaint of disappointed hopes, every sign of exhaustion and longing for peace on our part, or that of our allies, any talk of the alleged impossibility of standing another winter campaign can only have the effect of prolonging the war."

The wording of the Chancellor's reply, dated June 25, revealed extraordinary depression. His way of thinking differed from ours. He could find no way out of the situation, and still less could he summon up the energy to act. He was afraid of that "helots' peace," but talked about a peace by understanding, although he considered England's readiness for peace to be the necessary condition precedent, and despaired of getting Lloyd George to agree to it.

However, his view of internal conditions soon became more hopeful, as we may see from a telegram to the Emperor of July 5.

In the mean while, on June 27, the Field-Marshal had himself written to the Emperor: "Our greatest anxiety at this moment, however, is the decline in the national spirit. It must be revived, or we shall lose the war. Even our allies need a powerful tonic, otherwise there is a danger of their deserting us. For this it is necessary to solve those economic problems which are the most difficult and are of the greatest importance for the future. . . . The question arises whether the Chancellor is capable of solving these problems—and they must be correctly solved or we are lost!"

An outward indication of the falling-off of our spiritual capacity for war was afforded at the session of the Main Committee of the Reichstag on July 6. Deputy Erzberger made a speech which utterly surprised us, in which he maintained that the submarine war was perfectly hopeless, and that it was quite impossible for us to win the war at all. On this the spirit of the Reichstag broke down completely. The Imperial Chancellor had apparently been under a delusion when he changed his mind so suddenly on July 5. Now it was perfectly clear how far we had sunk. If things continued in this way in Germany, if nothing was done to encourage and strengthen the people, then, indeed, military defeat was inevitable.

The War Minister agreed with us as to the bad effect of the events in Berlin on our military position, and considered it necessary for the Field-Marshal to make a report to the Emperor on the subject. So the Field-Marshal and I proceeded to Berlin on the evening of the 6th. The Emperor, however, regarded those events as an entirely domestic affair, which had nothing to do with the military authorities, and further considered that the latter should, constitutionally, be represented by the War Minister. So our presence in Berlin on the 7th produced no result in any direction, and we returned to Kreuznach that evening.

The situation in Berlin became more acute. On July 8 the Chancellor, although at that time he accurately gaged the enemy's destructive intentions, agreed to the peace resolution which was to be put forward by the Majority parties, and at the same time definitely promised them to apply the Reichstag franchise law to the elections for the Prussian House of Representatives. Both these measures must have strengthened the enemy's will to an incalculable extent. On the afternoon of the 10th the Imperial Chancellor felt obliged to hand in his resignation, which was, however, refused on the 11th.

At Kreuznach we thought for a time that Prince von Bülow would succeed him. Further confusion was caused when suddenly the Austro-Hungarian Government openly sided with the Imperial Chancellor, Von Bethmann, and against Prince von Bülow.

The Emperor had decided that Chancellor von Bethmann was to stay; and the Crown Prince, who had arrived in Berlin, had given way. After all that had happened I could no longer believe that the Chancellor was the right man to perform the task demanded of him by this war, and lead the country out of the depths of its depression to victory. It had become evident to me that, in order to conquer in the field, the General Staff needed the co-operation of the statesmen at home, and the better acquainted I became with the general situation after assuming duty the more convinced I was. This co-operation we had not obtained; national thought and feeling at home had fallen off. The political leaders lacked creative force; they had no ideal which would take hold of the people and thus develop its own powers.

In 1914 we were aglow with patriotism, self-sacrifice, and confidence in our own strength. We now needed fresh energy and impulse to make the German people forget the years of suffering and distress, of bitterness and disappointment; replenish it with holy ardor, strength, and confidence, and enable it to imbue its fighting forces with fresh enthusiasm. The Imperial Chancellor underestimated the value of these moral forces. But the German people had to go on starving.

The Chancellor had permitted the enemy's refusal of our peace offer to pass by without letting the people know that, owing to the enemy's will, no just peace was possible; but that, on the contrary, as he believed and put it himself, a "helots' peace" was to be our lot. He had failed to imbue them with fresh warlike resolution, and call upon them to fight for life and honor against a strong-willed enemy, striving for our destruction.

No, he himself despaired of victory, and allowed the talk of an unattainable peace by understanding to shake our nerve, while it put all the trumps into the enemy's hand.

England's defiance of the laws of nations in employing the blockade against our very flesh and blood was not met by fiery protest; the heart of the people was not filled with strong, manly hatred; its holy ire was not directed against the inhuman enemy. Far from it. Discontent with the conditions at home, which were directly caused by the blockade, was permitted to develop its force internally, increase the effect of the blockade, and disintegrate our national life.

The inhuman ill-treatment of our prisoners, the very flesh of our flesh, was not allowed to arouse any feelings which could be vented outside—though not, of course, against the prisoners in our hands. Instead, every expression of anger was suppressed and the seeds of bitterness were sown.

When Wilson, on the entry of the United States into the war, attempted to drive a wedge between the Emperor, the princes, and the people, the Chancellor did not arise to protect his Imperial Master. The Reichstag protested, but the Imperial Chancellor held his peace. He never called upon the people to defend the monarchical idea, which, then as now, had its roots firmly fixed in millions of German hearts—he never prevented the ax being laid to the tree of the Imperial Office and the glory of the Empire.

Moreover, the political leaders lacked the strength to govern with firmness. At that time the mass of the people were not yet greedy for cheap phrases. They wanted to be sure that no unfair privileges were allowed as to living and conduct, and that in these respects everything was justly and equitably regulated. They also wanted peace, but never a peace such as we are now getting, and could only have got even then. The Government had lost the determination to win and its faith in German strength, which had so brilliantly manifested itself in the past three years, and had commenced to totter only for want of leading. So the army did not receive what it needed for victory. I no longer believed that a change would take place under that Chancellor. The hope of being able to collaborate in complete accord with the Imperial Chancellor, which I had cherished when I went to General Headquarters, had broken down. So I wrote out my resignation.

The constitutional problems did not affect my military action. Personally, I considered the barrier which the Imperial Chancellor had erected between the Emperor and the people to be deplorable. The Emperor could not become sufficiently acquainted with men. Several times, though in vain, I had asked Chancellor von Bethmann to let him meet leading men; it could only serve to smooth matters over in a satisfactory manner. For this reason I thought it advantageous to include Parliamentary Secretaries of State in the Cabinet. I hoped, too, that through them the country would be more likely to receive what it needed for the war.

The Field-Marshal joined me and submitted his resignation at the same time. Our applications were despatched to Berlin on the evening of the 12th, after we had sent a preliminary notification to General von Lyncker in the afternoon. Simultaneously we received an urgent telegram from the War Minister, who considered it necessary, in view of the military situation, for the Field-Marshal to make a further personal report in Berlin. The Emperor also wished to see us.

In the mean time the Crown Prince had had a conference on the morning of the 12th with the party leaders of the Reichstag, the majority of whom either declared themselves in favor of the immediate resignation of the Chancellor or else asserted that they attached no importance to his remaining in office. No one took his side.

On the Crown Prince's report the Emperor now decided to accept the resignation of Chancellor von Bethmann.

When we arrived in Berlin on the 13th the Emperor had already given his decision. I hoped that the man who was to assume office would be capable of concentrating the whole energy of the German people for a united effort.

On our first visit to Berlin, July 7, the Field-Marshal and I had been prepared to meet members of the Reichstag at the General Staff offices and give them information about the military situation in an informal manner. I was anxious to reassure them. This conversation took place in the afternoon of the 13th. Before the conference began, the Secretary of State, Doctor Helfferich, and Under-Secretary of State, Wahnschaffe, talked with me in a very excited manner about the possibility of a peace resolution.

Our defensive attitude throughout the first half of 1917, the various failures near Arras, in the Wytschaete salient and in Galicia, where we had not yet attacked, the absence up to date of any decisive result from the submarine war, and our serious situation as regards food and raw materials, had caused great anxiety. These were the matters we were to discuss. But every one was thinking about the peace resolution which the Reichstag was to introduce, with the co-operation of Count Czernin, possibly even at his instigation. This gave rise in Berlin to the completely erroneous idea that we had come to take part in the deliberations on the peace resolution. As a matter of fact, the deputies kept on coming back to it.

We summed up our view of the situation more or less to the effect that on land it was serious, but secure. We simply must hold out, since our enemies did not want peace. The ammunition-supply had improved, and there was sufficient raw material. We made no reference to the impending operations in Galicia, both for the sake of secrecy and because their development could not possibly be foreseen. We had faith in the success of the submarine war, although up to date it had not produced the decisive effect that we had hoped for. In discussing the possibility of transferring the American Army to France we put forward the naval opinion that it could be considered feasible only to a limited extent. To the peace resolution we were unable to give any support; we explained that it did not meet with our views, since it was bound to exercise an adverse influence on the spirit of the troops and on the determination of the people, while the enemy would construe it as a confession of weakness. Its full effect must therefore be injurious. We also pointed out the evil consequences that might result from it in Bulgaria, where the demands for peace went very far.

The text of my argument was this: We shall win if the army is backed up by a united people. That is where the people's representatives must help.

The meeting was quite informal. Herr von Helfferich requested the deputies to take no steps with regard to the peace resolution for the present. He invited them to meet him at the Ministry of the Interior the next day and the day after for a conference, at which the new Imperial Chancellor would be present. The gentlemen accepted. However, early the next morning the peace resolution appeared in the *Vorwärts*. At the suggestion of Under-Secretary of State Wahnschaffe, I had tried to prevent it, and had asked Deputy Südekum to exert his influence on *Vorwärts* in the same sense. The publication could, however, no longer be delayed. With that the Majority parties in the Reichstag had absolutely committed themselves. Further discussion could serve no useful purpose.

Doctor Michaelis became Imperial Chancellor. Herr von Valentini, Chief of the Emperor's Civil Cabinet, had given the Field-Marshal the names of several gentlemen of whom His Majesty would select one. Prince von Bülow, whom the Field-Marshal had on occasion suggested to the Emperor, was not among them. Count Hertling had refused, and declared he could not co-operate with the General Staff, at which I was not particularly surprised.

From correspondence I had had with him through the Bavarian War Minister, Von Hellingrath, I had unfortunately acquired the conviction that he and every one else in Munich regarded the General Staff in the same light as did the Wilhelmstrasse. Count Hertling became Chancellor later, and on his retirement he expressed to me his satisfaction at the hearty co-operation that had marked the relations between his office and General Headquarters. The Field-Marshal told Herr von Valentini that he should welcome any gentleman His Majesty might nominate. I was surprised to find that the authorities concerned did not have a successor to the Imperial Chancellor always in readiness, and that, in a matter of such decisive importance for its destiny, Germany had to live from hand to mouth.

The path of our internal development had not afforded scope for the growth of strong personalities. It was quite striking to see how the officer class, the members of which were always thought to be the most narrow-minded, had produced men of decision, while the civil official class, on the contrary, had, unfortunately, so conspicuously failed in this respect. Men who were prominent in public life kept out of the way, and followed their own professions. There may have been men of strong character in the Reichstag who could have guided the destiny of the country. The party system prevented their coming to the front. We were poor in men. Our political system had not produced new creative brains, and by its barrenness it pronounced its own sentence.

Our participation in further parliamentary discussions of the peace resolution at the Ministry of the Interior had been suggested by the new Imperial Chancellor. I requested him to dispense with our attendance. I was convinced that we had fulfilled our task the day before, and that it would only drag us into political controversy. The Chancellor persisted. As far as possible, we wished to support him in taking over his burdensome heritage, and therefore decided to comply. At the same time, we were desirous of showing Doctor Michaelis what value we attached to confidential collaboration with the Imperial Government. Both the Field-Marshal and I frequently wrote in this sense to the new Chancellor.

At the meeting we thought it most remarkable that the Majority parties based their demand for the peace resolution on the spirit of the country at the moment. Only by this means could the masses be rendered capable of holding out, if the wished-for peace did not materialize. This was a melancholy picture, far worse than I had expected. At the same time, the hope of a collapse of the enemy was expressed. The Russian Socialists were said to be desirous of forcing the other states of the Entente to stop the war. Otherwise no new points were raised.

As senior representative of the General Staff, the Field-Marshal again spoke against the resolution. I merely pointed out to the gentlemen sitting next to me that the resolution contained not a single allusion to the army. They therefore included a sentence expressing the thanks of the people to the army.

When we left I requested Deputy Erzberger to stop

the peace resolution. Beyond that I felt that my
presence had not been necessary at this discussion of
the question, and that I should have done better not
to go. I said so later, among others, to the Deputy
Müller-Meiningen.

From the tribune of the Reichstag the peace resolution went out into the world. As anticipated, it produced on our enemies no political effect whatever;
they took it as a confession of weakness. Bulgaria and
Turkey began to doubt our victory. Nor was the
effect in the country what the movers had hoped.

Instead of drawing the proper conclusion from the
refusal of the enemy, and strengthening the fighting
spirit of the people, the Government gave no thought
to the enemy, but entangled itself further and further
in the unfortunate idea of a peace by understanding
that could be had at any time. This was to prove the
curse of the peace resolution. The General Staff considered it a mistake from the military point of view.
But the Field-Marshal and I authorized the Imperial
Chancellor to announce our concurrence in his attitude
toward it, because he wished to avoid a conflict with
the majority of the Reichstag in the interests of the
prosecution of the war. And so we also shouldered
the responsibility for the resolution, which we thought
a lesser evil than internal confusion. To that pitch
had things come in Germany. We hoped the new
Imperial Chancellor might improve matters, even if
only gradually, and therefore thought it necessary to
meet his wishes.

In Berlin the deterioration of morale at home had
literally thrust itself upon my notice. I could not fold
my hands and watch the spirit of our people fall still
further and undermine our fighting capacity altogether.
Consequently, I laid before the new Chancellor the
request I had made to his predecessor, in the previous

December, that the direction of the press and the education of public opinion should be put into the hands of an authority under his immediate control. He promised to discuss this application at the end of August.

## VIII

The spirit of the people at home rendered action imperative. We had the best prospects of winning the war, but it was not over, and what we had won had to be kept. The popular state of mind jeopardized everything. The Quartermaster-General wrote on July 25, "It is certain that the Independent Social Democrats are carrying on an agitation in the army which is in the highest degree detrimental to discipline." That this was the case at that early date is corroborated by the leader of the Independent Social Democratic party, Ledebour.

Speaking at a conference of the Soldiers' and Workmen's Councils in connection with the events that took place November 5–9, 1918, he said:

"These four days up to November 9 were utilized by Scheidemann and his associates to reap the fruit of nearly two years' work by the Independents."

Another leader, Richard Müller, asserted, "The preparations for revolution were made as long ago as June 1916, though the object was at the time not so clearly apparent."

The Independent Socialists had definitely paved the way for revolution for a long time. The majority of the Reichstag, and a section of the press and the public, unfortunately, helped on this work, often unconsciously.

In July 1917 I had definitely come to the conclusion that under the circumstances General Headquarters could not remain inactive until the end of August. Whatever it could do to revive our spiritual capacity

for war must be undertaken at once. I was aware
that, so long as the Government did not itself take
energetic steps in this direction, whatever we did would
only be patchwork.

Nor, owing to the slowness and confusion of ideas
prevailing in the Civil Government, had I any guaranty
that the work would be done thoroughly, even if the
new Chancellor were to take charge of the work of
educating public opinion personally. It was not easy
for him either to carry through innovations and establish some entirely new machinery, since most of the
Government departments were dominated by the same
spirit which had hitherto radiated from the Imperial
Chancellor's office, or, at any rate, did not oppose it,
which was, in its effects, the same thing.

For a long time past I had been thinking over the
problem of diffusing a knowledge of the national aims
and needs in the army. It now became a burning
question.

In accordance with the proposal submitted to me by
Lieutenant-Colonel Nicolai, General Headquarters arranged for patriotic instruction in the field army. But
this was only a poor substitute for the work of enlightening public opinion at home—work which was done so
consistently and effectively in the Entente countries.

The importance of patriotic instruction, or, as we
first called it, the "work of enlightenment among the
troops," was summed up in the following sentences:

"The German Army, owing to the spirit which
animates it, is superior to its enemies and a powerful
support to its allies.

"At the beginning of the war the foundations of this
spirit were enthusiasm and the discipline which had
been inculcated during prolonged peace training. The
three years of war have changed and enlarged these
foundations. A comprehensible longing for home, fam-

ily, and calling may weaken its war resolution and take the edge off the will to hold out till the final victory is gained.

"The long duration of the war has also brought with it want and sacrifice in increasing measure, both at home and in the army.  The more these burdens oppress the spirit of the army the more must the foundations of fighting power be laid upon conviction, sense of duty, and definite resolve.

"To supply this need is the task of patriotic instruction in the army."

On September 15, 1917, I wrote:

"The enemy's determination to destroy us and the necessity for us to go on fighting are less obvious to the troops employed on the lines of communication, on garrison duty, and at home, than to the fighting forces themselves.  For this reason special attention must be given to the morale of the troops on the lines of communication, and patriotic instruction must be specially fostered among them.

"Attention is drawn in the General Instructions to the relationship between the home and the army. From the spiritual point of view and for the fulfilment of the national tasks, the people and the army are inseparable.  Consequently, great importance attaches to the cultivation of patriotic feeling among the people at home, a duty which is carried on in conjunction with the civil authorities.  The prosecution of this task must be regarded as one of the most important duties of the home commands."

I intentionally extended this patriotic instruction to the home territory, although in other respects I refrained from direct action there.  But I could not sit still and let everything slide before my very eyes. I expected to produce a stimulating effect, but received not the very slightest assistance from the civil authorities, although the Imperial Chancellor, Doctor Michaelis, and Secretary of State von Kühlmann recognized that some sort of machinery had to be created in order to raise the national spirit. An impression prevailed that nothing should be undertaken which might inflame national passions, for we had reached a point at which the development of national feeling was regarded as a damnable crime.

The War Minister agreed to the work of patriotic instruction being extended to the domain of the detached corps commanders. In the summer of 1918, at his request, he was accorded wide powers in this respect.

As the first object of instruction I recommended discussion of the causes of the war, Germany's economic development and its importance, the consequences of a lost war, especially for the German workman, and the necessity for continuing the struggle until we had broken the will of our enemies and created a safe foundation for further economic development.

I further laid stress on our justifiable hope of final victory, and the need for leadership and authority on the one hand and subordination on the other.

"Consideration of self must be suppressed in view of the great common aim. Strikes endanger the success of the war and are paid for by the blood of the troops. Dreams of peace prolong the war, and so does discontent. Unity at home makes us strong; everything else is weakening."

I designated as our object in the war the "safeguarding of our future," and closed with the words, "Army and people must unite in backing up the leaders of the Empire with all their strength until peace is finally concluded."

These instructions were based on the military situation at the time. They were the natural countermeasure to the wretched ideas prevailing at home. I believed in our final victory, and feared disaster. I did all I could to show the people how serious was the situation without still further depressing them. I set great value on the moral factor, like many others, but among them were men who designedly undermined the fighting capacity of the German people and with it the discipline in the army. Between these two extremes stood the great bulk of the nation, who had no conception of the spirit of their own people nor of that of the enemy.

Again and again the War Press Office directed the authorities responsible for the work of enlightenment to describe the dangers of a lost war.

Patriotic instruction was to be kept away from all party intrigue. In this I included attack or defense of the peace resolution and discussion of our war aims. I tolerated no departure from this principle. But I had no objection to superior officers expressing their own opinion on war aims to their men in a calm and objective manner, provided the latter approached them on the subject in a spirit of confidence.

It was a bad sign that in October this subject of instruction was approached in the Reichstag solely from the point of view of narrow party politics, while its real significance was misunderstood. The regulations for the instruction were closely examined, and nothing objectionable was found in them. I was curious to see whether any demand for Government action would be put forward, or whether it might feel itself called upon to take up the matter. But the Reichstag was content merely to criticize; useful work was no part of its program. The Government was glad to have steered past an obvious reef. But the public remained ignorant of the dangers which menaced it.

There were still men in Germany who had correctly
gaged the enemy's mind. They desired to strengthen
the fighting spirit and founded the Patriotic party
(*Vaterlandspartei*). I had no connection with it. But
its work was most welcome to me in the interest of the
war; that their objects went too far did not matter.
The storms of war will see to it that no trees grow
up to the sky.

I began to hope that the Patriotic party would at
last achieve some good, but my hope was of short
duration, for it was soon dragged into the orbit of
internal politics. Well, we were going in for internal
politics instead of war politics. Its name may have
been unfortunate, and various circumstances attending
its foundation may have been detrimental to the cause,
but its energy was broken by its opponents and by the
Government. In this Count Hertling not only followed the lead of the Majority parties; to my horror,
it coincided with his own private opinions. Instead
of providing allies for those who were carrying on the
war, the Government took away those they had without filling their place itself. Such was the state of
affairs. The Lord in Heaven forsook His German
nation because it had forsaken itself.

I attached importance to gaining a personal knowledge of the working of patriotic instruction. Accordingly, I arranged for the Propaganda Officer at Saarbrücken to give a lecture at Kreuznach of the same
nature as he was delivering in public. The lecturer,
Lieutenant Schmetzer, described the effects of an
unsuccessful war on our working-classes most effectively.
He showed that they would be deprived of work and
food unless they became the slaves of international
capital. I can only say that all of us who heard the
lecture were deeply impressed. I considered it to be
of general interest, especially for the Secretary of

State for Foreign Affairs, and had it repeated in his presence. Unfortunately, the hopes I had based on it were not realized.

It was not to be expected that the regimental officers, particularly the juvenile company commanders, who were fully occupied with their daily duties, would display a sufficient grasp of the possibilities and requirements of patriotic instruction. I therefore wished it to be directed by officers who were in touch with the state of feeling both in the army and at home, and who were particularly qualified to enter into the way of thinking of the men at the front. They in turn were to get into touch with suitable officers, non-commissioned officers, and men, and obtain the assistance of men from home. We were confronted with an entirely novel task, and had to overcome suspicion and numerous difficulties in the army itself. Nor was it easy to find suitable propaganda officers. Much time was bound to elapse before all was working smoothly.

Even after patriotic instruction was instituted, I continued to receive reports from the army headquarters as to the spirit and feeling of the army, and made use of every opportunity of obtaining an insight into its state of mind. Incidentally, I heard that the chaplains were fulfilling their responsible office with devotion and ability, and afforded valuable support to the troops in the trenches.

In the corps commands at home, the work was naturally even more difficult than in the army. There also men of all parties helped us. The Government, however, stood absolutely aloof.

The soldier was particularly concerned about his future after the war. This was natural, considering the economic conditions at home, the ever-increasing selfishness, and the ruthless profiteering. While I was still Chief of Staff to the Commander-in-chief in the East,

at a time when conditions at home had not yet becom
acute, I had, by means of communications to the arm
newspapers, endeavored to inform the troops of wha
was being done for disabled men and for dependents
I took much interest in these questions, and observe
with regret that the people at home showed less an
less gratitude toward the disabled, and that the feeling
of the latter were very often not adequately considered
The question was one that concerned the whole Ger
man people, and should not have been exploited fo
party purposes.

The care for the soldier and for the dependents c
the fallen was to me of vital importance. It could bes
be assured by final victory, which alone would plac
it upon a sound foundation. But I wanted to do some
thing more personal than that. A fund for the dis
abled was started in May 1918, in which I collaborate
and which at that time was named after me. Th
Ludendorff Fund was a brilliant success. It wa
originated by an enthusiastic German lady, Fräulei
Emma Tscheuschner, who was most energetically as
sisted in her great work by Director Henrich, and i
raised far more than 150,000,000 marks ($37,500,000)
a hitherto unequaled result. During the revolutio
it was renamed the "National Fund." Did the na
tional delegates and the first Government of the Ger
man Republic object to my name being connected wit
a charitable institution which, mainly on account o
my name, had brought in such great sums, and b
which so many disabled men are benefited? I leav
this action to be judged by humanity and by the dis
abled who enjoy well-earned benefits from the "Luden
dorff Fund," should they ever hear my name.

What has happened to the fund under its new nam
I do not know in detail. It is not in accordance wit
my ideas that advances have been made from it t

ake the place of State aid. That was not the intention.
I wanted to help, and it goes through me now like a
knife to see disabled soldiers, who are unable to earn
their living, going begging. That also, however, passes
or gratitude and the national sense of duty.

It seemed to me a particularly important branch of
he care of the disabled to discover how brave men
who had lost limbs could be re-educated so as to recover their joy in life and work, and thus be reinstated
n their former surroundings and given back to the
country. All endeavors toward this object, as well as
he progress made in the manufacture of artificial limbs,
. followed with active interest.

Care for the soldier included not only provision for
he dependents and the disabled, but also arrangements
or insuring economic security after the war for the
ound men who wished to work. That was a duty of
he State and the people at home toward the class
hat had unselfishly done so much for them. Soldiers
ught to have been given cheap houses and cheap land,
vith proprietary rights, in which speculation should
aave been forbidden to come in. This, of course,
could be effected only very gradually, and should not
nvolve harshness to the original owner nor loss of his
ights. I was much impressed by the opinions of the
and-reformer, Mr. Damaschke, on the need for reduc-
ng the cost of housing, especially for the working-classes,
nd for excluding profiteering, and also by his historical
reatment of the subject. The information he gave
bout the scarcity of houses after the war of 1870—71
eemed to me of the greatest importance. General
Headquarters approached the Imperial Chancellor,
pointed out the influence of the housing question on the
fter-effects of the war as regards national recuperation,
nd requested him to bring in a bill to safeguard the
ights and properties of soldiers. We also asked that

means might be provided for building small house and for securing them against speculation. General Headquarters induced the Chief Sanitary Officer Generalstabsarzt von Schjerning, to take an interest in the whole policy of distribution of the population to which he and his assistants, especially Oberstabsarzt Doctor Hochheimer, devoted themselves with great enthusiasm. Their ideas were embodied in a memoir which was also sent to the Imperial Chancellor.

After the war I wanted to bring up a contented generation, capable of self-defense. In the Baltic littoral I wanted to create a settlement area for soldiers and for the large number of Germans who were expected to re-emigrate from Russia. The vast uninhabited and untilled areas in those parts provided room for German settlements without crowding the inhabitants. Alsace Lorraine also was to be used for settlements, and in this way this ancient German territory would at last regain its German character. A wide field of labor of the greatest national importance was before us General Hahndorff took up these questions in a far-sighted manner. Co-operative settlement-companies assisted by the most experienced men in Germany were started and set to work at once. At that time people got wildly excited about the settlement-companies. The soundness of the fundamental idea was proved later. One of the first measures of the republican Government was to draft a settlement-law, of which the guiding principles were taken from the edicts for Courland drafted by Prof. Ludwig Bernhard on behalf of General Headquarters. Its practical application is now impossible, owing to the extraordinary rise in prices and to the difficulty of obtaining building materials. In the matter, also, of helping the war victims, the revolutionists have watered down the original schemes; they have taken instead of given.

Money has been wasted, but the deserving soldier got none of it.

We also provided for the students and advanced school-boys who were on active service, and whose future became more and more precarious as time went on. I hoped that the assistance afforded to them would prove of special benefit to the country. The Prussian Minister of Education, Doctor Schmidt, felt strongly on this subject and took the lead in the work.

## IX

Besides the actual conduct of the war and the big questions connected with it, I had a great many other duties to attend to at Kreuznach; they were apparently unimportant, but yet formed part of the whole process. Life had settled down to the same sort of routine as at other headquarters. The Field-Marshal and I, as well as other officers, lived in a villa which had once formed the home of the Emperor William I, that great monarch and judge of men, under whose scepter Germany's dream of union had been realized. Our office was in the Oranienhof. The distance to it was short, and my regular walks to and fro afforded an opportunity to many kindly disposed people who wished to please me by their greetings and at times by gifts of flowers. Otherwise I led a secluded existence, because—I know men.

Every day I went for exercise to the "Rose-garden" above the town, or perhaps merely into the grounds near the Oranienhof, rarely anywhere else. In the spring of 1918 this beautiful *Rosengarten* and the garden in front of the Oranienhof were destroyed in a few hours by tearing floods. As the revolution passed over Germany in the autumn, so the flood passed over Kreuznach in the spring. What had taken the townspeople many years and an infinite amount of trouble was demolished in a few hours. It happened very quickly. The clearing up of the gardens and houses and the removal of the dirt and mud began at once, but it took a long, long time, and traces of the flood remained everywhere. Was that an omen?

We had many visitors who came and went, and in spite of my enormous burden of work I had to find time to spare for all of them. I had also to confer with the representatives of the Prussian and Bavarian War Ministers on the maintenance and increase of the fighting capacity of the army. The feeling at home and reinforcements were matters which never disappeared from the agenda. Questions relating to the future of the army were also dealt with. Ideas on disarmament were as prevalent as those on peace by understanding, and as little in accord with the existing state of affairs. To disarm before changing the whole existing order of the world seemed to me, as a practical man, just as impossible as it did to the democratic Governments of England, France, and the United States. Food and other problems of the home country often came before me. In a word, all the fundamental elements of warfare were continuously dealt with, revised, and, as far as I was able, organized to meet our requirements. Applications for what we could not supply from our own resources were submitted to the Imperial Government; with what sad results I have shown in reference to our most pressing need, that of arousing the warlike ardor of the German people.

As regards war-policy, I had mainly to deal with the Dobrudja, the territory under the Commander-in-chief in the East, and Alsace-Lorraine.

In the Dobrudja the struggle between the Bulgarians and the German lines-of-communication headquarters continued, with all its many side-issues. In June the

King of Bulgaria came to Kreuznach with Radoslavoff, who now tried to get the lines-of-communication area placed under Bulgarian administration, which amounted to his obtaining the Dobrudja for Bulgaria. This led once more to a great deal of argument. I raised the question of Germany exploiting the rich coal-fields of Serbia for the common benefit of the Quadruple Alliance during the war; some notes were made, but nothing more was done. It was a waste of time while my thoughts were so fully engaged with events at the front. Owing to the enormous restraint I had often to impose upon myself, this extra work was an intolerable thing to expect of any man. So stern a course of self-education would do many people good. In the present case General Headquarters succeeded in defeating the Bulgarian project, or at any rate in shelving the question indefinitely. Even now the Government failed to induce M. Radoslavoff to recall the representative of the United States from Sofia, assuming, that is, that it really made another serious attempt to do so.

I had left the territory of the Commander-in-chief in the East at the end of August 1916. The administrative system I had introduced was adapted only to military needs; it continued to work well in 1917. Its operations had now to be more developed on the political side.

It was to be expected that the proclamation of the Kingdom of Poland on November 5 would have a depressing effect on the Lithuanians and would produce a Pan-Polish agitation in the territory under the Commander-in-chief in the East. The guiding principles laid down for an impartial treatment of questions of nationality were by themselves no longer sufficient.

At my request Secretary of State von Jagow published an official announcement in the papers of the occupied territory, with the object of calming the

Lithuanians. This announcement appeared simultaneously with the proclamation of the Kingdom of Poland. The Lithuanian movement, which had hitherto emanated exclusively from Switzerland, now began to be manifest in the country itself, and the Pan-Polish movement, of which the object was the union of Lithuania with Poland, grew at the same time. We had no reason to permit these agitations. Poland had clearly shown, in the matter of raising the army, that it was merely a political war-profiteer. We could no longer consider anything but our own future, and the dangers which might threaten us from Poland. In accordance with our previous policy, the Commander-in-chief in the East was therefore instructed that any strengthening of the Poles, which could only come about at the cost of other nations, was undesirable.

The Lithuanians entered the lists against the Poles by expressing their feelings and wishes more forcibly. In March 1917 they submitted their views on the subject to the Commander-in-chief in the East. The latter now sent in a memorandum on the methods to be followed by German policy in the territory under his administration. We passed the memorandum on to the Imperial Chancellor, with the request that he might give a definite decision as to the policy to be adopted in regard to the nationalities in the area administered by the Commander - in - chief in the East. General Headquarters considered it out of the question to pursue a purely Polish policy. The establishment of a Poland that would surround East and West Prussia was incompatible with the security of Germany. German rule in the territory under the Commander-in-chief in the East must be based on the Lithuanians and the White Ruthenes. At the same time we suggested a conference on these questions, the early solution of which I very greatly desired. In this, as in all other matters, I maintained that the Imperial Chancellor must lay down the guiding principles of policy, with the sole limitation that they must be compatible with military security. The execution of the political instructions was in this case the duty of General Headquarters and of the Commander-in-chief in the East.

On April 5 we had the first conference with representatives of the Imperial Chancellor, under the presidency of the Quartermaster-General, General Hahndorff, at Bingen.

The Field-Marshal and I considered that the territory administered by the Commander-in-chief in the East should finally be divided into a Duchy of Courland and a Grand Duchy of Lithuania, both with the further object of adjusting their respective interests, in the closest relationship to Germany, and uniting them under the personal sovereignty of His Majesty, either in his capacity as King of Prussia or Emperor of Germany. In this way Germany would gain a military defense against further surprise attacks by Russia, and also land for the settlement of our troops after the war.

The boundaries of Courland were already fixed.

The delimitation of Lithuania was difficult. Generally speaking, the mass of the Lithuanian people, though interspersed with big Polish landowners, lives north of the line Dvinsk-Vilna-Olita-Suwalki. South of it they radiate into the country of the White Ruthenes, which, however, is permeated by Poles and very Polish in spirit. Vilna, Grodno, and other towns were Polish. The solid mass of Polish population only began at Bialystok. Jews were to be found all through Lithuania. Germans lived mainly on the East Prussian border. In the territory under the Commander-in-chief in the East, south of Courland, the Lithuanians were slightly the more numerous, and so formed a counterpoise to the Poles. They were menaced by them in precisely the same way as we were on our eastern borders, and so were our natural allies, whom we must seek to strengthen and attach to ourselves by every possible means. On April 5 my argument did not go as far as this. My immediate object was to obtain the Imperial Chancellor's consent to a pronounced pro-Lithuanian policy. Nothing definite resulted from this conference.

On April 23 a second conference took place at Kreuznach. After the outbreak of the revolution, Russia had made extensive promises to the Lithuanians. Now even the Imperial Chancellor admitted the necessity of formulating a clear line of policy with regard to them. On April 30 a general agreement was reached to the effect that in the whole of the territory under the Commander-in-chief in the East our action was to be based on the following principles: Everything German was to receive favorable treatment, but even the merest appearance of forcible Germanization, of which I had never approved, was to be avoided. The word "Germanize" has always been abhorrent to me. The Lithuanians were to be won over by all possible means, and the White Ruthenes in the northern district to be brought more in touch with them. In consideration of the Poles the latter object was not to be pursued in the south.

Polish propaganda was to be prevented, but without coming into conflict with the policy of the Governor-General of Warsaw by combating it in public.

The enunciation of these principles did not finally commit the Imperial Government, but it did enable us to follow a settled policy with regard to the Lithuanians. On May 30 the Commander-in-chief in the East, in agreement with the Government, published a decree permitting the formation of a Lithuanian Confidential

Council, in which the Lithuanians were to form the majority, the other nationalities being represented by single members. The Confidential Council was intended to be the official channel by which the wishes of the Lithuanians were to be communicated to the administration.

The general conditions made it more and more imperative clearly to define our intentions in the eastern territories. The catchword "peace without annexations" and "self-determination of small nations," which had been invented by hostile propaganda, were likely to lead to a solution of the Lithuanian problem which would be detrimental to German interests. It opened the way for the Poles to become supreme in districts where they had not hitherto been so.

On July 21, when the Imperial Chancellor, Doctor Michaelis, had just attained his exalted position, General Headquarters approached the Foreign Office with the proposal to pursue a policy of local nationalism in Courland and Lithuania, that in Lithuania being definitely Lithuanian in character. We made a final attempt to carry out our ideas with regard to these two countries. In both of them "Local Councils" were to be instituted.

On July 25 Secretary of State Zimmermann agreed to our policy being initiated at once. Our success in Galicia had cleared up the situation still further. The Secretary of State merely dissuaded us, "in view of the impossibility of foreseeing the future," from "binding ourselves publicly, or even only mentally, to the definite project of a personal union." Later on, however, he declared that he "by no means intended definitely to decline that form of organization." When the Government would publicly announce this policy was its own affair; I was content with having obtained its consent to a definite policy. I expressed my satisfaction at our having reached an agreement as to the immediate policy to be followed in the territory under the Commander-in-chief in the East. The latter received instructions early in August with a view to the formation of "Local Councils."

I hoped that, with the necessary firmness and perseverance, we should attain our object, and that by this arrangement the Lithuanians would obtain their rights better than by joining either Russia or Poland. Competent judges among them had perceived that they could maintain their nationality only with the aid of Germany. Among these were the clergy, whose superior intelligence, and the fact that we had promoted the return of the Bishop of Kovno, made them well disposed toward us. The Lithuanian democracy believed in the power of the catchword "self-determination," although, in the case of the mixed population of the country, it could not possibly be applied with justice. Being tied up in political theories, they did not see the Polish danger which actually menaces their land.

The third problem which occupied me in the summer of 1917 was that of Alsace-Lorraine. General Headquarters could of course approach it only from that point of view which it was its duty to represent, namely, the military one. The impressions I had gained as a brigade commander at Strasburg, and the many sad experiences of this war relating to Alsace-Lorraine, had fully convinced me that its position as Imperial territory (*Reichland*) was an anomaly which did not accord with the interests of the inhabitants. There was far too much meddling in its affairs by the Reichstag. The policy followed was weak and ill-defined and could not satisfy anybody. I strove for a union of the country with Prussia, which by no means involved "Prussianizing" its inhabitants. Prussia had absorbed

the Rhine Province, of which the population had
retained its typical character and developed vigorously;
why should not the same path lead to the happiness
of the people of Alsace-Lorraine, who are by character
and economic conditions closely allied to Germany?
Other solutions also seemed possible.  Whatever happened, it was necessary to make certain of insuring
unity of command over the troops on the frontier, of
the frontier protection system, and of the railways.
On carefully examining the question it was found to be
very difficult to achieve this end by any other than the
"Prussian" solution.

From the military point of view I expressed the
opinion that the granting of autonomy was the least
satisfactory solution.  But, whichever one was to be
adopted, the fundamental principle was really to oppose
the unjustifiable French influence and to replace it by
the German; in my view this involved the employment
of German clergy and civil officials.  The clergy was
still recruited from French institutions, as also were
some bodies of Sisters and female teachers.  This was
really scandalous.  Was not Germany just as well
able to provide clergy and teachers?  The civil officials
ought also to have been imbued with German feeling.
There was no need to select the notorious "East
Elbians," who had done so much for Germany's greatness, but whose natural hardness might possibly render
them unsuitable for Alsace-Lorraine.  The Rhine Province and South Germany could meet the demand.

Finally, French property in Alsace-Lorraine ought
to be transferred to German possession, a transaction
which the Entente had declared to be in accordance
with the usage of war.  In this way we should also
acquire land for settling German soldiers.

The attack upon private property was one of the
abominations of this war.  In 1870–71 Germans had

been deported from France, an action which was at the time considered a special offense against international law, but France had left their private property untouched. Very soon after this war began, England had proceeded to liquidate German businesses, and by so doing had made plain why it had joined in the war. It wanted to remove the inconvenient German competition throughout the world, and its example was followed by the other Powers of the Entente. The black-lists served the same purpose; they were also intended partly to increase the severity of the blockade. They caused the greatest suffering among the neutral countries, who said nothing. The war of nations produced ever greater abominations.

It seemed to me necessary that the highest military and civil authorities should be in agreement as to the future of Alsace-Lorraine. Field-Marshal Duke Albrecht of Württemberg, who had represented the military authority in Alsace-Lorraine since the spring of 1917, required clear instructions. I therefore suggested to the Government that a conference should be held. It took place. Nothing definite was achieved.

# FIGHTING IN FLANDERS AND THE COLLAPSE OF RUSSIA, SUMMER AND AUTUMN 1917

Battles in Flanders, at Verdun, the Eleventh Isonzo Battle, the Occupation of Riga—Preparations for the Offensive in Italy—The Third Flanders Battle—The Battle Around the Laffaux Salient and Cambrai—The Campaign in Italy, 1917—The Macedonian and Turkish Theaters of War—The Campaign Against the Baltic Islands and the Armistice in the East—Peace Questions—The Internal Condition of Germany—Reasons for the Peace Negotiations in the East.

I

FOLLOWING on the prelude in the Wytschaete salient on June 7 the battle of Flanders began on July 31, after an artillery preparation lasting several days. This formed the second great strategic action of the Entente in 1917; it was its bid for final victory and for our submarine base in Flanders. The fighting spread over large portions of the Western front, the Italian and Macedonian fronts, and finally as far as Palestine.

The fighting on the Western front became more severe and costly than any the German Army had yet experienced. In spite of this, the Western armies could not be reinforced from the East, for there, at last, heavy work was to be done. Russia and Rumania were to be defeated, in order to enable us to force a decision in the West in 1918 by means of an attack on France combined with the submarine war, in case the latter should not achieve the desired result by itself. The situation required that I myself should undertake a great responsibility, so great that it shook even me. However, I had to do it, for in 1918 the dangers might otherwise become too much for us. It was, of course, obvious that General Headquarters did not withhold from the armies of the West a single man who was not urgently needed elsewhere. During the further course of events the German Crown Prince often told me not to let the tension in the West become too great. I knew well that General Headquarters, in imposing this enormous strain on the Western front, had in view the possible situation in 1918. I saw what the danger would be if the submarine war did not work, after all. But I am not one of those who give way in the face of dangers; I was put into my position in order to overcome them and to employ every means to prevent a great misfortune overtaking our country.

In the East we had to keep on hammering at Russia in order to bring about the fall of the Colossus. While the operations in eastern Galicia were yet in progress, I had telephoned to Colonel Hoffmann to ask his view of a passage of the Dvina above Riga. For that he, of course, wanted troops, which were at the time still engaged in Galicia. The Colonel was all for it at once, and the Commander-in-chief in the East issued the first preparatory orders without delay. In the first days of August it became evident that our advance would have to be stopped in eastern Galicia and the Bukovina, and that the offensive could not be resumed there until the railways had been repaired; he was therefore instructed to carry out the passage of the Dvina. At the time I believed it might take place about August 20, and hoped that some troops would soon become available from there. By the middle or end of September, after the repair of the railways south of the Dniester, I thought we might be able to com-

nence operations from the Bukovina across the Sereth
nto Moldavia. For that purpose the troops would
have to be railed back again from Riga to the south.

From July 31 till well into September was a period of
tremendous anxiety. On July 31 the English, assisted
by a few French divisions on their left, had attacked on
a front of about fifteen miles. They had employed
such quantities of artillery and ammunition as had
been rare, even in the West. At many points along
the whole front the enemy had penetrated with tanks.
Cavalry divisions were in readiness to push through.
With the assistance of the counter-attack divisions
(Eingreifsdivision) the Fourth Army, whose Chief of
Staff was now Colonel von Loszberg, succeeded in
checking the hostile success and localizing its effect.
But, besides a loss of from one and a quarter to two
and a half miles of ground along the whole front, it
caused us very considerable losses in prisoners and
stores and a heavy expenditure of reserves.

In August fighting broke out on many parts of the
Western front. In Flanders the Entente attacked
again on the 10th, although it must have suffered
severely on July 31. August 10 was a success for us,
but on the 16th we sustained another great blow. The
English pressed us beyond Poelcapelle, and even with
an extreme exertion of strength on our part they could
be pushed back only a short distance! During the
following days fighting continued with diminished
intensity. The 22d was another day of heavy fighting.
August 25 concluded the second phase of the Flanders
battle. It had cost us heavily.

Further to the south several English divisions broke
into our position north of Lens on August 15, and
captured an important height.

On the old battle-field of Arras on both banks of the
Scarpe a hostile attack failed on the 9th.

Toward the end of August the Siegfried line nor'
of St.-Quentin was unsuccessfully attacked by tl
French. It was not a serious affair.

Subsidiary French attacks were made on the rid;
of the Chemin des Dames.

The main French effort took place at Verdun c
August 21 and 22. The Fifth Army was not surprise
As had been provided for weeks beforehand, certa
areas, such as the Talou ridge, were abandoned :
time. The assault, which was not accompanied l
tanks, again penetrated far into our positions. C
the left bank, close to the Meuse, one division ha
failed, nor had we been fortunate on the right banl
and yet both here and in Flanders everything possib
had probably been done to avoid failure. The 21;
and 26th also brought success to the enemy and lo;
to us. The French Army was once more capable c
the offensive. It had quickly overcome its depression
Just at this time the statesmen in Paris put forwar
peace conditions which did not accord with the militar
situation.

The costly August battles in Flanders and at Verdu
imposed a heavy strain on the Western troops. I
spite of all the concrete protection they seemed mor
or less powerless under the enormous weight of th
enemy's artillery. At some points they no longe
displayed that firmness which I, in common with th
local commanders, had hoped for.

The enemy contrived to adapt himself to our method
of employing counter-attack divisions. There were n
more attacks with unlimited objective, such as Genera
Nivelle had made in the Aisne-Champagne battle. H
was ready for our counter-attacks, and prepared fo
them by exercising restraint in the exploitation c
success. In other directions, of course, this suited u
very well.

FIG. 21. BATTLE IN FLANDERS, 1917

I myself was being put to a terrible strain. The
state of affairs in the West appeared to prevent the
execution of our plans elsewhere. Our wastage had
been so high as to cause grave misgivings, and had
exceeded all expectation. The attack on the Dvina
had to be postponed repeatedly. Indeed, it became
a question whether we could continue to bear the
responsibility of retaining those divisions in the East.

The Crown Prince was not alone in his anxiety

EXPLANATION

▬▬▬ German line before the French attack on August 20, 1917.

◀▬ ▬ ▬ German line at the end of August 1917.

FIG. 22.  BATTLES BEFORE VERDUN, AUGUST 1917

several chiefs of staff of very cool judgment shook
their heads. But, in estimating the strength of our
enemies, I always said to myself that in this war the
only alternatives were victory or defeat, that their
determination to destroy us made any intermediate
solution impossible. In spite of all, I was convinced
that the Western front would stand even more battering, though fate might have even greater trials in
store for it. This was another case where human wisdom failed.

General Headquarters allowed the Dvina attack

FIG. 23.  THE ELEVENTH BATTLE OF ISONZO, AUG. AND SEPT. 1917

from which it expected great results, owing to th
proximity of Petrograd, to proceed, although it did no
intend to push it very far. From the purely strategica
point of view it was intended merely as a means to
wholesale improvement of our position, which woul
enable us to economize troops.

The offensive in Moldavia was still kept in view a
a second decisive stroke. But this operation, whicl
was delayed by difficulties in railway construction
came to nothing.

At the end of August the eleventh battle of the Isonz
had begun on a front of forty-five miles and prove(
successful for the Italians. Early in September th
fighting was continued with determination. The Ital
ians were again successful. The Austro-Hungariar
Armies had indeed held their ground, but their losse
in the Carso Mountains had been so heavy and the\
were so shaken that the responsible military and po
litical authorities of the Dual Monarchy were con
vinced that they would not be able to stand a con
tinuation of the battle and a twelfth attack on the
Isonzo. The Austrian Army on the Italian front needec
stiffening by German troops. We could not carr\
our attack into Moldavia, and to throw in Germar
divisions into Italy for a pure defensive was not a
measure which accorded with our critical situation
General Headquarters had to take steps to carry out
some offensive, if possible even a whole operation, sc
as to bring about an improvement in the general situation somehow.

To abandon the operation in Moldavia was a disappointment. It seemed to me more important than
one in Italy. It might, considering the situation in
Russia, prove a decisive step toward ending the war
on the Eastern front. It could not then be seen that
this object could be attained without considerable

military effort, owing to the disintegration of the Russian state and army. The attack on Italy might, no doubt, become effective and immediately relieve the Western front; but whether it would, in conjunction with the shortage of coal, produce a crisis in Italy could not be foretold. The general opinion was that it would not.

In spite of the difference in the value of the possible results in the middle of September, it became necessary to decide for the attack on Italy in order to prevent the collapse of Austria-Hungary. We had now only to examine how Russia, after the attack on Riga, could be damaged further in a way likely to accelerate her dissolution. Moltke's saying, "Strategy is a system of expedients," remains as true as ever.

At the end of August and early in September I had much to bear. I had a great deal of business with Berlin. On a journey to the West I met with a railway accident. Another train ran into the coach in which I was dining with my officers, and overturned it. But that caused only a momentary fright. A severe blow was the death of my eldest son, or, I should say, the eldest son of my wife by her first marriage. I have no children of my own. I was deeply attached to my son, as to all my stepchildren, and had seen him at Lille only a short time before, fresh and strong, and full of enthusiasm for his profession and his country.

He was shot down over the Channel. Not till weeks afterward did we find his body washed up on the Dutch coast.

This high tension was followed by a period of quiet, commencing in Flanders at the end of August, at Verdun and in Italy at the beginning and middle of September. How long it would last no one knew.

Between August 30 and September 8 the Entente had also made heavy attacks on several parts of the

Macedonian front, but without success. Local engagements in the mountains west of Lake Ochrida had an important bearing on the main operations in so much as they forced the Bulgarians to extend their line.

In Rumania there was some fighting between the Sereth and the frontier mountains. Otherwise there was but little activity on the whole Eastern front right

EXPLANATION

German line before the attack on Sept. 1, 1917.
German line on Sept. 1, 1917.
German position after the attack.

FIG. 24.   RIGA, 1917

up to Riga. A local attack by German troops near Czernowitz was intended merely to rectify our line, which was urgently necessary.

The front between the Carpathians and Tarnopol was now thinned out in order to obtain reserves for the next operations.

On September 1 we effected the passage of the Dvina at Uxküll, southeast of Riga, opposite a strong enemy position. Helped by various superior commands, General von Hutier, commanding the Eighth Army, and his Chief of Staff, General von Sauberzweig, had made very thorough preparations. The passage was successful. The Russians had evacuated the bridge-head on the left bank in time, and, with few exceptions, offered but slight resistance here also. I breathed again when the blow had at last fallen. We soon halted the Eighth Army, and behind the farthest point of its advance it at once set about fortifying a position on the shortest line between the Dvina and the Gulf of Riga. Two divisions left immediately for the Western front in order to relieve others for Italy. The Eastern front had to send considerable forces there. In spite of our intention to strike at Italy and the extremely critical situation in the West, where fighting might flame up again at any moment, the Commander-in-chief in the East still retained a certain surplus in order to keep Russia busy. It was a poor substitute for the offensive in Moldavia, but still better than nothing. If, after the event, I am charged with dispersion of force, I must put up with it. Things do not always work according to plan—and I achieved my object.

## II

Apart from the lack of vigor shown by the troops, the defect of the Austro-Hungarian offensive from the Tyrol in 1916 was that the forces with which it was undertaken were too weak for the point at which it was made, and that the army on the Isonzo did not attack at the same time. From a military point of view it was tempting to dally once more with these ideas and possibilities, but in September 1917 I had to base our plan of campaign on the fact that the Austro-Hungarian Armies were very exhausted at the moment and that Germany could not spare more than six or eight divisions. With such forces an attack from the Tyrol would have been absurd. They could achieve results only by striking at a point where the enemy was particularly weak and not expecting attack. If, furthermore, the selected point admitted of a strategic exploitation of the break-through, as had been the case in eastern Galicia, every immediate requirement would be met. Further developments would have to be left to careful preparation and the decision of arms.

The front between Flitsch and Canale was suitable for attack, although the difficulties of the ground seemed almost insurmountable and the communications on the Austrian side were as bad as could be imagined. But the Italians themselves were not expecting to be attacked there, and were holding the line with weak forces. If we succeeded in surprising them and bursting over the mountains north of Cividale toward Udine the Italian line on the Isonzo would totter.

We could now begin to consider the operation itself. The warmest supporter of the plan was Lieutenant-Colonel Wetzell. It was first necessary to determine whether the attack on this front was possible at all, and if so, how it could be made. With the consent of General von Arz, Gen. Krafft von Dellmensingen, who was then Chief of the General Staff in the army group of Duke Albrecht, and Major Freiherr von Willisen were ordered to reconnoiter the ground. Their report showed the attack to be feasible and formed the basis of further decisions by General Headquarters. I now gave myself up completely to this new great task.

General von Krafft and Major von Willisen had also made some excellent suggestions for the equipment of the troops. On this subject General Headquarters at once communicated with the Austrian General Headquarters, who were asked particularly to provide pack transport and mountain artillery for the German formations. Both before and during the war the German Army was often in difficulties for want of mountain artillery, and a certain amount was provided. But, of course, what we had was insufficient for this campaign. Austria-Hungary was perfectly well able to help, and there was no reason why we should always provide everything ourselves.

The selection of the troops was most important. The first to be chosen were units like the Alpine Corps, which had gained experience in mountain warfare in the Carpathians, and were suitably equipped. These were the 117th and 200th Infantry Divisions, at that time in Bukovina, which were to be set free by the Austro-Hungarian troops in that area, taking over their front.

Generally speaking, General Headquarters wanted to employ divisions which had fought only on the Western front, or had suffered particularly severely in operations in other theaters. But, owing to the importance of the Western front, and the small numbers that could be drawn from it, the wishes of many formations to fight in other localities, and be employed in an offensive, could be met only to a small extent. The choice now fell upon the 5th, 12th, and 26th (Württemberg) Divisions and a few Jäger Battalions, which were later formed into the German Jäger Division. Six to seven divisions were made available against Italy; two were taken from the Western front, where they were replaced by the two from Riga.

In addition, the East was to release two more divisions, which, if the situation at all permitted, were to be sent later to Italy, otherwise to the West.

The divisions detailed were also provided with German formations of artillery, engineers, trench mortars, aeroplanes, balloons, signals, motor and horse transport, and lines-of-communication establishments; everything, in a word, which an army needs. The troops were given such mountain equipment as was necessary by the Intendant-Generals and their respective War Ministries. Training in mountain warfare began at once. The artillery required special training in shooting in mountainous districts.

It was arranged with General von Arz that the Germans, with a contingent of Austro-Hungarian troops, were to form the Fourteenth Army, under General Otto von Below, who had hitherto commanded the Sixth Army. General von Krafft became his Chief of Staff, and Major von Willisen joined the Fourteenth Army Headquarters as Senior General Staff Officer.

In the Sixth Army, General von Below was succeeded by General von Quest, a man of clear judgment and a resolute leader. In the army group of Duke Albrecht, General von Krafft was replaced by Colonel Heye, who had for a long time served with distinction as Chief of Staff to General von Woyrsch.

The preparations for the operation had involved a great deal of business with the Austro-Hungarian General Headquarters at Baden. General von Waldstätten was often at Kreuznach. From the outset it was agreed that the German Army should make the main attack, on which everything depended. It was therefore assembled at the decisive point on both sides of Tolmino. The German Jägers were moved into the Flitsch Valley.

The Emperor Charles wished the operation to be conducted by the Austro-Hungarian High Command. I had, however, a sufficient voice for our own General Staff through our preparations, the interspersion of a German army command, and a system of telephonic communications.

Unfortunately, it was clear that the operation could not begin until after the middle of October.

The operations in the East continued in September. The bridge-head of Jakobstadt was captured on the 21st by a powerful and well-planned attack. It was to be followed by the capture of the islands of Ösel, Moon, and Dagö. This would require one division and a brigade of cyclists, which were temporarily withdrawn from the coast of Flanders. The operation had been in preparation in conjunction with the navy since the middle of September. At the end of the month the fleet, transports, and landing-force were ready at Libau. Owing to unfavorable winds, the execution of the landing was also delayed until the middle of October.

The postponement of the operation against Italy and the attack on the islands until the middle and end of October was to prove another enormous burden for us.

After a period of profound quiet in the West, which led some to hope that the battle of Flanders was over, another terrific assault was made on our lines on September 20. The third bloody act of the battle had begun. The main force of the attack was directed against the Passchendaele-Gheluvelt line. Obviously the English were trying to gain the high ground between Ypres and the Roulers-Menin line, which affords an extensive view in both directions. These heights were also exceptionally important for us, as they afforded us ground observation posts and a certain amount of cover from hostile view.

The enemy's onslaught on the 20th was successful, which proved the superiority of the attack over the defense. Its strength did not consist in the tanks. We found them inconvenient, but put them out of action all the same. The power of the attack lay in

the artillery, and in the fact that ours did not do
enough damage to the hostile infantry as it was
assembling, and, above all, at the actual time of the
assault.

Another English attack on the 21st was repulsed,
but the 26th proved a day of heavy fighting, accompanied by every circumstance that could cause us loss.
We might be able to stand the loss of ground, but the
reduction of our fighting strength was again all the
heavier. Once more we were involved in a terrific
struggle in the West, and had to prepare for a continuation of the attacks on many parts of the front.

October came, and with it one of the hardest months
of the war. The world at large—which began in my
immediate neighborhood—saw only Tarnopol, Czernowitz, Riga, and later Ösel, Udine, the Tagliamento,
and the Piave. It did not see my anxiety, nor my
deep sympathy with the sufferings of our troops in the
West. My head was in the East and in Italy, my
heart on the Western front. My will had to bring
head and heart together. I had not known what joy
meant for many a long day.

The actions in the third battle of Flanders had presented the same set-piece characteristics as those in
the second and the fighting at Verdun. The depth of
penetration was limited so as to secure immunity from
our counter-attacks, and the latter were then broken
up by the massed fire of artillery.

After each attack I discussed the tactical phenomena
with General von Kuhl and Colonel von Loszberg,
sometimes at the front, sometimes on the telephone.
This time I again went to Flanders in order to talk over
the same questions with officers who had taken part
in the fighting. Our defensive tactics had to be
developed further, somehow or other. We were all
agreed on that. The only thing was, it was so infinitely

difficult to hit on the right remedy. We could proceed only by careful experiment. The proposals of the officers on the spot tended rather in the direction of our former tactics; they amounted to a slight, but only a slight, reinforcement of our front lines, and the abandonment of the counter-attack by the counter-attack divisions, local counter-attacks being substituted for this. These local counter-attacks were to be made by a division in the second line, to be brought close up and spread over a wide front, before the enemy's attack began. So, while the front line was to be held rather more densely once more, in order to gain in power, the whole battle-field was to be given more depth than ever. General Headquarters would thus, generally speaking, have to provide a second division for every fighting division in the front line, an unheard-of expenditure of force. That the employment of a second division in rear of practically every one in the front line would increase the power of the defense was a simple sum in arithmetic. But the second sum was equally simple—that our lines on other fronts would have to be thinned out even more than they had been hitherto. I would see what I could do. I agreed to the tactical changes, although misgivings were expressed among my staff at this departure from the "defensive battle." I thought I ought to give way to the experience of officers at the front.

Another tactical detail which was emphasized everywhere was the value of ground observation for artillery. Only by that means could the attacking hostile infantry be annihilated, particularly after penetrating our front, or fire be concentrated on decisive points of the battle-field.

As to the tanks, opinion was unanimous; they were not thought particularly dangerous. I purposely made use of the expression "tank-fright," but the officers from the front would not admit there was any such thing.

I need not say that from the first the Fourth Army was as well supplied as possible with artillery, ammunition, aircraft, and other weapons; and Colonel von Loszberg, who always wanted a lot, was in the end satisfied with his army group and with me.

The officers in the West followed the Eastern and Italian operations with ever-increasing anxiety.

Early in October the artillery action revived, and on the 2d and 3d artillery engagements of great violence took place. The infantry battle commenced on the morning of the 4th. It was extraordinarily severe, and again we came through it only with enormous loss. It was evident that the idea of holding the front line more densely, adopted at my last visit to the front in September, was not the remedy. I now followed my own judgment without asking for further outside opinions, and recommended the Fourth Army to form an advanced zone—that is to say, a narrow strip between the enemy's front line and the line which our troops were to hold by mobile defense. The enemy would have to cross this strip in making his attack, and our artillery would have time to get on to him before he could reach our main line of resistance. The great difficulty lay in withdrawing the garrison of the advanced zone in case of attack, and in bringing the artillery barrage back to our own line. The term "advanced zone" has been defined in various ways, and ideas often become confused. The principle of it was simple. The Fourth Army complied with my suggestion somewhat reluctantly, and did not accept it with conviction for some time. I never ceased to lay stress on the principles of the employment of artillery in masses and the utmost possible concentration of artillery fire.

There were further severe engagements on October 9 and 12. The line held better than on the 4th, although in some places the enemy penetrated to a considerable distance. The wastage in the big actions of the fourth battle of Flanders was extraordinarily great. In the West we began to be short of troops. The two divisions that had been held in readiness in the East, and were already on the way to Italy, were diverted to Flanders. The attack on Ösel, at any rate, had commenced, but the Italian operation could not be started before the 22d, and the weather held it up until the 24th. These days were the culminating point of the crisis.

### III

The fifth act of the great drama in Flanders opened on October 22. Enormous masses of ammunition, such as the human mind had never imagined before the war, were hurled upon the bodies of men who passed a miserable existence scattered about in mud-filled shell-holes. The horror of the shell-hole area of Verdun was surpassed. It was no longer life at all. It was mere unspeakable suffering. And through this world of mud the attackers dragged themselves, slowly but steadily, and in dense masses. Caught in the advanced zone of our hail of fire they often collapsed, and the lonely man in the shell-hole breathed again. Then the mass came on again. Rifle and machine gun jammed with the mud. Man fought against man, and only too often the mass was successful.

What the German soldier experienced, achieved, and suffered in the Flanders battle will be his everlasting monument of bronze, erected by himself in the enemy's land.

The enemy's losses were also heavy. When we occupied the battle-field in the spring of 1918 we en-

countered the horrible spectacle of many unburied
corpses. They lay there in thousands. Two-thirds of
them were enemies, one-third German soldiers who
had found a hero's grave there.

And yet it must be admitted that certain units no
longer triumphed over the demoralizing effects of the
defensive battle as they had done formerly.

On October 26 and 30 and November 6 and 10 the
fighting was again of the severest description. The
enemy charged like a wild bull against the iron wall
which kept him from our submarine bases. He threw
his weight against Houthulst Forest, Poelcapelle,
Passchendaele, Becelaere, Gheluvelt, and Zandvoorde.
He dented it in many places, and it seemed as if he must
knock it down. But it held, although a faint tremor
ran through its foundations.

The impressions I received continuously were very
terrible. In a tactical sense, everything possible had
been done. The advanced zone was good. The effectiveness of our artillery had considerably improved.
Behind almost every division in the front line there
was another in support; and we still had reserves in the
third line. We knew that the enemy suffered heavily.
But we also knew he was extraordinarily strong and,
what was equally important, had an extraordinarily
stubborn will. Lloyd George wanted victory. He held
England in his hand. Only one thing we did not know—
how long the battle would continue. The enemy must
tire at some time.

The French had attacked simultaneously. For this
they had selected the favorable salient southwest of
Laon, known as the Laffaux corner. We discovered
their intention early in October; the army took all
measures for defense, and was supplied with everything
it deemed necessary. In spite of other advice, it wished
to hold the salient, feeling confident of success. It

made all its arrangements with meticulous care. All the same, General Headquarters ought to have ordered the evacuation of the salient.

The French attack on October 22 was successful. One division succumbed to the effects of an exceptionally heavy gas-bombardment, and gave way before the hostile assault. The enemy advanced toward Chavignon and so caused a narrow but deep indentation in the salient. This forced us to order its evacuation, and the

**EXPLANATION**

━━━ German line before Oct. 22, 1917.
➤ Direction of main attack of the French, Oct. 22, 1917.
×××× German line, Oct. 23, 1917.
━ ━ German line, Oct. 26, 1917.
•••• German line, Nov. 2, 1917.

1 : 300000

FIG. 25. BATTLE AT THE LAFFAUX CORNER, OCT. 22

line was withdrawn behind the Oise-Aisne Canal. The losses were very serious; once more several divisions were destroyed.

This withdrawal of our line inevitably entailed the evacuation of the Chemin des Dames ridge. It was ordered, and carried out on the night of November 21, after the stores and equipment had been removed. In itself it was of no consequence whether we stood north or south of the Ailette, but, after having fought all through the summer for possession of the Chemin des Dames, it was very difficult to order it to be given up. To hold on, however, would only have involved continuous wastage.

In pushing on toward the canal on the 23d the enemy gained further success, but later on all his attacks, which curled round toward the north and also extended farther toward the east, were repulsed.

As at Verdun in August, the French, supported by remarkable masses of artillery, had fought very vigorously.

While the October battles continued in the West until the combatants were exhausted, in the East the expedition against the islands had terminated in our favor. The campaign against Italy had begun. There our troops raced from victory to victory.

In the West the crisis caused by the battle of Flanders, the battle of the Laffaux salient, and their after-effects, passed away. We were expecting a continuation of the attacks in Flanders and on the French front when, on November 20, we were surprised by a fresh blow at Cambrai.

The Siegfried position was but weakly held. The fighting farther north, particularly the heavy concentration in Flanders, had induced the army group of Prince Rupprecht, with the consent of General Headquarters, to weaken the troops holding the Siegfried line—tired or Landwehr divisions—more and more. This brought about a serious element of danger, which we at once endeavored to make good. As things were, we had commenced the relief of tired Western divisions by strong Eastern ones in the East, and the 107th Division, which had entrained in the East about the middle of November, was intended for the neighborhood of Cambrai. Its leading troops had just arrived when the blow fell.

Under cover of darkness and the great Havrincourt

Wood, the English had, during several nights, concentrated a considerable number of tanks and cavalry divisions between the two roads converging on Cambrai from Bapaume and Péronne. On the morning of the 20th, after a short, heavy bombardment, they advanced to the attack. The tanks overcame obstacles and trenches, and so opened the way for the infantry and cavalry divisions. When, soon after 8 A.M., I spoke with the Chief of Staff of the Second Army he reported that the enemy had already broken into our line at several points. I at once ordered several divisions which were more or less rested, in the rear of the group of the German Crown Prince, to be railed to the neighborhood of Cambrai and south of it, and requested the group of Prince Rupprecht to move forces to the north of Cambrai. General von Kuhl had left by car for the Fourth Army before hearing about the battle on the Second Army front. The divisions of this group were thereby delayed.

The order for a unit to entrain is by no means the same thing as its arrival. It has to march to the entraining stations, where trains have to be got ready for it. On the various lines the trains can follow each other only at certain definite intervals of time, and the normal duration of the journey has to be added to all this. So it generally took two or three days for a division, using some thirty trains, to reach its destination. It could seldom be done in less.

The first reinforcements could not reach Cambrai by train before the morning of the 21st; not until the 23d would sufficient troops be collected to oppose the attack. The lack of motor transport for moving troops was now much felt.

It was not until noon that I obtained a clear idea of the extent of the enemy's success. It made me very anxious. Everything possible, however, was already

FIG. 26.   CAMBRAI, 1917

being done. So here again I had to leave things to take their course.

The English Army Commander did not exploit his

great initial success, or we should not have been able to limit the extent of the gap. If he had done so, what would have been the judgment on the Italian campaign? That was the sort of war we had to wage against the world. As a matter of fact, the blow was parried on the afternoon of the 22d and on the 23d, on the line Moeubres-Bourlon-Fontaine-Noyelles-Masnières. Even the troops which had been run over by tanks on the first day fought well, and so did the newly arrived 107th Infantry Division. To its intervention the early check to the enemy's attack is mainly due. It was immediately decided, if possible, to take the English attack in flank. In theory, a decision of that kind is easy to make; but in practice its execution was enormously difficult in the West. The assembling of the troops, their disposal for attack, and bringing up the huge quantities of ammunition required take time. In the mean while, the defense itself consumes troops.

At other points the English and French Armies undertook nothing of importance. In the re-entrant in our line the fighting died down without the employment of excessive numbers on our part. By the evening of the 29th the commander of the Second Army, General von der Marwitz, had collected enough troops for a counter-attack. The main effort was to be made on the southern part of the battle-field, in the direction of Bauteux and Gouzeaucourt, while a subsidiary attack was to be made west of Bourlon in a direct southerly direction. This time the English were surprised. Our attack on the 30th was well supported by artillery and succeeded, though not quite so well as I had hoped. But it was, at any rate, at last an offensive victory on the Western front. The foresight of the Chief of Staff of the Second Army, Lieutenant-Colonel Stapff, and the energy of the commander had earned their just reward. The success was the more remarkable because it was in the main achieved by half-tired troops who had not been specially trained for attack.

There was only one serious feature. The success had not been as complete as it might have been, because a good division, instead of pressing on, stopped to go through an enemy supply-depot.

The English brought up reserves and counter-attacked. The battle went on until December 5, and during its course we regained a good deal of the ground we had lost and some new ground as well. We had won a complete victory over a considerable part of the British Army. It was a good ending to the extremely heavy fighting of 1917. Our action had given us valuable hints for an offensive battle in the West, if we wished to undertake one in 1918.

Neither the English nor the French attacked again in France. The second strategic scheme of 1917 had also resulted in failure for them. A quiet period, which our exhaustion rendered so imperatively necessary, supervened at last in the West.

## IV

The offensive against Italy at Tolmino began on October 24.

The Flitsch group, under the Austro-Hungarian General von Krausz, and the Fourteenth German Army were to seize the mountain range which follows the right bank of the Isonzo from about Flitsch to Canale, and reaches its highest point in Mount Matajur, 5,420 feet, southwest of Caporetto. While all the other divisions were to ascend the range, the 12th, under General Lequis, was to move from Tolmino on Caporetto and then advance round the Matajur by the valley road toward Cividale.

The army group of General Boroevic was to join

in the advance of the Fourteenth Army, moving in a westerly direction from the Carso Mountains.

The deployment of the Fourteenth Army had proved very difficult. Only two mountain roads were available, and they were very narrow in places, so that movement in one direction only was possible. All the care and intelligence of the German staff-officer was needed to insure the movements taking place without friction and being completed on time. First of all the artillery and trench-mortars, with large supplies of ammunition, were moved up in good time, under the feeble protection of a few Austro-Hungarian battalions. The infantry divisions were moved up last of all.

The deployment took days and was betrayed to the Italians. The desperate hostile attacks in the West in the second half of October had already some connection with our plans in Italy. Our weakness in the West was to be taken advantage of. Tactically, Cadorna seems to have taken no steps. Possibly he thought the attack was hopeless.

After a few hours' bombardment by artillery and trench-mortars with high-explosive and gas shells, the ascent of the mountains began on the morning of the 24th, while the 12th Division pushed ahead in the valley toward and beyond Caporetto with the greatest energy. On the 25th the decisive mountain range was already in our hands, and the Matajur was taken from several sides.

On the 27th we had already gained more ground in the mountains toward the upper Tagliamento, and occupied Cividale. The Italian north front on the Carinthian frontier, and the Isonzo front both began to give way. Unfortunately Boroevic's group did not follow up with enough energy, so that more Italians escaped than should have been the case,

EXPLANATION

▬▬▬▶ Front of the confed-
erated armies at the
beginning of the at-
tack, Oct. 24, 1917.
⇢⇢⇢➤ Direction of attack.
●●●●●● Position, Oct. 30.
×××× Position, Nov. 6.
▬ ▬ ▬ Line reached by the
attack.

FIG. 27.  ITALIAN CAMPAIGN, 1917

FIG. 27.  ITALIAN CAMPAIGN, 1917

General von Below was instructed to keep his right wing in the mountains, but to advance with his left by Udine and press toward Codroifo and the south, so as to strike a decisive blow at the whole enemy force to the east of the Tagliamento. In this way another 60,000 Italians were captured east of that river, which was reached on December 1 along its whole course below Tolmezzo.

November 30 was a good day for a change. In France there was the victory of Cambrai, and in Italy this fine success. As early as November I had requested General von Arz to reinforce General von Conrad's group in the Tyrol from that of General Boroevic, and to make an energetic attack there, either down the Brenta or in the Asiago-Arsiero area. Now that the operation we had planned had succeeded, General von Boroevic was too strong, General von Conrad too weak. General von Arz consented. But the railways were too bad, and no movement worth mentioning could be effected.

The Tagliamento was crossed December 6, and the Piave, from the Montello downward, was reached on the 11th. Other troops pressed on in the mountains toward Feltre. Before this advance the Italian Army on the upper Piave hurriedly fell back from the mountains *via* Belluno.

The right wing of the Fourteenth Army now was deflected through Feltre toward the mountains between the Brenta and the Piave, in order to secure the descent into the plain. Elsewhere the Piave, being in flood, brought our advance to a halt. Beyond the Piave the Italians once more stood their ground in fair order. The first English and French reinforcements joined them.

Here, just as in August in the Bukovina and eastern Galicia, the railways in rear of the armies had to be repaired before we could think of resuming operations in the plain. The weather in the mountains became unfavorable, and the fighting there proved very exhausting. The troops continued to gain ground, but they did not succeed in capturing the critical Monte Grappa *massif*. The impulse of the offensive, begun on the Isonzo, had come to a natural end. Reinforcements would even now have carried it on some way, but General von Conrad had insufficient artillery, and his infantry was not strong enough to attack.

His advance began on December 4, much too late to affect the main operation, and very soon came to a standstill. The German General Staff would have been glad to send a division from the Western front to the Trentino, but could not spare it in November. When this was eventually done it was too late. Here again the railways were too bad.

Early in December, after a discussion with General von Krafft, I came to the conclusion that nothing further was to be gained by continuing the operation beyond the Piave. We therefore suggested to General von Arz that he should order it to stop and arrange for the German troops to be transported to the West.

The operation against Italy had achieved all that could possibly be expected of it. The Italian Army was thoroughly beaten and needed the support of its allies. Both the Austro-Hungarian Army and the Western front had been relieved. Austria-Hungary and her army had taken on a new lease of life. As Russia now concluded an armistice, the Dual Monarchy appeared to be coming round to a more warlike frame of mind again. We were no longer told, as we used to be, that her army would have to drop out of the war at the beginning of winter. This campaign had once more revealed its poor fighting capacity. It badly needed the approaching period of rest for recuperation and training.   Success had stimulated it.

German leadership and German troops had gained fresh laurels, and given further proofs of their superiority in the war of movement.   On occasions our full force had not been developed, owing to incidents arising from the lack of experience of young troops.


v


After the outburst of activity in September, another period of quiet set in on the Macedonian front, which was to last for some considerable time.   General von Scholtz was untiring in his efforts to train the Bulgarian troops and keep them fit for battle.   All German commands in Macedonia were working for the same end.   The Bulgarian General Staff, however, as before, took no interest in these important questions.

In the mean time the Entente had not slackened in its endeavors to secure the services of the royal Greek Army.   King Constantine had been deposed, and his son, Alexander, had succeeded him.   Venizelos ruled the country.   The Greek Army had been mobilized, but the formation of troops fit for the battle-line proceeded only slowly.

In Palestine and Mesopotamia Turkish affairs became steadily worse.

Operations against Bagdad were to begin in the autumn of 1917 or the spring of 1918.   A start had been made with the preparations, but in spite of the improvement in the traffic, which resulted from the opening of the tunnels, little progress was made.   The service remained bad and irregular.   The local commanders, however, believed that, with the assistance given them by our General Staff, they would be able to overcome all these difficulties. In this they displayed too much confidence in the Turks.

The strategical pivot of the enterprise against Bagdad was the security of the front in Palestine. I continually drew Enver's attention to this point, and very often requested him to reinforce that front and pay particular attention to improving the service on the Syrian railways. General Headquarters gave him all the help it could. What we gave him was not excessive, and this fell into the hands of incompetent Turks.

Colonel von Kresz was the leading spirit in all endeavors to improve the condition of the Turkish Armies in Palestine. As I afterward discovered, he had a better idea of the troubles and anxieties of the local headquarters than the gentlemen in Constantinople. The latter had far too optimistic an idea of the situation, and communicated it to their General Staff.

The authorities in Constantinople gradually came round to the idea of strengthening the Palestine front, but now thought of achieving that object by an offensive. The operation against Bagdad was ingloriously consigned to the waste-paper basket, and an attack in Palestine substituted for it. The army group headquarters of Von Falkenhayn was brought to this theater.

In view of the poor communications and the condition of the Turkish troops, Colonel von Kresz had doubted the possibility of their taking the offensive, and events proved that he was right. Instead of the Turks, the English attacked.

After the failure of their attack on Gaza in March the Colonel had attempted to operate against their communications in the Sinai Peninsula by means of raids and aircraft. He did once succeed in damaging their pipe-line, but he was unable to do either it or the railway any serious harm.

FIG. 28. PALESTINE

At the end of August large masses of English cavalry advanced on Beersheba so as to work round the left flank of the Gaza front and reach the water-supply of Jerusalem. This enterprise failed, as did others on

October 2 and 18. Not till November 2 did the English succeed in capturing Beersheba. Simultaneously, with the assistance of the fleet, they attacked Gaza. The Turkish Army was forced to retire and was drawn up on the line Jaffa-Hebron-Dead Sea in order to protect Jerusalem. The English Army followed slowly. On the 17th it took Jaffa and deployed strong forces toward Jerusalem as well. On this line the Turks did not fight it out, but fell back to a position south of Nabulus, between the sea and the Jordan. English troops occupied Jerusalem on December 9. The Turkish Army had suffered heavy losses. Its ability to offer further resistance could be considered only slight. However, the German Asiatic Corps arrived in Palestine by degrees and gave our ally some stiffening.

The defeats of the Turks greatly influenced the attitude of the Arabs, who sided more and more with England.

After occupying Bagdad the English extended the area under their control farther up the Euphrates and Tigris. In October they held the line Ramadieh-Samara, and in November they gained more ground toward Mosul.

On both fronts, in Palestine as in Mesopotamia, the strength of the Turks had considerably decreased. It was evident that the position there could be maintained only by means of further reinforcements.

The Russo-Turkish front continued inactive. At my request, Enver was going to send reinforcements from there to Mesopotamia, but whether the troops ever started could not be ascertained.

VI

On the Rumanian front the fighting continued without result into September, when it died down.

On the Eastern front all was quiet. In the middle of October we withdrew our advanced troops east of Riga to their permanent positions. Along these extended fronts active communications between the two lines of trenches gradually were established. We continued our endeavors to increase the desire for peace in the Russian Army.

On October 11 the fleet left Libau for the attack on the islands lying off the Gulf of Riga. The blow was aimed at Petrograd, and, since very many people have no idea of time and space, it was bound to make a profound impression there. It was a peculiar satisfaction to me that in this way the fleet obtained an opportunity for active work.

During its long period of rest, events had occurred which threw a most disquieting light not only on the agitation which the Independent Socialists had carried on among certain portions of the navy, but also on the state of public opinion in Germany, and, therefore, on our fighting power. The aims of a small fraction of the people had been accomplished in the navy. The outward conditions of its existence and its constant touch with the home country had favored the spread of revolutionary ideas. Many, and often the best, of the regular officers and engineers of some length of service had been detached for duty with submarines, or in the high-seas fleet, and this had not been good for discipline. A renewal of active operations could not fail to improve and fortify the spirit of the navy.

The tasks of the Navy were to provide transports, cover the sea-passage and the landing, co-operate in the operations from seaward, and maintain the communications of the expeditionary force with Libau.

This force, consisting of the 42d Infantry Division and the Cyclists' Brigade, was commanded by General von Kathen, whose Chief of Staff was Colonel von

FIG. 29. DAGÖ-ÖSEL

Tschischwitz. So the conduct of the operation **had** been intrusted to particularly capable hands.

The landing-place reconnoitered and selected **was** Tagga Bay, on the northwest corner of Ösel Island.

After neutralizing the batteries on the Sworbe Peninsula—the southern extremity of Ösel—the fleet steamed into the Gulf of Riga, and then advanced into Moon Sound, while torpedo craft steamed round the north side of the island. They were to bombard the long causeway which connects Ösel and Moon and cut off the enemy's retreat from Ösel. They were also to push into Moon Sound from the north. The navy hoped to force an action on those portions of the enemy's naval forces which had their permanent stations there, or to cut them off altogether. The object of the troops landed on Ösel was to seize the causeway as soon as possible, capture the whole island, and so take the defenders of the Sworbe Peninsula in rear.

This plan succeeded, and only a small part of the garrison escaped by way of the causeway. On the 16th Ösel was in our possession, and Moon fell on the 18th. Soon afterward we also secured Dagö. The navy found an opportunity of engaging hostile craft.

This ended the fighting on the Eastern front for the time being.

How far these last attacks accelerated matters in Russia I do not know. The fact is that simultaneously with the rise of the Bolshevists in the autumn the disintegration of the Russian Army proceeded very rapidly. The officers lost their privileged position, and all authority was taken from them. They were not to be regarded as more important than the men in the ranks; in a little while they were regarded as less and had no rights at all. These measures were approved by many people in Russia. For there, as elsewhere, there were many short-sighted individuals who could not see that the strength of the army, and all social order, rests on authority, and that by shaking the authority of the officers they were undermining the social order of the whole world.

Hetman Skropadsky told me that he never noticed how his corps, which he had commanded in the war, dissolved. It simply vanished all at once. This simple story made a tremendous impression on me.

In the army the Russian Revolution did not stop at depriving the officer of his rights. It set up the Soldiers' Council in the place of authority, and went even farther. It disarmed all but the proletarian soldiers and created the Red Guard. In the purely political sphere it acted in the same way. The *bourgeois* counted for nothing at all; the proletarian Workmen's Council was predominant.

The proletarian Society of Workers and Soldiers was now, by means of its councils, to govern and reorganize the world. All that had existed hitherto was ruthlessly destroyed. Civilization was disintegrated. Private property was to be limited and the joy of work to be killed. Woman became public property. Bestial instincts soon became uppermost. The chaos developed more and more into the bloody dictatorship of a few men, who relied on troops faithful to themselves, and on whose passions, even when they were Chinese mercenaries, they placed no restraint. The country, dominated by this dictatorship, was ruined, but that meant nothing to those in power.

A curious state of affairs was thus created. Those who never could cry out enough about violation of rights and against war paid no regard to the rights of the majority, but violated them more than any Government had done, called the people to arms and made war, not against external enemies at first, it is true, but generally against every existing institution. Those who disagreed with them heard no word of reconciliation or understanding.

And soon all those who had previously done their utmost to destroy authority in the army and the nation recognized the danger into which they had plunged themselves and their whole country. Unfortunately, it was found impossible in Russia to arm all the anti-Bolshevist parties and make them sink their sectarian differences and unite for the regeneration of the country.

The peasants and the middle class found themselves exposed, unarmed, to violation by their oppressors, and fell a prey to anarchist disruption. Who knows when, if ever, they will recover their vitality? We can see no signs of it, and merely to hope for it seems almost dangerous self-deception. Possibly, like many people in Germany in the spring of 1919, they looked upon Bolshevism with fatalistic equanimity, as an inevitable doom which must of itself produce salvation. That is a cowardly thought, and in Russia it had terrible consequences. Salvation from Bolshevism is not to be found in looking on and doing nothing, but in strong and wise action, accurate gaging of the enemy's strength and weakness, and also in far-sighted economic reforms which would have been imperative after the war in any event.

From October 1917 on, Bolshevism in Russia obtained an ever firmer hold.

I could not doubt that the disintegration of the Russian Army and nation involved an extraordinary risk for Germany and Austria-Hungary. All the greater was my anxiety when I thought of the weakness of our Government and theirs.

By sending Lenin to Russia our Government had, moreover, assumed a great responsibility. From a military point of view his journey was justified, for Russia had to be laid low. But our Government should have seen to it that we also were not involved in her fall.

The events in Russia gave me no cause for complete satisfaction. They considerably eased the military situation, but elements of the greatest danger still remained.

As early as the summer I had drafted the armistice conditions. They were based on the desire to come to an understanding with Russia, for the needs of the war demanded peace in the East.

The fundamental idea of the armistice was to cease hostilities on the lines which each army held at the time. I demanded no cession of territory or surrender of arms. The conditions contained nothing that might make the armistice or the future peace more difficult. The draft was submitted to the Imperial Government and the allied Headquarters and was agreed to. Minor changes involved no alteration in principle. It was agreed with the Imperial Government that if the armistice was negotiated between the contending armies, the conduct was to be in the hands of General Headquarters, assisted by a representative of the Imperial Chancellor. The latter agreed to include a representative of General Headquarters in the Commission to be appointed for the peace negotiations; he was, of course, to be the subordinate, not the equal, of the Chancellor's plenipotentiary.

I had everything ready in case the Russians should make advances. By November the Russian Army was so far corroded by Bolshevism that General Headquarters could seriously think of weakening the Eastern front in order to strengthen the West. We had then about eighty divisions there, one-third of our whole force. I now proposed that the Austro-Hungarian troops should take over a larger part of the line. We discussed with their Headquarters and with the Commander-in-chief in the East how we could set free the greatest number of German troops on the fronts in Transylvania (Siebenbürgen), the Bukovina, and eastern Galicia. General von Arz also agreed to send Austro-Hungarian troops from Italy to the East. These measures would, of course, be carried out only in the somewhat remote future. But it was necessary to make preparation now, so that all movements might be completed by the coming spring, the decisive period for us. Otherwise the scheme would have been impracticable, owing to the bad condition of the railways and the critical state of transportation in the occupied territory and Germany. But conditions in Russia prevented our taking too drastic decisions as yet.

From the end of November onward troop-trains were incessantly passing from East to West. It was no longer a case of replacing tired divisions in the West by fresh ones, but of really adding to the number of combatants in the West.

The training of the troops in the East for the Western conditions was pushed on, and the same was done in Rumania.

The idea of making an attack in France in 1918 occupied many of our generals as early as November, myself perhaps most of all. I therefore eagerly awaited the day when the Russian Government would ask for an armistice. At the front numerous local truces were made in November. Larger and larger formations made overtures to us, and already individual Russian Armies made proposals for ceasing hostilities. Peace negotiations were attempted at Dvinsk (Dünaburg), but came to nothing. In some places armistices were denounced. It was a confusing picture, half peace, half war.

On November 26 the Russian Commander-in-chief, People's Commissary Krylenko, inquired by wireless whether we were prepared to conclude an armistice. We agreed. On December 21 the Russian delegates crossed the German lines. Negotiations began without delay at Brest-Litovsk, where the Commander-in-chief in the East still had his Headquarters. At the same time the four allied Powers sent their representatives. By December 7 a ten days' truce was agreed upon.

General Hoffmann conducted these negotiations very skilfully and kept the Bolshevist representatives to the point. The discussion was limited to the matter in hand. The Russians returned temporarily to Petrograd with the draft agreement in order to obtain fresh instructions. Negotiations were reopened on the 12th, and the armistice was signed on the 15th. It was to begin at the termination of the truce at noon on the 17th, and continue until noon on January 14, 1918. If not rejected in seven days it would continue automatically.

The original draft had not been fundamentally modified; the Russian front had not changed, and no neutral zone was created. The respective wire entanglements were considered as the boundaries. Indeed, at the request of the Russians, communication between the two fronts had been arranged at certain points of passage. We clearly perceived their intention of carrying on propaganda. The Commander-in-chief in the East was positive that he could frustrate this attempt by suitable measures. We therefore accepted this condition merely to make an end of the business. The agreement was officially binding on the whole Russian front, but the power of the Government of Councils did not extend so far.

It therefore became necessary to enter upon special negotiations on the same basis in Rumania and Asia Minor. These were also brought to a successful conclusion. The armistice of Focsani was concluded on December 9. It is useful to compare our conditions with those which the determination of the Entente to destroy us imposed upon the Powers of the Quadruple Alliance.

After three years of titanic contest, quiet reigned
along the whole front.  What German leadership and
German troops accomplished in fighting throughout
this long period against enormous superiority will
always fill a glorious page in the history of our country
and of the German manhood which fought and bled
here.

For the previous six months I had devoted myself,
and made others devote all their energies, to the attainment of the object we had now achieved.  The Western
front had held, the Italian Army was defeated, and the
Austro-Hungarian Armies in Italy had been imbued
with fresh vigor.  Negotiations were to begin at
Brest-Litovsk about Christmas.  We had some prospect of gaining the final victory.

It was only in Asia Minor that all had not gone well,
but, compared with the great events in Europe, that
was of quite subsidiary importance.

The troops and leaders who had fought in the West
could proudly say that their achievements had laid
the foundation of this mighty result.  By their steadfastness the campaign in the East and in Italy had been
won.  Here also the German had done a hero's work.

As in the year before, the co-operation between our
General Staff and the allies had produced great results.

The Entente was impressed by this change in the
situation.  It still had hopes of America.  But in
spite of that, feeling in France had remained shaken
since the battle on the Aisne and in Champagne.  In
November Clemenceau became Prime Minister.  He
was the strongest man in France.  He had been through
1870–71 and had since then been one of the most ardent
protagonists of the *Revanche*.  Clemenceau knew what
he wanted.  His policy was a war policy; he suppressed every sign of peace agitation and strengthened
the spirit of his country.  His proceedings against

Caillaux showed clearly what we were to expect of him. He, too, thought only of victory, and, like Lloyd George, had his country behind him. The enemy's conduct of the war gained immensely in vigor. In America also the fighting spirit became more and more pronounced. There, too, the Government took action against all thought of peace with the greatest ruthlessness. Under the powerful influence of Clemenceau and Lloyd George, Italy survived the impression produced by her defeat, which had been at first very deep. In the hostile democratic states the Government assumed more and more the character of a dictatorship.

VII

The peace resolution of the German Reichstag moved the Vatican to take special steps in the direction of peace. The Papal peace note of August 1 appeared in the middle of that month and was addressed to the heads of the various states at war.

The note pronounced entirely in favor of a peace without annexations or indemnities and expected us to make considerable sacrifices, while the Entente got off very cheaply. German public opinion received it in the same way as the peace resolution in July. The press of the Right declined it, that of the Majority parties was in favor of it and invited the enemy to follow the sounder view and accept it also. The press of the Entente unanimously refused it, and adhered to that attitude, and the Governments did the same.

The Imperial Chancellor, Doctor Michaelis, read his answer aloud to us at Kreuznach. I anticipated no results from this attempt at peace. Nor did the answer accord with my views. But I put my objections aside and made only unimportant counter-proposals. I could only wait and see what would come of these purely theoretical endeavors to make peace, notwithstanding my aversion to the perpetual peace talk on account of its evil influence on the conduct of the war. Looking back, I regret that I did not oppose all these ideas with more energy. To conclude peace, which I equally desired, was the business of diplomacy, but to be always talking to the public about it could do us no good so long as the enemy remained determined to destroy us. The foresight of the Entente in this respect was exemplary.

Our reply, like that of Austria-Hungary, accepted the Pope's advances, although many points were diplomatically evaded. By a reference to the peace resolution of the Reichstag, which was included at the desire of the seven members who assisted in drawing it up, our position was clearly defined.

The reply of the Entente amounted to a refusal; otherwise it was not to the point. The Pope's step was entirely unsuccessful. It was always the same old story—the German people honestly desired peace, but the Entente refused it. In their quiet but penetrating propaganda the Entente nations were continually making our public and neutral countries repeat the catchword, "Peace by understanding and reconciliation," but they always avoided committing themselves to it. Now, as ever, they pursued but one idea, to destroy Germany.

The Pope's step could not succeed. It is curious now to observe the way in which the Pope was excluded from the negotiations at Versailles. The Entente was not grateful to him.

At his accession I had informed Doctor Michaelis that Herr Hugo Stinnes was in communication with the Japanese ambassador in Stockholm and had told me he had some hope. He said he was about to leave for Stockholm and was likely to see the ambassador.

The Imperial Chancellor thereupon received Herr Stinnes. I took no further interest in the matter.

Suddenly, at the end of August or early in September, we heard there was an opportunity of opening discussion with the Entente. The Imperial Chancellor and Herr von Kü:lmann, who had become Secretary of State for Foreign Affairs, when he was appointed, told us it was a secret. I had heard from Colonel von Haeften that reports had come through neutral countries, in connection with a speech by Mr. Asquith, the former British Premier, and later statements by Lloyd George, that England expected us to make a statement about Belgium. Now the Chancellor told me that England had suggested the possibility of some sort of discussion. I was naturally pleased; if England had now become ready for peace, its prospects were brighter than before, when we alone made the approaches. I therefore considered the question of peace more favorably than I had done hitherto.

The talk of peace led to various discussions with the Imperial Chancellor on the question of Belgium.

We laid down as our goal the economic attachment of Belgium to the German Empire, in view of the close relationship that had existed before the war. The Imperial Government thought that this gave it some basis on which to enter into communication with England. I expected that the Secretary of State would make a public declaration in this sense in the form of a speech in the Reichstag at the end of September. On September 20 Colonel von Haeften had a fairly long discussion with him about it. But the Secretary of State did not agree, and remarked, "Who ever told you that I am prepared to sell the horse 'Belgium'? It is for me to decide that. At present the horse is not for sale at all."

In his speech on October 9 he did not mention Belgium, but amid the boisterous applause of the Reichstag alluded to Alsace-Lorraine in the following terms: "As long as a German fist can hold a rifle, the integrity of the German dominions, which we have received as a glorious heritage from our fathers, can never become the object of any negotiations or concessions."

That did not bring us a single step forward, as far as England was concerned.

We heard no more of the prospects of peace. On inquiry the General Staff received no definite answer from Secretary of State von Kühlmann. I was disappointed, and regretted having momentarily believed in it. It was only for that reason that I had requested the Imperial Chancellor to refrain from a great speech which he wished to deliver at the end of September, as it seemed conceivable that it might lessen the possibility of peace. It would have been better for him to have spoken. It seems doubtful, however, whether he would have succeeded in uniting the whole Reichstag and people, in view of his relations with the various political parties. He opposed their desire for power, and his attitude toward the Reichstag itself was that of a stranger.

I also entertained some hopes of the efforts being made by the representative of the Foreign Office in Brussels, Herr von der Lancken, who sought to get into touch with French statesmen. He went to Switzerland, but the gentleman from France stayed away.

I also heard casually that Herr von Kühlmann was in communication regarding peace questions with the Spanish ambassador in Brussels.

Such were the possibilities of peace of which I received information during 1917. Of President Wilson's so-called offer, which Herr Jaffé brought to the Foreign Office from Munich, I heard from the papers only after my resignation.

In connection with these mysterious peace rumors a Crown Council was held at Berlin on September 11. I considered it my duty, and it was within my province, once more to point out clearly what, according to the experience of this war, was necessary in order to secure Germany's future, and on this occasion, and later on in the autumn of 1917, I committed myself to the following opinions:

"According to the statements of the departments concerned, the food and coal situation at home is difficult. As regards coal this is unfortunately due in part to neglect in previous months. Our financial system is enormously strained. The Majority in the Reichstag has rendered the situation at home deplorable. The labor question, and therefore the recruiting question also, have become acute. But I consider that these internal difficulties must be overcome by firm statesmanship on the part of the present Government. It is possible."

In considering the requirements imposed upon us by the necessities of strategic and military economics, I based my considerations on our pre-war situation and developments during the war. A three years' war was possible only because we had abundant coal in Germany, and so much iron and food that, together with what we could obtain from occupied territory and neutral countries, and in spite of the hostile blockade, we could, by practising the most rigid economy, manage to exist.

Only by offensive action in this war which had been pressed upon us, and by expanding to the east and west, had we been able to exist; we should certainly have been lost had we remained within our frontiers.

Defeat was inevitable if the enemy should succeed in occupying German territory for any length of time; we might starve, and the back of our military economic system would be broken. The importance in war of coal, iron, and food was known before this war; but how absolutely decisive they would actually become was demonstrated to all the world only as hostilities proceeded. Before the war we had recognized the exposed position of the coal-fields of Upper Silesia, and when we demanded the "milliard of marks" measures were taken to protect them. Our sources of strength in the west were considered to be secured by our strategical deployment.

No less unfavorable than our strategic situation in the center of Europe was the position of our iron and coal fields, which were mostly near our frontiers. Every other country was better off in that way. The coal and iron of Upper Silesia were right on the Russian border. In the west, the iron of Lorraine and the coal of Saarbrücken were just as exposed. The industrial area of the Lower Rhine and of Westphalia was quite unprotected against Belgium. In comparison with these areas, the lignite deposits of central Germany were unimportant.

Destructive weapons had been perfected in the war. The range of guns had considerably increased, and the power of aircraft had been greatly extended. On the other hand, their employment was limited by certain fundamental conditions. Every shot out of a long gun did not stop all activity within range. That we learned in the spring of 1918 when bombarding the French coal-mines, and on other occasions. Aircraft are dependent upon the weather; otherwise we would have hit London more often. With these reservations I had to allow for all the new means of warfare in considering the characteristics of any future war. I took as a basis the same frontiers and the same political situation as in 1914.

It was to be expected that the enemy would, at the

latest, directly after the order to mobilize, attack our military factories with numerous aircraft well supplied with ammunition. A certain degree of security could be obtained by concentrating strong aircraft forces on the frontier and good anti-aircraft protection, but these measures would not prevent attack or bomb-dropping. Nor could any protection be provided against distant hostile guns. This sudden attack would be followed up by the main mass of the army. The course of the operations could not be foreseen in detail. But one could anticipate with certainty that our war industry would suffer at least partial restriction everywhere, which would on the whole prove decisive, and that a great proportion of our laboring classes would be very hard hit. Without being unduly pessimistic, I could foresee that we might in certain circumstances lose the war in the first days. We should be killed like rats in a trap.

It was not possible to follow out all the conclusions which this led to—e.g., we could not aim at pushing our frontiers far into the interior of France. We must be content with meeting our most pressing needs. A protective belt of a few miles would have to suffice for safeguarding the Upper Silesian coal-field and the iron-mines of Lorraine from the immediate effects of the operations. The fact that both coal and ore are found in these belts both in Poland and near Briey did not influence me. That these measures were insufficient by themselves, but would have to be supplemented by elaborate military defenses in time of peace, was obvious. Whatever we might do, the security of these two sources of strength would be inadequate, and it was therefore imperative to insure the reliable protection of the industrial area of Westphalia and the Lower Rhine. I had become acquainted with its importance as a peace and war industry when acting as Regimental

Commander at Düsseldorf, and now again as First
Quartermaster-General. The only possible conclusion
was that Belgium must on no account be allowed to
become a hostile area of deployment. Its neutrality
I considered to be a mere phantom on which no practical man would rely. We must insure that its economic
interests became identical with those of Germany, with
which it was already united by such strong commercial
ties. It was to remain an independent state in which
the Flemings also should enjoy their rights. The violation of this ancient Germanic race is another of the
enormities of human history. For the first few years
I considered it would be necessary to maintain a
German army of occupation. The Meuse at Liège
could be given up, if at all, only after Belgium had
completed its economic union with Germany and, in
accordance with its real interests, taken its place on
our side.

The idea of German naval bases on the coast of
Flanders did not appeal to me. It had not been
thought out and was not the outcome of a definite
military policy. I wrote as follows: "We would become quite secure—*i.e.*, as regards the industrial area of
the Lower Rhine, especially if the Channel Tunnel
scheme is executed—only by occupying the whole of
Belgium and establishing our army on the coast of
Flanders. This object is unattainable at present.
The question is whether we should continue the war
for the sake of achieving it. In my opinion we ought
to do so if the English keep a strip of French territory—
*e.g.*, Calais. If they do not, the acquisition of the coast
of Flanders is not a sufficient reason for us to prolong
the war through the winter."

The retention of Calais by England was at that time
discussed in my presence more than once; that is why
I mentioned it.

I thought it important to bring Luxemburg into closer relationship to the Empire.

When we had arranged matters in the west more or less in the manner indicated, we should have achieved what was necessary in that quarter for Germany's military and economic security.

In the east the whole German frontier was as unfavorable as possible, not only on account of the Upper Silesian coal-field. The campaign of 1914 had shown the difficulty of holding the country east of the Vistula. East Prussia, after its severe suffering, was certainly entitled to a protective belt.

The Polish re-entrant had proved exceedingly detrimental to our defense.

The full force of this disadvantage had again been felt in the autumn of 1914 when Grand Duke Nicholas struck his great blow at the Prussian frontier. To eliminate the danger altogether by territorial acquisitions appeared impossible. It was, however, strategically necessary to widen the narrow neck between Danzig and Thorn toward the south and to provide a protective belt for the Upper Silesian coal-field.

The desired union with Courland and Lithuania would not improve the frontier. But, once we had secured the protective belt east of the Vistula in the south and the widening of the neck on the south side of Thorn, a great deal could be made good by completing the railway system. Courland and Lithuania would improve our food-supply, in case we should, in a future war, have to rely once more on our own resources.

This rearrangement of the Eastern frontier would in this region also secure what seemed essential to the military and economic security of Germany; provided always that the so-called "Austro-Polish solution" did not eventuate, and that Poland established economic relations with Germany, and perhaps later with Russia.

My hopes went a step farther. The inhabitants of Courland and Lithuania were to bring Germany additional man-power. That men meant power I felt more and more every day. It was in men that the superiority of the Entente consisted. The population of those countries could retain their nationality under the German Empire. An increase of the Polish population, which would accrue in the defensive belt, was undesirable, but this grave objection would have to give way before military necessity. The German settlement, which we hoped would take place on a great scale, and the collection of Germans from abroad in those extensive eastern territories, which the Imperial Chancellor had tried to establish as far back as 1915 in certain frontier areas, would in the future provide further increase.

For the benefit of Germany's economic position in relation to the rest of the world I contemplated commercial advantages in Rumania and the Balkans, and above all the return of our colonies, or their combination in one united colonial territory.

I was averse to the Central-European economic union; it did not appear possible of realization, as it postulated too great a position of superiority for Germany.

War contributions I never took seriously into account.

These were the military necessities I aimed at; it was not, however, at all certain if we could achieve them. If we could not, our demands would still not be unnecessary; but the failure to secure them would be a disadvantage which would have to be accepted and remedied by greater safeguards in time of peace.

I never, on my own initiative, expressed in public my ideas regarding the conditions of peace. But, at the request of the Imperial Chancellor, Doctor Michaelis, I discussed them with several representatives of the most diverging political opinions.

My views on peace never formed the basis of any discussion with the enemy, as the Government never got so far as that. Later on, in the first negotiations at Brest-Litovsk, and at Bucharest, the Government went its own way, which did not coincide with mine.

The discussions on war aims between the Imperial Chancellor and General Headquarters were purely academic. Every one knew that the terms of peace would be decided by the way the war ended, and by nothing else, and that we should have to make up our minds according to circumstances.

When concrete cases had to be dealt with, as in drafting the reply to Wilson on January 29, 1917, our attitude toward Russia in the early summer or toward England in August and September of the same year, or finally in drawing up the terms of the armistice in the East, we acted according to the circumstances of the time. I did not think of taking my stand on purely theoretical ground.

As long as the enemy persisted in his determination to destroy us, this war could end only in victory or defeat. In any case, the Government was unable to indicate any other way of finishing it and obtaining peace.

To assert that we could have had peace earlier on some condition or other is a scandalous piece of frivolity and a wilful misleading of the German people. The Entente never made an offer; it never dreamt of giving us anything; it was not even satisfied with the conditions existing before the war; it wanted only to take. Well, then, did any single German put forward the idea that we should sacrifice Alsace-Lorraine, the Province of Posen, or our colonies? Imperial Chancellor von Bethmann did in the autumn of 1916 allude casually to the cession or exchange of a few localities in Lorraine and the Sundgau (part of Alsace).

Were we to hold a plebiscite in our country, as a peace offering? That idea was surely not evolved in a German brain. If we wanted to render our defense even more difficult and weaken our political and economic position, we ought to have taken it up. That is the kind of thing we are experiencing now.

The war was begun; our duty now was to seek a decision by force, or to accept a defeat which we had strength to avert. If only Germany would realize this now, that it has been clearly shown that all the Entente's catchwords about self-determination of peoples, no annexations or indemnities, disarmament, freedom of the seas, were mere figments of the imagination and will ever remain so. Every human life is a battle on a small scale; within the various states parties struggle for supremacy, and so it is in the world of nations— so it will ever be. That is a natural law. Enlightenment and a higher morality can alleviate the struggle for power, as well as the means of waging it, but can never destroy the desire for power itself, for that goes against human nature and in the long run against nature itself. Nature is war. If that which is strong and good does not win, then the ignoble powers gain supremacy. If we want the good to survive we must be prepared to defend it, by fighting and even by violence. Even goodness can live only if it is strong.


VIII

The internal conditions in Germany continued to develop unsatisfactorily. In the Reichstag the struggle for power between the parties and the Government became more acute. This vice of "Parliamentarism," carried on by professional politicians and concealed under catchwords of every kind, grew daily more naked and unashamed. Doctor Michaelis opposed it with determination and thus very soon became the victim of his own actions. He wore out his strength in this struggle and had no time to work for the war.

In the answer of the United States to the Papal note, Wilson had again attempted to interfere in Germany's internal affairs and to divide Government and people; this aroused protest in the Reichstag. But even thus we could not muster the strength to repudiate his action with the righteous indignation it deserved.

The occurrences in the navy in the summer of 1917 showed clearly how far the spirit of revolution had spread. The idea was to enforce peace by a naval strike. These conditions were not duly appreciated; the first warning was unheeded.

The attitude of the Government was not strong; it revealed the uncertainty of one that is conscious of its own weakness. Doctor Michaelis did certainly perceive the dangerous influence which the Independent Socialists exercised on the conduct of the war, but he did not prevent their revolutionary activity. Their press, whose evil influence could be proved, was allowed to go on writing.

The Reichstag displayed no understanding of its duties in connection with the war. Well-known members protected those representatives whose close connection with affairs in the navy was proved, who were fighting for revolution and destroying discipline. The German people were not sufficiently informed of the serious nature of these events.

In the navy also they were dealt with in a way that was bound to do immense harm; in the army, too, they were discussed, and the settlement of the matter made a deep impression.

After a temporary rise the warlike spirit of Germany had fallen since July to a disquietingly low level. The spirit which was to disarm the German people in the summer of 1918 and in 1919 became apparent. Our offers to undertake the direction of the press and of internal propaganda were not met in a manner at all compatible with the seriousness of the situation, and this in spite of the revolutionary turmoil in Russia and the naval mutiny.

After discussion with the War Ministry, General Headquarters considered it imperative to create an organization for dealing with the instigators of revolution. Proposals to this effect went to Berlin, where they were discussed with the Imperial authorities. Again nothing could be achieved. The representative of General Headquarters now suggested that this office should be established as part of the General Staff in Berlin. Every one agreed to this. Its duty was limited to establishing facts; but its field very soon became almost entirely political. It was significant that in spite of this the Government refused to take over the new department, which I considered to be the right procedure and had already recommended. General Headquarters had thus no alternative but to assume another function that was no part of its duty.

The anomalies of our way of carrying on war-time government became more and more apparent and were bound to cause increasing irritation.

Our economic position had also become more acute and raw materials became scarcer.

We had managed to struggle through the food troubles, but it had been very difficult. In the winter of 1916–17 there had been no means of carting potatoes. We had to fall back on kohlrabi. At that time many people were hungry. In spring and summer supplies improved; but they had sufficed only with the aid of Rumanian wheat and maize. By early threshing on a considerable scale we might yet tide over a period between the old harvest and the new. But that meant anticipating our credit.

Forage had become very scarce; grazing started early and helped a good deal. The oat harvest had been bad and the hay crop scanty. Evidently the forage problem was going to become worse.

The coal-supply seemed more certain than in the winter of 1916–17; that of house-coal was tolerable.

The stocks of oil were uncommonly low; it was urgently necessary to increase the supply from Rumania. In the country they would again have dark winter nights.

At the time of Doctor Michaelis's resignation the prospects for the future were exceedingly serious. I hoped that the collapse of Russia, about which there could no longer be any doubt, would at last remove the danger. That, in conjunction with our brilliant successes in Italy, and our heroism on the Western front, were surely enough to rouse us and to prevent disappointment at the absence of complete success in the submarine war. The nations of the Entente could not point to similar results at that time. They had had nothing but failures, but they were as determined as their Governments, and with strong national feeling backed up the great men who led them so vigorously. Opposing tendencies were suppressed. Germany, unfortunately for itself, had taken another road. The Reichstag opposed united government, and the opponents of war gained ground among the people. The political leadership of the Chancellors was a failure. Thus the balance of internal conditions in the various states that were at war altered to our disadvantage. The enemy's hope of our internal collapse balanced his military disappointments. We could not entertain such hopes in respect of our strongest enemies, and so, although the military situation was in our favor, there existed a profoundly different spirit in the contending nations.

At the end of October Count von Hertling succeeded Doctor Michaelis. He was the first Chancellor to be nominated by the Crown with the consent of the majority in the Reichstag, so far had the balance of power been altered in favor of Parliament, and the same process was illustrated by several other ministerial appointments. From this time onward the Reichstag majority was even more than formerly jointly responsible for the country's misfortune.

General Headquarters did not hear of the nomination until it had become an accomplished fact. In the mean time Count von Hertling had come to think better of us. He was unknown to me. We expected of him the fulfilment of the tasks which fell to the Government in the prosecution of the war. These were, strong internal government, raising the warlike spirit of the people; the execution of the proposals as to recruiting which we had already made to Doctor Michaelis; and finally, the development of propaganda against the enemy.

Once more I entered into communication with the War Minister and the head of the War Department,[1] which had been for a considerable time in the hands of General von Scheüch, regarding the need of supplying the army more liberally, but could not bring them to a decision. No doubt both these gentlemen were suffering from the influence of the unsettled economic conditions, which, instead of overcoming, they allowed to paralyze them.

I constantly recurred to the subject which had prompted my proposals of the autumn of 1916, namely, the necessity for utilizing all the forces of the country to achieve victory. It had become perfectly evident that the Auxiliary Service act did not fulfil its object;

---

[1] The German word is *Kriegsamt*—it is not the same as the *Ministerium*, which corresponds to the administrative side of the War Office.

on the contrary, it did harm. Besides that, it failed to place the working capacity of the individual at the disposal of the country and to return the reclaimed men to the army in sufficient numbers. The question of drawing the employers and work-people closer together, which was so immensely important for the transition period, and for the maintenance of order after the war, had made no progress.

At the request of General von Scheüch, the Field-Marshal and I received the representatives of the free Unions (*freie Gewerkschaften*), and later those of the Christian Unions (*Christliche Gewerkschaften*) and the Employers' Associations (*Angestelltenverbände*). We told these gentlemen how necessary it was to maintain and raise the spirit of the people at home, as otherwise that of the army must inevitably suffer. It was not our business to deal with the Auxiliary Service act itself. They promised to assist in improving the morale and denounced the strikes; to my satisfaction, they realized their great responsibility. They made a number of suggestions regarding working conditions at home which, though they did not immediately concern me, interested me considerably, and were passed on to the Government departments concerned with the request that they might be adopted. I hope that in our discussion I clearly explained to them the connection between the army and the people at home, and that they grasped the great importance I attached to the effect of internal conditions of the country on the conduct of the war. They were our guests at dinner and no doubt felt that we treated men of different opinions to our own with respect and aimed at securing collaboration for the good of the country. The stupid gossip about our seeing none but the "captains of industry" died down somewhat after this visit. We had quite different ideas. We regarded ourselves as the leaders of the whole nation in arms, and not only a part of the nation, which was at that time still capable of defense. In this also we were, though not openly, in opposition to the Government, which depended consciously and emphatically only upon that section of the people represented by the Left Majority of the Reichstag and had more or less democratic and radical ideas, while the other section was completely eliminated. The manner in which the law was weakened in favor of the Left, whereby strikes were facilitated and those who were willing to work rendered defenseless, and young men were allowed to combine and to run wild instead of being educated, and the punitive measures promulgated simultaneously against the Right, show clearly the road the Government traveled.

I discussed with the War Minister the regretable phenomena at home, and among other things I pointed out that I did not consider the supervision of the press to be adequate. The state of affairs in the Garrison Army was discussed. The training and discipline of the men were not up to the required standard, saluting had become slack and was generally omitted. No doubt the Garrison Army had to contend with great difficulties. The shortage of suitable officers was increasing. The army at the front could not spare fit officers, but there were, after all, a number of unfit officers available who still retained their strength of will. But they, too, were trying to get to the front, which they were often forced to do by the extremely low rates of pay prevailing at home. In this respect, too, nothing but drastic innovations could have brought any improvement. However, conditions in the training units led the War Ministry to reinforce the recruiting depots of the Field Army as far as possible, so as in this way to get the recruits away from home sooner and bring them into touch with the front and thus make them into reliable soldiers. The contingent of 1899 was transferred to the recruiting depots during the winter of 1917–18.

I had again examined the question of insuring the drafts required to continue the war. I considered it so important that I thought the people must at last take an active part in it. It could be solved in a satisfactory manner only if the nation could be made to see the situation clearly and to decide its own fate for itself. On September 10, 1917, General Headquarters had made serious representations on the subject to the Imperial Chancellor. The Field-Marshal had written:

"The drafts for the Field Army are at present insufficient; in particular, all branches are alarmingly short of trained reinforcements. . . .

"If we fail to provide the necessary drafts the success of the war will be jeopardized."

We considered that, besides raising the warlike spirit and further propaganda, it was necessary, in order to secure drafts, to improve the Auxiliary Service act, increase the output of labor, draw the largest possible number of fit men from the factories not later than the spring of 1918, and prolong the term of service. The document ended as follows: "But this it is my duty to emphasize—the situation must become critical if we do not act with energy and at once. If we do, the army will yet bring the war to a satisfactory conclusion.

"An enormous responsibility rests, therefore, on all departments concerned with the questions discussed above. In particular the Reichstag, the trades-unions, etc., must not be left in doubt that they, too, will incur the most serious blame by hesitation or refusal.

"It is unnecessary to point out that, after months of delay, immediate action is necessary."

But this letter also produced no result. Whether the Reichstag was ever informed of it I do not know.

After I had come to know the Imperial Chancellor, Count von Hertling, I became convinced, and had to reckon with the fact, that he, too, was no War Chancellor. His platform was entirely that of the Majority, of which he was in a sense the product, and his program was peace by understanding. He said so clearly and distinctly in his first great speeches, without finding any sort of echo in the countries of the Entente. He called himself the "Reconciliation Chancellor." I think the time was not yet ripe for reconciliation. We needed a Chancellor who would live only for the duties of his exalted position as War Minister, act with energy, and make the country see the dangers which threatened it. All this was contrary to the nature of Count von Hertling. He was skilful in manipulating the parties of the Reichstag, but gave in to them even in cases where the war demanded different action. Honest intentions had induced him to accept office; but the times demanded a strong personality. The burden was too great for a man of great age and frail physique. Was I once more to tell that to His Majesty? Who was to become Chancellor, since His Majesty had so often pronounced against Prince von Bülow and Grand Admiral von Tirpitz? Who was the man who would throw himself into the breach and join in the fight, who would unite and lead the people by the compelling powers of his aims? Many had already approached me with the suggestion that I should become Chancellor. This, though well meant, was a mistaken idea. The work I had to compass was enormous. In order to carry on the World War I had to govern the instrument. This alone required an unusual capacity for work. It was inconceivable that I should take over in addition the conduct of a Government which, on account of its extremely clumsy working methods, required even more than one man's whole time and strength. Lloyd

George and Clemenceau might be dictators, but the details of the war did not concern them. Germany's dictator would have to be in Berlin, not at General Headquarters. He would have to be a man with an intimate knowledge of all home conditions. Such a man Berlin might have followed. I could not take over the task; of that I became convinced after a severe mental struggle. I was not deterred by fear of responsibility, but by the knowledge that the strength of one man would be insufficient to lead at the same time the people at home and the army at the front in this world-wide war of nations and overcome all the opposition and friction which, as a notorious representative of militarism, I should everywhere have encountered. Circumstances were very different from what they had been in previous wars. The analogies which were suggested to me at that time did not fit at all; times and circumstances could in no way be compared. Frederick the Great was a monarch and possessed his authority by the grace of God. Napoleon knew, at any rate, at the outset of his dazzling career, that he had all France behind him. One thing, however, was certain—the power must be in my hands.

There was no alternative. I must, in addition to my tremendous task at the front, continue the struggle with the Government in order to obtain what the army needed for its last and final victory. I knew how arduous it would be, but hoped that the fall of Russia would make a satisfactory solution possible. This was where the situation differed from the time of the resignation of the first War Chancellor in July 1917.

## IX

Besides the problems of peace, the most important political question was the Austro-Polish one. Count

Czernin had succeeded first of all in winning round the Emperor, and then the Imperial Chancellor and Secretary of State von Kühlmann, to his way of thinking. Directly after Count von Hertling had been won over, a Crown Council was convened to deal with this matter, which the Field-Marshal and I were ordered to attend. The Imperial Chancellor and the Secretary of State were Bavarians, the Vice-Chancellor, Von Payer, a Württemberger. They were strangers to the conditions of the Eastern provinces of Prussia and favored the Austro-Polish solution; the other ministers and Secretaries of State agreed in the main with them. The Field-Marshal and I expressed serious dissent, based upon military objections. My arguments are corroborated by the conditions which now prevail and which illustrate in another form the danger I anticipated.

But the Field-Marshal and I were outvoted. The Emperor ordered us to report what military arrangements would make the Austro-Polish solution acceptable to us.

We therefore sought a way out of the difficulty; it could be found only in a still wider protective belt along the whole Prussian frontier.

In the mean time, in the territory under the Commander-in-chief in the East, matters had developed as a result of the instructions issued in August, in a favorable manner in Courland; in Lithuania, however, the situation had become unsatisfactory.

In September, in accordance with the instructions of the Commander-in-chief, Major von Goszler had succeeded in forming a Local Council at Mitau. He was able to revive to some extent the historic constitutional life of Courland. The nobles had the sense to follow his lead, and invited the Letts to take part in forming the Local Council. They accepted. All those who think that the destruction of all existing institutions spells the salvation of a country considered that the Letts had been offered too little. It was indeed not much. But it did pave the way for steady future development; at any rate, the Letts no longer stood aside. The Local Council assembled with due ceremonial at Mitau, and requested His Majesty in an address to protect Courland and accept the dignity of the Dukedom. The reply of the Imperial Government was favorable, although it refrained from finally committing itself.

In Lithuania the confused wishes of the local democratic party were expressed with increasing insistence. The Local Council was formed at Vilna by transforming the old Confidential Council. But it proved incapable of performing its work, and political life stagnated.

Before he resigned, Doctor Michaelis had visited Lithuania and Courland, and I expected that now affairs in the East could be brought to a conclusion. At this request I intended to go to Berlin early in November. His sudden resignation destroyed my hopes.

Early in November I was in Berlin. The intended conference on questions relating to the territory under the Commander-in-chief in the East took place on the 4th, but under the presidency of the new Chancellor, Von Hertling. I intended to determine in his presence the fundamental principles of the relationship of Courland and Lithuania with Germany, and to assure myself that he agreed with the settlements arrived at with former Chancellors. At the same time I wished to strengthen the position of the administrators by seeing to it that they alone should be the deciding authority in those countries, and not any member of the Reichstag or the Imperial Chancellor or General Headquarters. As before, our policy in the territory of the Commander-in-chief in the East aimed at joining Courland and Lithuania to Germany by means of personal union under the House of Hohenzollern. I now considered it desirable in the interests of our future that the two Local Councils should make a declaration on the subject. In Courland most of the work was already done; nothing remained but formalities. In Vilna, on the other hand, extraordinary difficulties had still to be overcome. However, definite hopes were quite justified if the Administrator received clear instructions, and the vacillation in our dealings with Lithuania was put an end to. Then it was intended in both countries to prepare the main outlines of the internal constitution, as well as for the military, economic, and political union with Germany.

I met with no opposition at the Conference. The gentlemen sent by the Commander-in-chief in the East, who did not know Berlin as I did, were glad to be able at last to go on with their work. I was skeptical and it turned out I was right. The situation in Lithuania remained confused. The Lithuanians and Democrats began an agitation against the Administrator, Lieutenant-Colonel Prince von Isenburg. The complaints were usually alleged to be founded on the war conditions, for which the administration could not in any way be blamed. But the conviction was already formed, and as is usual in political differences, no statements of fact could prevail against it. The democratic Lithuanians of Vilna were listened to by our Majority parties, and these again by the Foreign Office. The Lithuanians lost the habit of regarding the Administrator as the embodiment of German authority, but very soon discovered that individual members were more powerful than the Government itself. These members again indulged their vanity by pursuing a Lithuanian policy of their own, although they did not know the country. The Government, anxiously engaged in preventing General Headquarters from starting a policy on its own account, of which it had no intention, allowed the members to do as they liked. Under its influence the Foreign Office continued to deal with the Lithuanian question in Berlin exclusively in accordance with the alleged requirements of the internal political situation in Germany, and not in accordance with those of the country itself. So in this case also party politics became the governing factor in matters of foreign policy. In this way it was impossible to bring about healthy conditions in Lithuania; every action of the Administrator, whose authority was being undermined from Berlin, was foredoomed to failure. In view of this, the Conference of November 4 was my last attempt to bring order into the Lithuanian muddle. I afterward restricted myself to preventing absolute damage.

Lieutenant-Colonel Prince von Isenburg found himself obliged to resign, when he saw that the main principles of the policy which he knew to be right were being forsaken. I regretted his departure.

About the middle of December the Lithuanians were led by the Imperial Chancellor to expect that their country would be recognized as free and independent, with its capital at Vilna. It would have to promise to conclude certain conventions with Germany. That sort of Lithuania was in a fair way to fall into the hands of the Poles, unless the conventions contained conditions which secured German influence. But the attitude of the Lithuanians gave little promise of that. What prospect there was was bound to decrease the more we gave way to their conflicting desires. Besides, some Lithuanians and one influential delegate from Württemberg wanted a Prince of the Royal House of Württemberg, while, on the other hand, the hopes of the Saxon House appear to have been raised also. Any prince at Vilna would have had the Polish nobility at his court, the officers of the army would have been Poles, and so would the majority of the civil officials. Only Prussian Germany (*Preussen-Deutschland*) could keep Lithuania for the Lithuanians, and provide officials and officers, which they themselves could not do in anything like sufficient numbers. States capable of an independent existence are not produced by political catchwords, nor are small nations kept alive thereby. I was, therefore, by no means pleased with this vague solution, which seemed so very dangerous for Germany's future. It was significant how quietly the Poles accepted it. They could afford to be satisfied.

General Headquarters maintained the view formerly approved by the Imperial Chancellor, that Lithuania should be closely joined to Germany, by personal union under the House of Hohenzollern.

The Eastern questions were again discussed at length in the conference which took place at Kreuznach on December 18 under the presidency of His Majesty, in order to determine the peace conditions to be presented to Russia. On this occasion the Emperor expressed his agreement with the protective belt on the Prusso-Polish frontier which we had stated to be just adequate without protest from the Imperial Councilor or the Secretary of State for Foreign Affairs. The Imperial Chancellor agreed with the idea of establishing personal union of Courland and Lithuania with Prussia or Germany, provided the Federal Princes agreed. His Majesty approved this opinion, and insisted on the necessity of allowing the nations of other races which might be included to develop according to their own character. As regards our policy toward the people of Courland and Lithuania, this involved safeguarding the results we had achieved hitherto, unless we wished to see fresh dangers arise on our eastern frontier in the future.

Regarding Esthonia and Livonia, His Majesty decided to suggest evacuation to the Russians, without demanding it, so as to allow these people to exercise their right of self-determination.

This provided the Foreign Secretary with the necessary basis on which to conduct the coming negotiations.

In the interval, a change had been made in the administration of the territory under the Commander-in-chief in the East. At the head of it were placed a special Administrative General, General Count von Waldersee, and a senior administrative official, Under-Secretary of State Freiherr von Falkenhausen. The intention was to provide better for meeting the political needs of the country and to comply with the wishes of the Imperial Chancellor. General Count von Waldersee and Under-Secretary of State von Falkenhausen carried out their duties with prudence and skill. But, lacking clear orders from Berlin, they could undertake no constructive work.

Under the Chancellorship of Count von Hertling the question of Alsace-Lorraine assumed another aspect, inasmuch as he was a decided supporter of the idea of dividing that country, in which case Bavaria was to get Alsace and Prussia Lorraine. Imperial Chancellor von Bethmann had already had discussions with Bavaria about it. I could not see what good could come of the idea, and feared that this particular solution would cause irritation, particularly in Württemberg. We could only ask the Chancellor to take the necessary steps for starting the discussions in which the fundamental principles of the questions would be laid down. Since then the whole business has been dormant. I had, at least, hoped that he would take advantage of his influence in Rome as an established leader of the Central party and former Bavarian Prime Minister to settle the ecclesiastical affairs of the Reichsland in a national German sense, but he achieved nothing.

# PREPARATIONS FOR THE 1918 OFFENSIVE IN THE WEST

The Determination to Launch the Offensive—The Peace Negotiations at Brest-Litovsk—Bolshevism—Peace with the Ukraine and the Ultimatum to Trotzky—Conferences in Hamburg—Resumption of Hostilities in the East—The Peace of Brest-Litovsk and the Preliminary Peace of Buftea—The Equipment and Training of the Troops for Attack—Support from the Allies—Our Situation as Regards Supplies—The Spirit of the Army.

I

OWING to the breakdown of Russia the military situation was more favorable to us at New-Year's 1918 than one could ever have expected. As in 1914 and 1915, we could think of deciding the war by an attack on land. Numerically we had never been so strong in comparison with our enemies.

The submarine war had not, up to date, produced those economic results which the Chief of the Naval Staff had expected and which I, relying on the opinions of the experts, had hoped for. I had continued to take an interest in the problem of providing submarines in spite of naval assurances that everything possible was being done. I actually received letters from Reichstag members who informed me that more could be built. I was pleased to get these letters, for they amounted to a recognition of my will to carry on the war with all possible energy. On the other hand, they surprised me. The building of submarines was constitutionally no business of mine. I had already been reproached by these gentlemen often enough for interfering in matters which did not concern me. It had, in fact, become quite the usual practice, when anything was needed to be done at home, to appeal to me. In this instance, of course, I could, unfortunately, do nothing except once more press the matter upon the naval authorities concerned. General Headquarters had long before issued orders that every application for individual men by name was to be complied with immediately. Further than that we could not go in releasing workmen. On the list of requirements for the supply of raw materials the construction of submarines was the first item. Everything connected with it was of decisive importance to us. The question was: What will be the rate of supply of submarines in the spring of 1918? Will the submarines, even if they have been unable to damage England decisively, have so far reduced tonnage that the new American troops cannot come over in a short time, and will they be able to strike at American transports while engaged generally in destroying hostile tonnage?

In July 1917 Deputy Erzberger had spoken with me about the bearing of world-tonnage on the effect of the submarine war, and had also expressed his opinions in the Reichstag. No doubt the world-tonnage did greatly influence its effect, but it was not alone decisive. If, for instance, England had to withdraw ships from the service between America and Australia in order to maintain the service with America, these ships could not be there as well; the Australian grain, on which England depended, remained in Australia, and the general supply available for the Entente fell short by that amount. In my opinion the expression "world-tonnage" does not fully answer the question why the submarine war did not conquer the Entente. England's economic situation was eased by increased agricultural production, and this delayed the effect

of the submarine war. Whether the construction of
new shipping in the Entente was greater than had
originally been assumed, and it thus received still
further stimulation, I cannot decide. But it was of
decisive importance that the Entente had had time in
two years of war to adapt its economic life to the circumstances and to perfect its means of defense. "But,"
says *The Economist* of September 7, 1918, "the fleet
(with American aid, certainly) mastered the submarine
danger and greatly reduced its efficiency." In war it
is even harder to see into the future than in peace,
especially when conditions are so complicated as in this
case. These conditions were not perceived by the
enemy, either. This explains why our Navy did not
obtain an absolutely clear view of all the determining
factors. Its responsible heads worked and calculated
dutifully and conscientiously. Although by October
1918 the submarines had not decided the war, their
achievements, nevertheless, were of great influence.
"It was the greatest danger that England ever faced,"
says *The Morning Post* of October 3, 1918. It would
also be a mistake to underestimate its effect on the
whole economic life of the Entente, and to disregard
the extent to which it eased the strain on the Western
front. It will be the task of history to clear up these
questions and to pursue this complicated problem
farther. The achievements of our submarine crews
will remain heroic deeds for all time, and the country
and the Navy may be proud of them.

About New Year's 1918 the opinion of the Navy was
as optimistic as ever. I had, however, become more
skeptical, and felt obliged to count on the new American
formations beginning to arrive in the spring of 1918.
In what numbers they would appear could not be
foreseen; but it might be taken as certain that they
would not balance the loss of Russia; further, the

relative strengths would be more in our favor in the spring than in the late summer and autumn, unless, indeed, we had by then gained a great victory.

In the late autumn, 1917, General Headquarters was confronted by the decisive question: Should it utilize the favorable conditions of the spring to strike a great blow in the West or should it deliberately restrict itself to the defensive and make only subsidiary attacks, say in Macedonia or Italy?

The Quadruple Alliance was held together only by the hope of a victory by the Germans.

The Austro-Hungarian Army was worn out; it had lost 1,800,000 prisoners; it was short of recruits. Its fighting value was slight, though against Italy it had, on the whole, sufficed. If Russia actually dropped out we might hope that the army would continue equal to the task that fell to it. Whether it could spare forces for other objects was doubtful. In 1917 we had already received an intimation from the Imperial and Royal Government that the army could go on fighting only for a limited period; we might anticipate something similar in 1918. We had to take into consideration that Austria-Hungary might actually arrive at the end of its military power. It was clear that its political power would not last one hour longer. Nothing but the army held the Dual Monarchy together.

The Bulgarian Army had sufficient recruits; it was, however, found necessary to enroll numerous men of other races. In 1917 the troops had fought tolerably well; their spirit had improved. The communications had been put properly in order behind their whole front. The influence of the German Group Headquarters and of the other German commands had become more pronounced; it extended, however, farther than the limits of actual direct German command. The training of the army as a whole was fur-

thered by means of schools established by Group Headquarters. Thanks to its past work, the latter could
anticipate the coming struggle with some confidence.
I often conversed with General Gantshev, and requested
him to do his part in promoting the improvement of the
Bulgarian Army. In view of the events of the previous
year he considered its position secure. It was only the
mobilization of the Greek Army that made him anxious.
That he could, of course, never ask for enough German
stores and German troops was his chief difficulty.
With every word he expressed the hope of a German
victory in the West.

Bulgaria had occupied all the territory it wanted to
keep when peace came; it was sure of its gains—it
thought no more of war, but only of enjoying in peace
and quietness what it had won. The people and the
army were tired of war. Radoslavoff's Government lost
ground, agitation against the Government and the war
began, at first with the object of giving other parties a
chance of feathering their nest. This increased the
danger of Entente influence gaining ground in Bulgaria,
a danger which was all the greater in that the present
Government had permitted agitation against us. The
irritation against us was further increased by the fact
that out of consideration for the rate of exchange we
did not take enough tobacco from them, and many
Bulgarians felt that they were losing money in consequence. The representative of the United States,
who sat tight in Sofia, took advantage of these conditions very cleverly, and held out prospects of large
profits in good Swiss francs. Many failed to resist this
temptation; they turned again to the Entente, with
whom at heart they had always been in sympathy.

The only conclusion I could come to about Bulgaria
was that it would remain faithful to us as long as all
went well with us. But if the prospects of victory

diminished, or still worse, if we suffered failure, then things were bound to turn out just as in fact they have. Why should there be any difference between the character of nations and that of men? I could believe in the steadfastness of the Bulgarian Army for just so long as I could believe in the faith of the Bulgarian nation.

Turkey was faithful to the alliance, but at the end of its strength; whether through its own fault or that of others was immaterial. Its man-power was greatly reduced, and the army existed to a certain extent only on paper. Palestine was sure to fall an easy prey to England unless the troops there were reinforced. Turkey's disintegration was bound to produce political results over a wide area, and must, therefore, be prevented, even though the decision of the war might be brought about elsewhere.

In Germany the national spirit appeared to be better than with our allies; nevertheless, it had sunk very low and feeling had become worse. I must admit I formed too favorable an estimate of our remaining energy. I hoped that the recruiting question would be put in order.

The army had come victoriously through 1917; but it had become apparent that the holding of the Western front purely by a defensive could no longer be counted on, in view of the enormous quantity of material of all kinds which the Entente had now at its disposal. Even where tactical conditions had been absolutely normal, and by no means so unfavorable as in the struggle for the Wytschaete salient or Laffaux corner, we had lost ground and suffered heavily. These losses had indeed been greater than we had incurred in well-conducted attacks. The enormous material resources of the enemy had given his attack a considerable preponderance over our defense, and this condition would become more and more apparent as our infantry approximated more nearly in character to a militia, as our best men became casualties, and as discipline declined.

It was also to be expected that the enemy would learn from past battles; he would probably attack on a broad front, as in the double battle of the Aisne and Champagne in April and May 1917, and aim at surprise. This he would be able to do by employing vast quantities of stores and equipment. These attacks would doubtless make far greater demands on us than any that had gone before.

The troops had borne the continuous defensive with uncommon difficulty. Skulkers were already numerous. They reappeared as soon as the battle was over, and it had become quite common for divisions which came out of action with desperately low effectives, to be considerably stronger after only a few days. Against the power of the hostile weapons the troops no longer displayed their old stubbornness in defense; they thought with horror of fresh defensive battles and longed for the war of movement. In this the Germans had achieved brilliant success in Rumania, eastern Galicia, Italy, and at Cambrai, and had once more proved their superiority, although their staying power was no longer what it had been in 1914. There had been incidents, too, which indicated that their cohesion was no longer the same. As they were depressed by defense, their spirits rose in the offensive. The interests of the army were best served by the offensive; in defense it was bound gradually to succumb to the ever-increasing hostile superiority in men and material. This feeling was shared by everybody. In the West it wanted the attack, and after Russia's collapse expected it with the most intense relief. Such was the feeling of the troops about attack and defense. It amounted to a definite conviction which possessed them completely that nothing but an attack could win the war. Many generals, among them the most distinguished, spoke in the same strain. Naturally, I did not allow myself to be influenced by this feeling; my sense of responsibility was far too great. I alone had to make the decision regarding that, of that I remained conscious throughout. The wishes of the troops and commanders merely indicated what the army felt regarding its own strength and weakness.

The condition of our allies and of ourselves and that of the army all called for an attack that would bring about an early decision. This was possible only on the Western front. All that had gone before was merely a means to the one end of creating a situation that would make it a feasible operation. Until now this situation had not arisen. We had been able to strike a blow at Italy with six or seven divisions, but for the Western front that was not a sufficient force. I set aside all idea of attacking in Macedonia or Italy. All that mattered was to get together enough troops for an attack in the West.

For this we needed enormous material resources and strong troops who, with their leaders, had been trained for the attack. If this could be effected in time we could—indeed, we must, attack. The attack is the strongest form of combat; it alone is decisive; military history proves it on every page. It is the symbol of superiority. Delay could only serve the enemy, since he was expecting reinforcements.

That the attack in the West would be one of the most difficult operations in history I was perfectly sure, and I did not hide the fact. The German nation, too, would have to give all it had. The greater the lack of men, the stronger must be its will, the more energetic the work of the Government in the service of the war.

General Headquarters would, as in the days of Tannenberg, have to get together for the decisive moment every man that could be spared from the various theaters. We could never be too strong. On the other hand, it would not do to forget that the European fronts are most intimately connected. A failure in Italy, in Macedonia, or in the East might check our operations in the West.

It was not necessary to leave German troops on the Italian front, and preparations were made for their departure about the new year. We retained only a certain interest in the military resources of the occupied portions of Italy, which then passed under Austro-Hungarian administration. From the Russo-Rumanian front, in spite of the objections of the Bulgarians, we moved Bulgarian troops to Macedonia, in order to relieve a few German formations.

The move from Galicia and the Bukovina to France and Belgium had been arranged for and a final decision as to the troops to be removed from the Eastern front and the Balkan Peninsula became urgently necessary. Before we could decide we had to obtain a clear idea of our future relationship to Russia and Rumania and of the attitude of Bolshevism toward the Entente and the Quadruple Alliance, both from the military and the revolutionary point of view. It was necessary for us to be placed in a position to do so as soon as possible. There still remained a great amount of transport work to accomplish. The American danger rendered it desirable to strike in the West as early as possible; the state of training of the army for attack enabled us to contemplate doing so about the middle of March. At that season, too, horses would find some grazing, which, in view of the shortage of forage, was a necessary provision.

If all went smoothly at Brest-Litovsk, if the people

there worked with real energy, we could expect to have our forces ready for a successful attack in the West by the time mentioned.  No delay could be justified.  It will be obvious with what interest we watched the peace negotiations.

II

The negotiations at Brest-Litovsk began on December 22, 1917.

Their progress was bound to exercise a determining influence on the military decisions, since we were still at war.  The really important matter was whether they were going to be conducted in such a manner that we could attack, and make certain of finishing the titanic struggle in our favor, after all, and so save ourselves from the tragedy of being defeated.

For the future of Germany it was all-important that the whole Eastern problem should be solved in a manner which satisfied the interests of Prussia and Germany, and as far as possible removed the danger threatening from Poland.  The decisions arrived at on December 18 at Kreuznach might yet assure this.

An exceptionally heavy responsibility rested on the negotiators, and this was by no means lessened by the feelings of the people at home, which had developed under the influence of hostile propaganda without having been counteracted, as it should have been, by a strong and determined Government.  There was a general misunderstanding of the enemy's determination, coupled with the fear of arousing his ill-will and thereby making peace more difficult, and this gave rise to hostile criticism whenever definite action was attempted, regardless of whether the interests of the country, or the prosecution of the war, and, therefore, the final peace would be hindered thereby.

The German Plenipotentiary at Brest-Litovsk was

Secretary of State von Kühlmann; under him was General Hoffmann, as special representative of General Headquarters. Austria-Hungary had sent Count Czernin. The other Powers of the Quadruple Alliance were also represented. Herr von Kühlmann declined the presidency; it was allotted to the different Powers in turn.

The Russian plenipotentiaries were conceded equal rights in every respect. They at once made proposals of their own.

On December 25 Count Czernin, in the name of the four allies, declared his agreement with the Russian proposal of peace without annexations by force and without indemnities.

On this basis the Entente Powers were also invited to join the general peace negotiations, being given till 10 P.M. on January 4 to decide.

Count Czernin, the leading diplomat of the Quadruple Alliance, declares in this connection, "Had the Entente at that time been prepared for a general peace, the principle of no annexations would have been accepted in its entirety."

The right of self-determination was applied in a manner that lacked clearness and did not accord with German interests.

Instead of simple and plain demands, a list of principles had been drawn up, the discussion of which was bound to take a very long time. The invitation to the Entente, too, could produce nothing but delay. There was no prospect of its being accepted. Nothing was in accordance with the decisions arrived at under the presidency of His Majesty on December 18. Our future in the East was rendered doubtful. How the Letts would now act one could not tell. The danger of the Lithuanians and White Ruthenes being betrayed to the Poles was immeasurably increased, and the latter, in accordance with Austrian interests, were correspondingly favored. The necessary military measures for securing the frontiers were not thought of. I spoke to General Hoffmann, regretting the way the negotiations were going. He very rightly said he thought matters had been settled in that way at Kreuznach on the 18th. I explained to him that we had not been in any way informed, and instructed him, now that the fourteen days' term had been fixed, to press Secretary of State von Kühlmann at least to secure our intentions regarding Courland and Lithuania, and make it possible for us to seize a protective belt in Poland, which we had so far, in accordance with His Majesty's instructions and with our agreement with the Imperial Chancellor, regarded as demands of the German Empire. On General Hoffmann's representation, Herr von Kühlmann now assumed a position in regard to Courland and Lithuania more in accord with the Kreuznach agreements; in this he, no doubt, placed himself to some extent in opposition to Count Czernin, who, in order to support Herr von Kühlmann, in the most incomprehensible manner threatened to conclude a separate peace on behalf of Austria-Hungary. During the whole proceedings the absence of previous agreement among the allies proved a stumbling-block.

The speeches of the Bolshevist representatives of Russia showed from the first that the Entente was anxious for the negotiations to be drawn out, and that they themselves still hoped that the Entente would help them to bring about a general revolution. They endeavored to develop the negotiations at Brest into a great propaganda for their ideas. This was all the more dangerous for our internal conditions, in that the destructive influence of Bolshevism on society was recognized by only a few. Above all, it was misunderstood and underestimated by the Majority parties in the Reichstag. All they saw in the utterances of the Bolshevists at Brest was a confirmation of their own pacifist ideals and the beginning of universal brotherhood. I took quite a different view. It was clear to me that, with or without the support of the Entente, Bolshevism was for us an uncommonly dangerous enemy which would have to be kept out by force of arms even if we did make peace.

At the end of December the delegates dispersed without having concluded any special agreements and went home in order to meet again in January at the end of the fourteeen days.

Early in January the Field-Marshal and I also went to Berlin in order to see Secretary of State von Kühlmann and urge him to hasten the negotiations. I also wanted to see General Hoffmann, who was in Berlin.

On January 2 there was a council in the presence of His Majesty. I pointed out that the intended blow in the West necessitated an early peace in the East, since the required transport of troops could not take place until it was in sight. On military grounds any attempt at dragging out the proceedings must be opposed. We were strong enough to prevent it. But Herr von Kühlmann received no special instructions to this effect.

Then the Polish frontier-belt was again dealt with. Count Czernin had utilized his time at Brest to induce Herr von Kühlmann to agree to its being narrowed, in contravention of the decision of December 18. The latter must have agreed to it, and obtained the consent of General Hoffmann, who was thereupon ordered to report on the matter to His Majesty. The latter, quoting General Hoffmann, adopted the view of the Secretary of State. Naturally it was for the Emperor to decide, but I was pained by the reasons given. I had believed that the Field-Marshal and I were His Majesty's responsible military advisers, and I regarded the extensive narrowing of the protective belt as a danger to the provinces of East and West Prussia. I considered it my duty again to emphasize my view, and gained the impression that I had aroused the Emperor's disapproval.

On the 4th I discussed my relationship to the Emperor with General von Lyncker. From what had occurred, I could infer only that His Majesty no longer gave me the confidence which I must demand to enable me to fulfil my arduous duties. I therefore placed myself at His Majesty's disposal for other employment. General von Lyncker advised me to talk it over with the Field-Marshal, who had returned to Kreuznach on the 3d. I agreed, and did so on the 5th. The Field-Marshal asked me to give up the idea, and said he would take the matter up himself, to which I consented.

Much to my regret, something became known in Berlin, and was connected with the Brest negotiations. That, however, was inaccurate. Now, as at the time of my resignation in 1918, it was a case of personal feeling against me on the part of His Majesty, which, coming as it did from my Emperor and Supreme War Lord, was unbearable, and caused me the deepest pain.

To my regret, on January 2 trouble arose also between me and General Hoffmann; but we settled it later.

In connection with these events the Field-Marshal submitted a memorandum to His Majesty on the 7th. He gave prominence to the responsibility resting on himself and on me for seeing to it that the peace should result in such a strengthening of the German people and such an improvement in its frontiers, that our enemies would not dare to let loose another war for a long time to come. The attainment of this object was jeopardized by the Secretary of State in departing from His Majesty's instructions of December 18 regarding the Polish frontier, supported though, indeed, he was by His Majesty's later decision.

The memorandum also alluded to what had occurred at the conference of January 2, and to the difficult position in which both the Field-Marshal and I found ourselves in regard to His Majesty. It ended as follows:

"As long as we discuss matters and no action is taken, the differences [with the Foreign Office] are not so apparent. But when, as now, action is taken against Austria in the Austro-Polish solution, or against the Russians at Brest, they become painfully evident. This will recur on every occasion, and so will the present situation in consequence.

"It is Your Majesty's exalted right to decide. But Your Majesty will not demand that upright men, who have faithfully served Your Majesty and the country, should lend their authority and their name to acts which, they are profoundly convinced, are dangerous to the Crown and Empire.

"Your Majesty will not expect me to submit proposals for operations which are among the most difficult in history, unless they are necessary for attaining definite objects of military policy.

"Most humbly I beg Your Majesty to decide on the fundamental principles. Personal considerations regarding General Ludendorff and myself cannot be allowed to count in matters touching the needs of the State."

His Majesty handed the paper to the Imperial Chancellor for reply. In the middle of January we had an interview with him.

Above all, he opposed the views that the Field-Marshal and I had a share in the responsibility for the peace terms. He insisted that the responsibility was his alone. The Field-Marshal did not intend now, any more than he had in the time of Chancellor von Beth-

mann-Hollweg, to impede the functions of the Imperial
Chancellor in any way. But in this matter our moral
responsibility was involved, of which we were profoundly conscious, and of which no one could relieve
us. It was further the case that in the army and among
the people, the Field-Marshal and I were very definitely
considered to share the responsibility for the peace.
That was the fault of the Government itself, which
often enough had proclaimed our agreement with its
views, or had shielded itself behind our objection to
plans and wishes which it had been unable to satisfy.

Count von Hertling himself had not done so; he was
obviously trying to free himself from supposed tutelage
of General Headquarters. I was, now and then, surprised at the way in which he did so. In the middle
of January, too, he expressed himself strongly to this
effect. Unfortunately, in public, the Government did
not state sufficiently clearly and emphatically that it,
and not General Ludendorff, was in supreme command.

As a matter of fact, there was no doubt whatever
as to the constitutional responsibility of the Imperial
Chancellor, and the silent moral joint responsibility
of the Field-Marshal and myself. But the more
clearly the Chancellor marked out the dividing-line
the heavier became his own responsibility.

We now learned also that Count von Hertling had expressly approved Count Czernin's Christmas speech.
So he was, as was his right, following his own policy
absolutely, and did not hold himself bound by any
agreement with us. What it was that caused him to
change his attitude in this way I cannot understand
to this day. We considered His Majesty's decision of
December 18 as binding, and could not but expect
that he would inform us of any change. Otherwise
grave misunderstanding and personal friction such as
had now occurred could not be avoided. They would,

however, have been avoided if we had been kept informed. The opinion of the Field-Marshal and myself would have remained the same, but it would have been differently expressed.

Neither the discussions nor the decision which His Majesty gave the Field-Marshal made any difference. In particular, we received no information as to the objects of military policy which were being pursued. Up till then Count von Hertling's object in the West had been to prevent Belgium becoming a concentration area for our enemies. This was also the view of General Headquarters.

### III

In the mean time the peace delegations reassembled at Brest. The Entente, of course, had not come. Many people were somewhat curious to see whether the Russians would return. They came under the leadership of Trotzky. They came under compulsion. The dissolution of their army was progressing rapidly; it was in a state of utter disorganization and wanted peace. Our military position was, therefore, as favorable as could be imagined; it was not even necessary for us to act as the Entente did toward Bulgaria, Austria-Hungary, and Germany; we had merely to enforce our simple demands with clearness and decision.

We made extensive concessions to the principle of self-determination. We dropped our contention that the people of the occupied countries, Courland and Lithuania, had already been permitted to avail themselves of this right, and allowed the inhabitants to be consulted again. All we demanded was that this should take place during our occupation. Trotzky maintained that we must first of all evacuate the country and that the people would exercise their right afterward.

To evacuate the country was a military absurdity; we needed it for our existence and had no mind to deliver it up to unscrupulous Bolshevism. We declined to evacuate it on this military ground, quite apart from the fact that no exercise of the right of self-determination was possible under the Bolshevist knout. On both these questions opinions are now probably clearer, and people may perhaps understand the view of General Headquarters. If we had left the country the armed forces of the Bolshevists would long ago have been in Germany. They were not the least interested in the right of self-determination; all they wanted was more power. They were politicians who govern by violence, and assumed that the territory evacuated by us would fall into their hands without further parley. They were, moreover, so nationally minded that they looked upon the severance of Courland, Lithuania, and Poland —self-determination notwithstanding—as a measure hostile to Russia.

Austria-Hungary had by far the greatest interest in the exercise of the right of self-determination in Poland at the expense of Russia. The Dual Monarchy hoped to gain political and economic strength from Poland.

The Turks wanted Batum and Kars, both of which had belonged to the Turkish Empire for a very long time. For us these wishes were of subordinate importance; but it was part of our duty as an ally to insist upon them.

Our purely military demands were so insignificant that they hardly counted. The demobilization was already making excellent progress; and we had not demanded the surrender of arms or ships.

We did not ask for Esthonia or Livonia, although we would have been glad to deliver our fellow-Germans and the other inhabitants from Bolshevism. This demand was not made, although it was down for discussion and became a military necessity against Bolshevism. Peace was not delayed by our demands, but merely by the revolutionary aims of the Bolshevists, and by want of resolution in our delegates, as well as by the attitude of Germany and Austria, where the people, being ignorant of the world, did not understand the inner meaning of the Russian Revolution. When on one occasion General Hoffmann adopted a more uncompromising attitude in order to shorten the negotions for military reasons and to restrict Trotzky's propaganda at the same time, there was a chorus of indignation in a large number of German and Austro-Hungarian papers and in all those others which, like the propaganda of the Entente, talked incessantly of peace by understanding. In these circumstances Trotzky would have been a fool to have given in on any point, but he was far too clever and energetic for that. His tone became more and more provoking, although he had no real power behind him; his demands became more and more insistent. He threatened to withdraw the Russian delegates on account of lack of sincerity on the part of the German and Austrian representatives and had the satisfaction of being requested to desist from this intention, which he can never seriously have entertained. Trotzky and the Entente were delighted with the prolongation of the negotiations; the former took every opportunity of delaying them; he even suggested transferring them to a neutral locality. He proclaimed his Bolshevist ideas by wireless to all the world, particularly to the German working-classes. The intention of the Bolshevists to revolutionize and destroy Germany became more and more obvious to every one who was not totally blind.

The negotiations made no progress; moreover, by the way they were being carried on at Brest we should not only never arrive at peace, but would undoubtedly bring about a further fall in our fighting capacity. All this time I was at Kreuznach, burning with impatience and urging General Hoffmann to hurry on the negotiations. He was well aware of the military necessity, but his position did not allow him to interfere with effect.

On January 18 Trotzky went to Petrograd, where the Bolshevists dispersed the Constituent Assembly. In that way they showed the world their idea of freedom of the people. But the Germans would neither see nor learn.

Trotzky had said he would be away only six days; he did not return until the 30th.

On January 23, at my request, the Field-Marshal declared, during a consultation at Berlin, that we must have the Eastern situation cleared up. Until it was it would be necessary to retain there good divisions that were fit for employment in the West. If the Russians delayed matters any further we ought to reopen hostilities. This would bring down the Bolshevist Government, and any others that might succeed it would have to make peace.

There were other reasons which made me press for an early conclusion. Count Czernin was right when he spoke ironically of a "spiritual wrestling-match." For him, indeed, at Brest, while the war was rushing on to its greatest decision, there was neither time nor place, nor yet a suitable opponent. What must the statesmen of the Entente think of our need of peace if we tamely submitted to this sort of treatment by Trotzky and his Bolshevist Government, a Government that had not even been recognized by any other State? They and their people could only gain enormously in strength and resolution by witnessing such a spectacle. How necessary must peace be to Germany when she literally ran after such people and put up with open propaganda against her and her army. This was bound to be the effect in every neutral and enemy country. How could the Entente leaders, above all men like Clemenceau and Lloyd George, be afraid of peace when we allowed ourselves to be treated thus by unarmed Russian anarchists? They would cease to feel any anxiety and come to the conclusion that they ran no risk from us at all. How that would affect the peace feeling among such enemies there could be no doubt.

Nor did the soldier at the front understand all this talk that went on for weeks on end, seemed to serve no practical object and produce no tangible result. What he had achieved at the expense of his last ounce of strength, and in a thousand forms of distress and danger, he naturally wished to see utilized with energy and to good purpose. And what was here at stake was the first peace, the result of which was awaited with no less interest at the front than it was at home. Surely we must at last take some decisive steps. That alone would clear matters up, both at home and abroad.

In the mean time it had become evident that Trotzky did not represent the whole of Russia, not to mention Rumania. On January 12 delegates arrived at Brest from the Ukraine, and took up a position completely opposed to the Bolshevists. They were supported mainly by General Hoffmann and gave the representatives of the Quadruple Alliance an opportunity of opening separate negotiations. These were of a practical nature, and were not lost in the mists of fantastic projects which take centuries to work out if they are ever worked out at all.

On January 30 negotiations with Trotzky were resumed at Brest.

Now began a most curious situation, for everything was ordered in accordance with his ideas.

However, the diplomats themselves now seemed to perceive that discussions with him led to no result. Secretary of State von Kühlmann and Count Czernin proceeded to interrupt the negotiations and were back in Berlin on February 4. Discussion with the Ukraine was continued on the principle that it bound itself to supply Austria-Hungary and Germany with large quantities of grain, in return for which it was to receive a favorable frontier against Poland in the disputed area of Cholm. In addition, Austria-Hungary promised to create a Ukrainian Crown-land in eastern Galicia.

In order to discuss the situation with Herr von Kühlmann and Count Czernin I had also gone to Berlin early in February. At our interviews on the 4th and 5th I received from the former a promise that he would break with Trotzky twenty-four hours after signing the peace with the Ukraine. From all I heard I was confirmed in my impression that Bolshevist Russia did not really want peace at all. It had set its hopes on the Entente and on the gradual spread of the revolution in Germany, and did not believe we would take any action. Its hopes must have been confirmed by the strikes which broke out in this connection in Berlin at the end of January 1918, against the will of prominent labor-leaders, so close, even then, was the connection between a part of our labor movement and the Bolshevists.

The men at the head of it, and the most influential part of the Socialist press, both of whom afterward opposed the Bolshevists, had not yet recognized that fact. At that time, it is true, the object was still to combat the common enemy, the established authority, and thus consciously or otherwise to undermine the foundations of the country. When afterward this object was attained and these people had themselves become the masters, the spark they had started had become a devouring fire.

At the discussion in Berlin, Count Czernin explained the reasons which had led him to agree to a peace with the Ukraine which was undoubtedly disadvantageous to the Dual Monarchy, and might be expected to arouse strong opposition from Poland. For this reason he requested us to keep the political settlement more or less secret. He said the food situation in Austria-Hungary was so bad that, owing to the ever-decreasing supply from Rumania, the people must starve unless they obtained corn from the Ukraine. The Austrian Director of Supplies, General Landwehr, supplemented this statement with details about the army and asked me if I could help. As, in spite of our own very serious situation, Herr von Waldow thought we could still help to a limited extent, I could raise no objection. What I then heard appeared to me most serious, and must have made a deep impression on the other gentlemen who had to deal with these matters.

Another matter we discussed was the old Austro-Polish solution. This time I was more of a listener. To my satisfaction the Secretaries of State von Stein and Count von Rödern, as well as several other gentlemen, opposed it on economic grounds. The protective belt was unimportant. The Austro-Hungarian ambassador, Prince Hohenlohe, for whom I have otherwise a warm regard, became irritated at the course of the conference and reproached me with throwing difficulties in the way of Austria - Hungary. I could only point out that on this occasion it was not I, but the others, who had objected to the Austro-Polish solution. The question of Poland remained in abeyance.

The terms of peace with Rumania were also briefly

discussed. In this case also I urged the need for energetic action.

Secretary of State von Kühlmann and Count Czernin returned to Brest after the discussion.

Peace with the Ukraine was signed there February 9. I now requested Herr von Kühlmann to carry out his promise of the 5th and break with Trotzky, but he declined.

On the same day a wireless message from the Russian Government called upon the German Army to refuse obedience to the Supreme War Lord.

At the request of the Field-Marshal the Emperor now instructed Herr von Kühlmann to present an ultimatum to Trotzky requiring acceptance of our former conditions, and further to demand the evacuation of the Baltic littoral. This latter instruction the Secretary of State thought he ought not to carry out, in view of the state of feeling at home and in Austria-Hungary. The Emperor agreed.

The Secretary of State now urged Trotzky to bring the negotiations to a conclusion. The latter, however, declined to be bound in any way, but declared at the same time that the war was at an end and that the demobilization of the Russian Army had been ordered.

This, of course, completed the confusion in the East. We could not possibly leave matters in this condition. At any moment fresh dangers might arise while we were fighting for our lives in the West. The military situation made it imperative clearly to define our future plans. This was to be achieved by a conference at Hamburg.

IV

The conference at Hamburg took place on February 13. It had a decisive influence on the events in the

East. The Imperial Chancellor, the Vice-Chancellor, Secretary of State von Kühlmann, the Field-Marshal, the Chief of the Naval Staff, and I took part in it. His Majesty the Emperor attended only at intervals.

Before this General Headquarters had despatched a number of telegrams to the Imperial Chancellor, asking for the armistice to be denounced. At the moment the Russian Army was no longer of any account; but the Entente was on the lookout to strengthen its front, and the Bolshevist leaders were men of action who would work by propaganda, and, if they were given time, by arms even without the Entente.

At any moment, somehow or somewhere, the Russian front might become strong again. Nor would Rumania ever make peace until Russia had shown the way. This would make any attack in the West hopeless. And with that we should miss the opportunity of victoriously finishing the World War, a war we were still waging, supported only by weak allies, against enemies superior in numbers. We also wanted the Ukraine as an auxiliary against the Bolshevists, so it must not on any account be surrendered to them. It had already appealed for help.

Whence were we to obtain the corn which, according to its experts, Austria-Hungary so badly needed? Germany could not supply it; but that is what it would have come to in the end. Germany herself was extremely short; the year before she had anticipated credits for early threshing, and now needed extra supplies herself. Rumania was no longer supplying the anticipated quantity. The prospects would be still worse if the coming harvest with us and our allies should be bad, as well as in Rumania, which, as a matter of fact, experienced a complete failure. Left entirely to herself, without any outside help, Germany could not exist, as was proved by the great distress in the winter of 1918–19. Disaster would certainly have come without help from the Ukraine, even if the destruction of public order had not been a contributing cause.

The peace with the Ukraine rested, owing to the Bolshevist influence, then, on a weak foundation. That we should have to assist there with military force in order to get corn, unless the peace was to become a futile farce, was evident to the representatives of the Quadruple Alliance.

In order to prevent the Bolshevists themselves from forming a new Eastern front against us, we had to inflict upon their troops a short but sharp blow, which would, in addition, bring in a great quantity of stores. For the moment no extensive operation was in contemplation.

In the Ukraine we had to suppress Bolshevism and create such conditions that we could get some military value out of it, and obtain corn and raw materials. In order to do that, it was necessary to penetrate deep into the country; there was no alternative.

In order to prevent Russia being reinforced by the Entente nations, which the latter were still endeavoring to do, it was necessary to hold up their troops and stores on the Murman coast. Otherwise England would certainly come to Petrograd and work against us from there. We must prevent her from obtaining a footing there and in the Gulf of Finland, and in striking at the Bolshevist troops we must advance through Livonia and Esthonia as far as Narva, in order to be able to act from that place in time, whenever necessary. In Finland, too, which had already called upon us for help, we might find an ally against the Bolshevists. In this way some effect would be produced against the Murmansk railway, and that on Petrograd would be increased. For some time past I had been in communication with a few Finnish gentlemen. Above all I would mention the first ambassador of the young Finnish State, Herr Hjelt, who served it with ardor. At the very beginning of the war a number of young Finns, who fervently loved their country, had been formed into a rifle battalion, which was employed at Mitau. Whether we should actually go so far as to undertake military operations in Finland was at that time doubtful. We supplied them with arms.

Our military and food situation required that the armistice should be denounced, and that the position should be definitely cleared up in the East, and rapid action taken.

To me, this new employment of military force was undesirable. But it was a military absurdity, or worse, to sit still and watch the enemy increase his strength; so it was necessary to act. That was demanded by the inexorable law of war. It would then be certain that we should obtain peace. That was all I wanted.

It was in this sense that I expressed myself to the Chancellor and Vice-Chancellor, and I pointed out to them the enormous difficulty of our task in the West. I also stated my belief that we should never get an honest peace from the Bolshevist leaders, but that they would, as before, certainly continue to work for the revolutionizing of Germany. This danger it was impossible to exaggerate. We could protect ourselves against Bolshevism only by placing a close cordon beyond our frontiers. It was no doubt a disadvantage to extend the containing line in the direction of the Gulf of Bothnia; but, owing to the large lakes, the line Dvinsk-Lake Peipus-Gulf of Finland did not require many more troops than that from Dvinsk to the Gulf of Riga. Any intermediate line would require far more. This was no case of a military operation without visible limits to its possible future expansion; it was a purely local and limited measure. I also laid

ress on the satisfaction I naturally felt at going to
the assistance of the people of Livonia and Esthonia,
specially those of our own German race, who were
calling to us for help against their Bolshevist oppressors.

At first the Imperial Chancellor and the Vice-Chancellor could not be got to agree to the denunciation of
the armistice. They based their refusal on the grounds
of internal politics and the condition of Austria-Hungary. Those arguments also determined the attitude of
Herr von Kühlmann. Reasons of foreign policy were
of no account. Gradually the first two gentlemen
were persuaded, and agreed to denounce the armistice,
specially in view of the food situation. Secretary of
State von Kühlmann remained obdurate. He declared,
however, that not he, but the Imperial Chancellor, was
constitutionally responsible, and that since the latter
had resolved to denounce the armistice he would not
refuse his further co-operation.

I could only assume that Secretary of State von
Kühlmann himself did not think his reasons for refusal very sound, otherwise, constitutional responsibility
notwithstanding, he would have been bound to draw
the appropriate conclusions as regards his own person.
The office of Secretary of State for Foreign Affairs was
surely such an exalted one that he dare not allow himself to be overridden in a matter of such grave importance. His conduct could not inspire in me that confidence which I should so much have wished to give
the head of the Foreign Office.

Unfortunately, this incident also impaired my relations with other gentlemen of the Foreign Office, some
of whom, especially among the non-professional diplomats, possessed capabilities of a high order. I regretted
these difficulties all the more because I was quite in-
different to the persons themselves, and was concerned
only with the cause. I was as strongly convinced that

this office needed reform as was the great majority of
the German people.

On the report of the Imperial Chancellor, His Majesty
agreed to the armistice being denounced or, as it was
thought more correct from the point of view of inter
national law, to the publication of the fact that, owing
to Trotzky's failure to sign the peace treaty, the armis
tice automatically came to an end

What method they chose was immaterial to me.

v

So hostilities recommenced along the whole front of
Great Russia on the afternoon of February 18 and the
morning of the 19th. Almost immediately the Bolshe
vist Government declared itself ready for peace by
wireless. Profiting by our recent experiences at Brest
we took care to put the affair on a totally different
footing. In concert with our allies and in agreement
with General Headquarters, the Government demanded
for our military security, but also in compliance with
the right of self-determination, that Russia should
recognize the independence of Finland, the Ukraine
and give up Courland, Lithuania, Poland, Batum, and
Kars. The future position of Esthonia and Livonia
was not yet settled; for the present they were to be
occupied by us.

The army of Great Russia was to be demobilized and
the fleet paid off. Russia was further to refrain from
all propaganda in Germany. A number of economic
questions, arrangements for exchange of prisoners, etc.
were left for later discussion. Our advance was to be
continued until these demands were finally agreed to
in further negotiations. Trotzky at once declared his
readiness to send new representatives to Brest; he
did not come himself, presumably because he saw there

as no possibility of carrying on propaganda from there
ny longer.

The Russian delegation arrived at Brest on February
8. No further negotiations took place. The Russian
lenipotentiaries, displaying dignity in the misfortune
1ey had brought upon themselves, declared that their
nly duty was to sign. At 5.30 P.M. on March 3 the
gning took place. Thus peace was concluded, and
ostilities ceased once more on the Russian front.

The conditions of the peace of Brest were aimed at
1e Bolshevists, whose revolutionary propaganda made
chronic state of warfare against them inevitable. It
as no desire of mine to destroy Russia or to weaken
er so that she could no longer exist. I hoped rather
1at the restoration of the Empire would be the work
f the Ukraine, and I should have preferred a Russo-
olish solution•of the Polish question to any other.
ithuania and Courland are not of vital importance to
ussia, any more than Batum and Kars. The loss of
sthonia and Livonia would be painful, but in this
istrict Russia was to receive every conceivable con-
ession. It was superfluous to discuss whether one
ould go even farther and return these two provinces
o an armed Russia; an armed Russia did not exist.
'herefore I supported in all sincerity the formation of
Baltic littoral. Otherwise the peace terms refrained
om any interference in the internal politics or economic
fe of Russia, and imposed no conditions that were in-
ompatible with the honor of an independent state or
educed the inhabitants to servitude.

It is instructive to compare the peace which Russia
1en received with the one she could have obtained,
nd the latter with the terms which we ourselves have
ad to accept, although we have never refused any
ffer of peace. The talk about the Brest "peace of
iolence" will in time cease, although part of the

German people are still confiding enough to repeat th
shibboleth, invented by hostile propaganda. If no
Russia emerges mutilated from the war, after her allie
for whom she has repeatedly pulled the chestnuts ou
of the fire since 1914, have won, that is another affai

The majority of the Reichstag approved the peace (
Brest; it also admitted that the treaty enabled th
right of self-determination to be exercised; the Ma
jority Socialists abstained from voting; only th
Independent Socialists voted against it.

Deputy Erzberger had already, on February 2
welcomed the peace, and declared that the conditior
conformed to the Peace Resolution of July 19.

Special commendation is due to the remarks (
Deputy Gröber on March 22; they displayed complet
comprehension of our position. He said:

"It is admitted that we cannot describe this peac
as a peace of understanding in the exact sense of th;
word. But I do not think its acceptance should b
made to depend entirely upon that. The question
not: is this a peace of understanding, or is it not?
is a more practical one. Could a treaty of peace hav
been concluded in any other way? I say it could no
and so, in the name of my friends, I declare that w
unanimously agree to the treaty.

"Gentlemen, the Russian delegation at Bres
Litovsk, under Trotzky's leadership, had obviously r
serious intention of coming to an understanding abou
peace; it intended to institute propaganda for i
Bolshevist ideas. For this purpose it prolonged th
negotiations as much as possible; why Trotzky eve
refused to agree to the proposed condition that v
should live together in peace and friendship in th
future! Even that was too much for him! And whi
the German delegates, with lamblike patience—to u
no other expression—strove in the sweat of their bro

ɔ push on the negotiations and bring them to a con-
lusion, we received from Russia, and from those who
ere in close contact with the Russian Government,
flammatory speeches and wireless messages of the
1ost violent description, which could evidently be
1id only at the door of Trotzky and his colleagues, and
hich meant nothing but contempt of all endeavors
ɔ bring about a real, decent peace. Trotzky was evi-
ently suffering from the delusion that he would suc-
eed in revolutionizing the other States, particularly
'oland, Germany, and England, and eventually the
hole world. In the end it was the Russian delegation,
nd not that of Germany, which caused the interruption
f the negotiations, and their final rupture, and literally
ɔrced Germany to resume the fight. . . .

"If, under such circumstances, when the Russian
overnment proposed to resume negotiations and con-
lude another armistice, the German Government and
s allies did not at once and unconditionally agree,
ut put forward demands to be definitely accepted or
ejected, and made the grant of an armistice and
esumption of negotiations dependent upon their
cceptance, such a step was, we are convinced, thor-
ughly justified, and even necessary, and no one has
1e right to reproach the Government on that ground."

These expressions were a valuable help to me, and I
ecognized that in this matter the majority of the
ation supported the Government. Unfortunately,
1e Reichstag soon neglected the revolutionary danger
hich was threatening us from Russia.

In their advance, our troops, the bulk of which were
andwehr, had in a surprisingly short time reached
Iarva, Pskof, Polotsk, Orsha, and Mogilef. The
ussians had made no resistance. The quantity of
tores we captured was extraordinarily great. The
opulace felt that it was delivered from Bolshevism.

The newly occupied territory was placed under th
administration of the Commander-in-chief in the East
We established a cordon to protect the frontier agains
Russia, in order to exploit the whole of the countr
economically, which was urgently necessary. At th
same time the influx of Bolshevist propaganda into th
occupied territory, and thence into Germany, had to b
prevented. I should then never have believed that i
would ultimately make its way into Berlin and Ger
many with Government sanction, and by officia
channels. General Headquarters would in that cas
have seen the futility of its efforts and would probabl
have saved men.

Measures were therefore put into operation whic
we and the Commander-in-chief in the East though
necessary for averting the Bolshevist danger.

Simultaneously with our advance into Bolshevis
Great Russia that into the Ukraine had begun. I wa
in constant communication with General von Ar
in order to arrange common action with him. All of
sudden the Emperor Charles drew back; he wante
to save his people the disappointment of learning tha
the peace with Russia had, after all, not materialized
Necessity, however, obliged him very soon to give hi
consent. I was surprised by the attitude of Austria
Hungary; it began by solemnly declaring that th
State must conclude an unfavorable peace in order t
exist, and now it did nothing to obtain the means o
subsistence which were at its disposal. The fina
adhesion of Austria-Hungary was a relief to me; alon
we could not possibly have solved the problem.

In the Ukraine also the advance proceeded rapidly
The main weight of our attack was directed on Kiev
which we occupied on March 1; that of the Austrian
on Odessa. The operations proceeded along the rail
ways; there were occasional fights between armore

trains; enormous spaces had hurriedly to be traversed by small forces. The Bolshevist troops offered very little resistance; the Czecho-Slovak troops—composed of Austro-Hungarian prisoners of war—fought much better, and fierce engagements with them took place. Operations and actual fighting continued into May.

The Commander-in-chief in the East at once proceeded to form two divisions in Germany from Russian prisoners of war of Ukrainian origin, who were selected by the War Ministry; unfortunately they did not turn out well. As soon as they arrived in the Ukraine they fell a prey to radical influences and had to be disbanded. That was very unpleasant. I had hoped that, just as the Entente had derived some benefit from its prisoners, we should at least obtain some assistance from the sons of the land we had liberated from Bolshevist dominion.

The Turks had also commenced their advance in Armenia at the close of the armistice and meant to continue it to Kars and Batum.

### VI

The peace negotiations with Rumania proceeded as unsatisfactorily as those with Bolshevist Russia.

After our experiences at Brest-Litovsk I had considered it imperative, in order to clear up the points of difference with Austria-Hungary, to institute detailed preliminary discussions regarding the negotiations with Rumania which should at first be confined to the Imperial authorities concerned.

The economic stipulations of the peace with Rumania would have special effect on the conduct of the war on account of the export of oil and grain for the use of the army and the nation. Later on these commodities would be of great importance to our economic life. In

January I had requested the Quartermaster-Genera
to discuss these points with the Imperial authorities i
Berlin, and with the Headquarters of Field-Marsha
von Mackensen, and to determine what our deman
should be. This work provided a foundation for th
peace negotiations later on. These negotiations wer
only in part of a military nature. They were mainl
concerned with the economic life of the people.

This preliminary work became all the more importan
as it was found necessary, in view of the offensive in th
West, to hurry on the conclusion of peace with Ru
mania. Taking our stand on the military situatio
alone, we could have made a peace such as the Entent
has imposed upon us—a peace of violence. But fo
that there was no reason. In our peace terms we had t
consider what the military situation might be up t
the time when a general peace would be concluded
we had no interest in weakening Rumania beyond tha
period.

It makes all the difference whether a country whic
is at war with all the world makes peace with one onl
of its opponents or with all. In the first case its de
mands must conform far more rigidly to the military sit
uation and to military requirements than after a genera
cessation of hostilities. It is different when there is a
intention, such as is now pursued by the Entente, no
only of weakening the enemy for decades to come, bu
of wiping states off the map and reducing whole nation
to a state of slavery in a way which up till now ha
been peculiar to the barbarous warfare of ancient day

To allow Bulgaria to absorb the whole Dobrudj
as the Bulgarians wished, was unfavorable to Ge
many's future. I should have preferred norther
Dobrudja to remain Rumanian; this was in accordanc
with the views I had held for the previous fifteen month
The rest I had to leave to the diplomats. It was the

FIG. 30. THE ADVANCE IN THE EAST, 1918.

duty to keep Bulgaria in the alliance, while averting all difficulties which might arise if the universal traffic route — Cernavoda-Constanza — fell into Bulgarian hands. Toward the end I thought of this area as a sort of free port under German administration.

We objected to extensive annexations by Hungary at Rumania's expense. For the better defense of the Hungarian frontier all that was needed was a slight adjustment at Orsova and in the angle of Moldavia south of Kirlibaba. More than that I did not consider justifiable.

General Headquarters had no objection to adding Bessarabia to Rumania nor to sparing the army. The hypothesis was, as agreed with Secretary of State von Kühlmann and Count Czernin, that Germany and Austria-Hungary would place a government in power in Rumania which suited us, and consisted mainly of men who were living at the time in the occupied territory. The Government, therefore, entered into the closest relations with those Rumanians who, from honest conviction, wished to side with Germany.

Another military condition was that, in order to exclude any chance of surprise by Rumania, the King and the royal family should leave the country until the general conclusion of peace.

The establishment of German political influence in Rumania was extremely inconvenient to Austria-Hungary. It was feared just as much as was any increase of Germany's economic interest. Count Czernin opposed both, and checkmated us at the end of January by sending Colonel Randa, the former military *attaché* in Rumania, to Jassy, to assure the King of his readiness to grant Rumania an honorable peace.

I heard of this mission at Kreuznach in a roundabout way, and was most disagreeably surprised. In our conferences on February 4 and 5 I pointed out its dangerous possibilities, but neither Count Czernin nor, to my amazement, Herr von Kühlmann took the matter up, from which I concluded that the Secretary of State was not only aware of it, but had given it his consent. Otherwise he would have been just as taken aback by this high-handed action of Count Czernin's as I was when I heard of it. That landed us in difficulties. Now that we had commenced to negotiate with the King, and thereby in a sense recognized him once more, we could no longer demand his abdication or his removal from the country. That, in fact, was Count Czernin's object. He needed the King to confirm Austria's position in Rumania, but Germany, by allowing the Quadruple Alliance to open discussions with the King, struck its most faithful supporters in Rumania a blow in the face and placed them in an intolerable position, the penalties of which they now have to suffer.

What had very serious consequences was that the diplomats kept on hinting to the Emperor and to General Headquarters that the Rumanians would probably remove their King themselves. This very adversely influenced our military measures. Hoping that the promised change in the Rumanian Government would result in the removal of their King, I omitted to demand the complete disarmament of the Rumanian Army.

These circumstances were responsible for those half-measures in the negotiations with Rumania which afterward characterized the peace itself.

The conduct of the negotiations was first intrusted to Field-Marshal von Mackensen, who very soon found himself everywhere impeded by Austria-Hungary. The military situation demanded that here, too, we should see clearly whether we should have to fight again or would obtain peace. The new Government was formed, but in no way corresponded with our interests, and so all through February the negotiations made no progress. On February 24 the diplomats took over the conduct of affairs, and more and more obviously it fell into the hands of Count Czernin. Secretary of State von Kühlmann did not take the prominent place which our prestige, our co-operation in the defeat of Rumania, and our military situation warranted. General von Arz might not care whether peace was made to-day or to-morrow; not so the German General Headquarters. I often requested the Imperial Chancellor to have the proceedings accelerated, and I gave instructions in the same sense to General Hell, Chief of the General Staff at Von Mackensen's Headquarters, who also represented General Headquarters. To the great detriment of the German cause, Colonel Hentsch, Chief of the General Staff of the Military Governor of Rumania, died at this time, and General Hell was not able to see this matter through. I had expected that in view of our extremely strong military position— since we could attack them from all sides—my insistence would lead to our dealing drastically with the Rumanians. But the Imperial Government thought fit to reply to my demand by giving way. This simple fact illustrates the fundamental difference between the ideas of the Government and my own.

On March 5 the preliminary peace of Buftea was concluded; its terms were embodied in the Treaty of Bucharest. By the end of March the negotiations were more or less completed.

The Dobrudja difficulty was not settled. The Turks, who had helped to conquer it, demanded from the Bulgarians, who wanted the whole of it, a compensation in the form of the return of the territory west of Adrianople and east of the Maritza, which they had ceded in 1914. I thought the Turkish demand just and reasonable. In spite of many proposals for mediation on the part of the diplomats, the two States could not agree. The southern part, nearly up to the Cernavoda-Constanza Railway, was given to the Bulgarians; the northern part became the common property of the Quadruple Alliance. But the allies agreed to keep open the Constanza route for Rumanian commerce. This was proposed by Radoslavoff himself; what induced him to do it I do not know. The result of this half-measure was unfortunate: it embittered the Bulgarians without satisfying the Turks.

Under pressure from Count Czernin, Rumania agreed to considerable cessions of territory to Hungary. General Hell was repeatedly instructed to oppose them, but could effect nothing.

Rumania was allowed to obtain a firm footing in Bessarabia.

According to the military terms, Rumania was to demobilize and reduce the army, and hand over a portion of its military equipment to be guarded by the allies. The French Military Mission was to be sent away through Russia. But it was left in possession of Moldavia, even as regards military control, and was allowed to keep a few mobile divisions for the occupation of Bessarabia. Germany and Austria-Hungary retained the right of occupying Wallachia with six divisions, of which four were to be German. Field-Marshal von Mackensen remained in Wallachia as administrator until the ratification of peace.

The economic arrangements with Rumania did not secure what I had hoped for. The conditions imposed were not particularly severe.

Besides the supply of oil and grain, the navigation of the Danube was very important. I hoped to secure advantages for the Bavarian Lloyd. The attitude of Austria-Hungary in this respect was again typical;

but so was that of our representatives. It required all the vigilance of the Director of Railways at General Headquarters to obtain even tolerable security for German interests on the Danube.

The question of the dynasty was no more settled than was that of allowing the ambassadors of the Entente to remain at Jassy. Everything remained as it was. At Jassy the old intrigues against us continued. We had left the Entente a citadel there. Only the Rumanian politicians who were hostile to us were sent to Switzerland, so that they could work against us the more effectively. The Rumanian people were to institute proceedings against Bratianu & Co., the instigators of the war; that was a farce.

The remembrance of those Bucharest negotiations is distasteful to me. On May 7 the treaty was at last signed. The diplomats allowed us to hope that they would pursue the question of the dynasty further. The peace was never ratified, for the defection of Bulgaria changed the situation in Rumania at a blow, and showed how our peace with her was inadequate for this World War.

That peace was also denounced in Germany as "a peace of violence," so permeated was popular thought by hostile propaganda, so little was our Government able to lead.

.        .        .        .        .        .        .

The situation on the Eastern front was extraordinarily eased by the Peace of Brest-Litovsk of March 3 and the preliminary peace of Buftea of March 5. A real peace with Russia had, however, not been arrived at. There was still the danger that a new Eastern front might be formed which the Entente and the Bolshevists, between whom there existed for the time a tacit understanding, were trying to bring about.

Only when the Soviet Government discovered that the Entente was its deadly enemy, and wished to place another Government in power which would be more useful in the war, did it break with the Entente and turn toward Germany, in order to strengthen its position internally, and fight Germany, no longer with arms, but by propaganda.

In Rumania the influence of the Entente was not completely broken; the situation was still obscure.

By our vigorous action against Russia in February and the strong line followed subsequently, and by the determined transfer of troops from East to West, any obvious disadvantages, due to the prolongation of the negotiations, had been avoided. The Rumanian divisions should, indeed, have arrived on the Western front earlier, but the attack there could still be carried out. More than forty divisions were transferred. Prior to this the older classes had been replaced by younger, and even the divisions remaining behind were much below strength, and subsequently surrendered their younger classes as drafts to the army in the West. What we had in the East was admittedly a strong force; yet all we had achieved there was an armed peace, and many elements of danger remained. During the spring and summer, when conditions had become more stable, the troops in the East were further reduced. The Commander-in-chief there was repeatedly asked for more, and sent whatever forces were available. General Headquarters knew that it was getting every man that could be spared. But the interminable spaces of the East, which cannot be measured by German standards, demanded a certain minimum of troops, without which we could not carry out the tasks required by our military and economic situation.

The four German and two Austro-Hungarian divisions which had been left in Rumania were the very

smallest force for the purpose. But even these four
German divisions had to send men during the spring.
Von Mackensen's group all too willingly gave all it
could to secure success in the West.

VII

The training of the army for the offensive was another
tremendous task. For this we had to utilize the winter
of 1917–18, as the previous one had been devoted to
training in defense.

In the same way in which tactical theories had then
been summarized in the "Defensive Battle," so now
the "Offensive Battle in Position Warfare" came into
being. We had to revive in the minds of the fighting
forces all those excellent offensive principles which
inspired our pre-war regulations. They had to be supplemented by more recent experience in actual battle.
Without checking the vigor of the attack we had to
keep down losses as much as possible. The whole line
of thought of the army had to be diverted from trench
warfare back to the offensive.

While in the defense the forces in a given sector were
more evenly distributed, in the attack the problem was
to discover some decisive point and arrange the distribution accordingly. In defense, commanding ground
had lost much of its value. The battle of Arras had
once more demonstrated it. Positions were held which
were completely open to the enemy's view. Often the
troops had thought they could not exist without the
possession of some height or other, but if they did not
get it they managed to continue the fight. In the
attack in the war of movement the capture of some
high ground brought about the tactical decision. Its
possession must therefore be striven for as a matter of
principle.

It was necessary to create anew a thorough understanding of the extent of front to be allotted in attack and to emphasize the principle that men must do the work not with their bodies alone, but with their weapons. The fighting-line must be kept thin, but must be constantly fed from behind. As in the defense, it was necessary in the attack to adopt loose formations and work out infantry group tactics clearly. We must not copy the enemy's mass tactics, which offer advantages only in the case of untrained troops.

In the infantry company the light machine gun had to become a thoroughly familiar weapon. It was, however, still regarded as an auxiliary weapon. The fact that the light machine gun was now the true "infantryman" while the "infantryman" of yesterday was nothing more than a "rifle-carrier," had not yet sunk deep into the mind and conscience of the infantry, let alone the rest of the army. Owing to its power compared with that of a rifle, the light machine gun, as its introduction became more general, was bound to become the main infantry weapon. This did not mean that the rifleman was not to shoot. Quite the contrary. The greatest stress was laid on that part of his duties.

The light machine gun and the rifleman formed the infantry group, which had to hang together in trouble and danger and the life-and-death struggle. Its fire power was further increased by quick-firing weapons of all kinds and various sorts of rifle grenades.

To the heavy machine gun, with its longer range and greater effect, fell the task of facilitating the approach of the groups to the enemy's position by keeping the latter under fire. Of course, it had to accompany the advance of the infantry. Therefore, although itself "infantry," it had already become a sort of "companion," or auxiliary arm, to the infantry.

The second auxiliary arm, of special use at short ranges against targets offering more than usual resistance, was the light trench mortar. Originally evolved for trench warfare, it had now to be made mobile and capable of direct fire by means of suitable sights. The light trench mortar was part of the infantry battalion, which became more and more the tactical unit of the division, just as the group within was the tactical unit of the battalion.

These "auxiliary" arms were not yet effective enough to enable the infantry to advance on its arduous way without excessive losses. Of course massed artillery prepared the attack. It could, however, do so only in a general way, and left untouched too many of the enemy's strong points, which had to be dealt with later in detail at the shortest ranges. In each division, therefore, field guns were withdrawn from their units for short-range work, and were attached to battalions or regiments [1] as infantry guns. The formation of special batteries of infantry guns had been started in the mean time, but little progress had been made.

In addition, each division had a company of medium trench mortars, which were also to be made as mobile as possible and allotted to battalions as required. Finally, there were the flame projectors, which could be brought into action at the shortest ranges against an enemy in blockhouses, dugouts, and cellars.

We had no tanks. They were merely an offensive weapon, and our attacks succeeded without them. That fact, however, could not release us from the duty of procuring everything that might make life easier for our infantry. I have already explained that our motor industry was already fully occupied in turning

[1] At this time the German regiments were composed of three battalions.

out lorries, and that we had not enough of them to enable us to keep our infantry away from the battle area in comfortable billets, and yet bring them up in time, as the Entente could do. I mentioned also that for that reason I attached the greatest importance to the provision of lorries. If our fuel situation was unfavorable, it must be improved, too. The construction of lorries could not be allowed to suffer. We could not possibly do enough toward supplying lorries for supply-work and for carrying infantry. The Army Headquarters was often enough troubled by lack of them. When the Chief of Staff complained to me of the difficulty of bringing up supplies, and particularly ammunition, attributing it to lack of lorries, and I maintained that they were available, I was then told that they had been used for carrying the infantry. General Headquarters was not able to get everything. However, the tank question had been carefully considered.

At Cambrai the tanks were very effective. But there they ran into a position held only lightly, chiefly by older men, but poorly equipped with artillery. In all other cases, although they had been a nuisance, they had achieved no decisive results. I took a much more serious view of "tank fright" than the troops themselves did. In the fighting around Bourlon and in Bourlon Wood our infantry had disposed of tanks at close quarters by multiple grenades.[1] Our artillery had shot them to pieces. Even the steel-cored bullets used by our machine guns had been good enough. The best weapons against tanks were good nerves, discipline, and intrepidity, which enabled many brave men to climb on to them, or destroy them by short-range fire. Not until our infantry lost its discipline and fighting capacity did the employment of massed tanks,

---

[1] The ordinary German stick grenade with a number of grenade heads attached to it.

combined with artificial smoke, produce a fatal effect on the course of events.

We formed detachments of captured tanks. I had a look at the first one in February 1918 at an exercise by one of the assault battalions. It did not impress me. Our own tank detachments suffered heavy losses in the fighting which followed without effecting anything.

The Director of Mechanical Transport in the Field had had early orders to start building tanks. The type he showed General Headquarters in the spring of 1917 did not meet requirements. I earnestly requested him to push on their construction energetically. Perhaps I ought to have made greater efforts; and possibly we should in that case have had a few more tanks for the decision in 1918; but I do not know what other claim could have been set aside to enable them to be built. We could not release any more workmen, and the people at home could not supply any more. Had any been available, we should have wanted them as recruits. We should never have been able to put masses of tanks into action in 1918—and tanks are effective only in masses.

When, toward the end of the war, the manufacturers were in a position to turn out tanks more rapidly and in greater numbers, General Headquarters ordered a considerable number from the War Department.

In order to provide aircraft support for the infantry, special battle aeroplane flights were formed. As had hitherto been done by individual airmen, they dived down from great heights and flew along at a low level, attacking with machine guns and light bombs the infantry lines, the artillery, and, as the practice extended, the enemy's reserves and transport columns, as well as columns of troops coming up from farther in rear. Originally intended to be an "auxiliary" arm to the infantry, these battle-flights were finally given important tactical tasks. Thus the air force gained a new field of activity of the greatest importance. The airmen, in the course of their duties, were not only reconnaissance troops who had to fight, they were not only bomb-carriers for destructive work far in the enemy's rear, but they had, like infantry, artillery, and all other arms, to take part in the fighting on the ground. Like the other combatant forces, they were a destructive arm in the great battle on land. This, indeed, became their main object, and the aerial combat was only a means of attaining it.

For the advance of the infantry in the offensive battle, the concentrated preparation by massed artillery was most important. It was necessary to bring up twenty to thirty batteries, about one hundred guns, to each kilometer (eleven hundred yards) of front to be attacked. No man had ever credited such figures before; still less had any one ever thought of the quantities of ammunition hurled upon the enemy. These were indeed massed effects! And yet the battle area was so vast that even these quantities of steel did not destroy all life; the infantry always found far too much to do.

These masses of guns and ammunition had to be got up close to the foremost lines; only then could they engage targets far behind the enemy's front line without having to change position as the battle progressed. At the same time, they had to be covered from view, both from the front and from the air. In these positions in the open it was not intended to fight an artillery duel for days on end; both guns and ammunition would have been annihilated. Nor was it possible to range, as we used to do; this would have attracted the enemy's attention, and the artillery action would have started before the battle itself under conditions unfavorable to us.

We had, therefore, to discover some means of dealing with this situation and insure an adequate effect without ranging. During the defensive battles we had already endeavored to do without constantly checking the barrage. The errors of the day (due to wind and atmospheric density), as well as the gun errors (due to size of chamber caused by wear, and other changes in the bore and carriage), were permanently determined and allowed for when firing. A system was now most carefully elaborated. The Artillery Meteorological Service was regulated on a general plan in combination with the general commanding the air forces. In this way all batteries could be informed of the errors of the day with the least possible delay. All guns were tested for individual errors behind the front. In this way it was possible to determine, by means of simple tables for any gun at any time, how much should be added to, or subtracted from, the normal elevation for any target. It was, of course, a necessary condition that ranges were accurately measured. Faultless maps, trigonometrical and topographical determination of all battery zero points on the ground, and the greatest care in marking targets on the maps, as determined by sound-ranging, field survey, and aerial photography —these were the necessary preliminaries, and an enormous work it was. The new procedure was strongly objected to, especially by some of the senior gunners. But it had to be adopted, nevertheless, and fulfilled all expectations.

The training and instruction of the troops in the new method were intrusted to Captain Pulkowsky, who carried out his duties with great energy and skill.

At the shortest ranges the effect of the artillery was to be supplemented by trench-mortars.

General Headquarters intended that after a short artillery bombardment, lasting only a few hours, the infantry, which was to be held in readiness in the forward positions, should advance to the assault.

This short storm of fire was expected to neutralize the enemy's artillery by means of gas, which spread over great areas, and keep his infantry in the dugouts.

At the beginning of the infantry assault, the artillery, while continuing to keep down that of the enemy, was to lay down a barrage in front of the infantry, and then pave the way for it like a gigantic roller.

The infantry had to keep close up to this wall of projectiles, and did so with admirable determination. The enemy, who came out of his dugouts when the barrage had passed, was now attacked by our infantry, assisted by auxiliary, or "companion," arms, under the protection of our artillery.

It was evident that the closer the infantry could keep to the barrage, the less time the enemy had to leave his dugouts, and the more chance there was of surprising him in them. Consequently, the barrage must not advance faster than the infantry could follow. This pace had to be fixed beforehand, for, in spite of hard thinking and experiments, it had been impossible to discover any means of controlling the barrage. The nature and state of the ground had also to be considered, as regards their effect on the advance of the infantry, and the consequent pace of the barrage. Stronger lines required a more prolonged bombardment, and the barrage had to dwell on them longer. So it came about that an advance of one kilometer (eleven hundred yards) required as much as one hour. It was always a great misfortune if the barrage got ahead; the attack was then held up only too easily. It could not be brought back again without great loss of time, and the infantry suffered losses which it was the duty of all commanders to avoid.

As the range increased the barrage became thinner,

as the shorter-range guns dropped out, and finally, beyond extreme range, it ceased, and the infantry lost its protection. By this time, some artillery must be already in action in more forward positions, from which to support the further advance. In spite of all auxiliary arms and its "infantry guns," the infantry could not do without it.

What form the fighting would take when the infantry emerged from the protection of the barrage it was quite impossible to foresee. It was necessary to prepare a regular scheme for bringing up a large force of artillery and even larger masses of ammunition. The latter, indeed, was the really important item; often too many guns were pushed up. It was bound to be unusually difficult to get many vehicles over our own and the enemy's system of trenches and wire, as well as shell-holes. It required careful preparation and a great quantity of gear to bridge this belt successfully.

General Headquarters laid great stress on the rule that the attack should be continued for several days on end by the divisions originally in the first line. I opposed the idea that they should be relieved by divisions in the second line on the second or third day. At the beginning of the war we had fought for weeks without relief. That was, indeed, beyond our present troops. But so frequent a change as many desired was not yet necessary.

The farther the attack advanced, the more clearly its character approximated to that of open warfare. In defensive fighting the senior commanders had to keep far behind, in order really to conduct the battle; but now their place was nearer the front; the more open the fighting the closer up they must get. The leader now had to make rapid decisions, and, if necessary, carry others away by his personal example.

Finally, as our operations progressed, we would come

up against a new front, which for the time we would not be able to overcome, as had happened in Rumania, eastern Galicia, and Italy. Then we should have to return to the defensive, and distribute our forces in depth. The right moment for this change was difficult to recognize; only too often we became involved in unnecessary fighting.

Our big attacks had clearly demonstrated the importance of supply, and attention was directed to it as a matter of course. All preparations had to be made to follow the attack across the fortified zones with railways, roads, and telephone lines, and to connect them up with those in the newly conquered territory.

In all the theaters of war training was carried out on these principles. To Rumania we sent a specially experienced general to train the troops there according to Western principles, so that, in spite of the belated conclusion of peace, they might soon become available for use in France.

In the West we revived courses of instruction for higher commanders and staff-officers, as well as for juniors down to group commanders, whose functions were so important a factor in success. Marked activity became apparent throughout the army. It commenced with recruit-training, and ended in exercises by formations of all branches, or on the ranges. The barrage was practised with live ammunition, and the infantry trained to follow close behind it. Now, as ever, all commanders regarded improved discipline as the foundation of our army and of all success. It was rated the more highly when it was realized that the home influence on the army was bad. As in peace, special importance was attached to individual training; exercises were seldom carried out by large forces of all branches.

Just as in the previous year everything had been

done to train the army for defensive fighting, so now it was trained for the attack. The country is indebted to the work of the officers and the well-thought-out scheme of training for the fact that our losses in killed and wounded, though very great, were much less than those of the enemy. According to a rough estimate, England and France have lost far more than two million killed, and Russia as many. Taking half the Russian casualties as having occurred on our front, which is probably too low an estimate, the enemy had far more than three million killed, as compared with two million Germans. I have included those killed on other fronts, both our own and the enemy's. This makes the proportion more favorable to us, and the more we know, the more favorable will it turn out to be. These numbers are terribly high, but they proved that we tried to fulfil our responsibilities toward the troops.

In preparing for attack we did not forget defense, as counter-attacks were to be expected. The principles of defense were retained; we only laid greater stress on anti-tank measures. Both in attack and defense the auxiliary arms served this purpose also. In the artillery, especially in the case of field guns and light trench mortars, training in direct individual fire at tanks was considered of decisive importance. The allotment of special ammunition to the heavy machine guns was increased more extensively. Experiments in destroying tanks with multiple grenades were carried out, and all experience gained in fighting them was communicated to the troops, whose opinions were called for. Our positions were examined as to their liability to attack by tanks; traps and stops were made, barricades constructed, mines put down, and anti-tank guns dug in at many points. Naturally, the extent of these defensive measures largely depended upon the available labor and the views of the troops as to the likelihood of tank attack.

The War Ministry kept us informed of the progress in the manufacture of anti-tank weapons, which it pushed on unceasingly.

Once more I spent much time at the front, and in active interchange of ideas with the various army headquarters on the tactics of offensive fighting and on the attack itself. Many proposals and counter-proposals, many pros and cons, were laid before me. I can still recall the discussions about the barrage and the advanced zone. As was my duty, I had to give the proper ultimate decision. The tactical principles were considered to be correct and readily accepted by the troops. They left room for individual action in all directions.

I was present at various exercises, and had conversations with many regimental officers. It was evidently not easy for the troops to adopt the necessary open formations. We urgently needed every moment of the time, right up to the middle of March, which was available for training.

## VIII

During January and February the divisions in the West that were intended for the attack were taken out of the line; some of them were replaced by those that had come from other theaters. From this time on they had to devote themselves entirely to training and equipment. We were unable to equip all divisions equally with stores and horses, and had in the beginning to confine ourselves to those which were destined to open the attack. Similar action was taken in regard to the formations not included in the divisions, such as army field artillery, heavy artillery, trench-mortars, etc. The horses of the shock divisions were given extra forage rations.

General Headquarters regretted that the distinction between "attack" and "trench" divisions became established in the army. We tried to eradicate it, without being able to alter the situation which gave rise to it.

In the mean time we had gradually got up everything that could be thought of as required for the attack. Some divisions were still on their way from the East.

We hoped that the forces we were collecting from all quarters would enable us to attack on a continuous front of over thirty miles (fifty kilometers), allotting twenty to thirty batteries, without trench - mortars, to each kilometer of front. By thinning out at suitable places we could extend the front still more. We had at that time twenty-five to thirty divisions more than the enemy on the whole Western front. But this was not the actual measure of our superiority, which was reduced by the numerous specialist arms and territorial troops of the enemy, of which we had not such large numbers. Even so, our superiority was greater than it had ever been, and afforded prospects of success. We thought of carrying out the attack with fifty or sixty divisions. In order to effect this the corresponding weakening of other parts of the Western front was unavoidable.

General Headquarters had also approached Austria-Hungary. The latter had sent batteries, but, unfortunately, with so small an amount of ammunition that the actual reinforcement did not amount to much. Austro-Hungarian divisions were not available. Their strengths were too low, and did not increase again until several hundred thousand men returned from captivity in Russia. The removal of German troops from the Italian and Eastern fronts, where they had held a very considerable portion of the line, made heavier demands on the Austrian troops, in spite of the altered situation.

General Headquarters would very much have liked to bring the Turkish 15th Corps over to the Western front; but the poor condition of the Turkish Army induced it to send the corps to Turkey. I regretted this afterward. Enver now had eyes only for the Caucasus, and therefore sent it to Batum, where it wasted its time doing nothing. It would have been more useful in the West.

Bulgaria wanted its troops on the Macedonian front; it could probably, as far as numbers were concerned, have sent troops to the West, but it could not appreciate the importance of a common prosecution of the war. In the past it had objected to crossing the Danube, and now only unwillingly released German troops from Macedonia, although it was merely a question of a few battalions of Jägers and some batteries and mountain machine gun formations. The Bulgarian troops that came to relieve them from the Dobrudja were considerably stronger, but even then we left some German troops beh nd. The stores belonging to the German formations were left in Bulgaria or replaced by special stocks.

We were well supplied with all stores required for carrying on operations in the West, but our recruiting situation was still very serious. Our representations had had no result. As a matter of fact, in the autumn of 1918, under the influence of recent events, the War Ministry did release men of the home army and the garrison troops who could have joined the field army sooner. General Headquarters still had a reserve of its own in the Eastern Army and the Army of Occupation in Rumania. As the situation became more settled all men under thirty-five were withdrawn from those formations, the strength of which was simultaneously reduced, so that their fighting value was greatly diminished by these measures. The special-arms and lines-

of-communication troops formed another, though limited, source of reinforcements. I also tried to extend
the system of replacing men by women, and a female
auxiliary telephone corps was to be started.

The recruiting situation need not have been so bad.
The loss by desertion was uncommonly high. The
number that got into neutral countries—*e.g.*, Holland—
ran into tens of thousands, and a far greater number
lived happily at home, tacitly tolerated by their fellow-
citizens and completely unmolested by the authorities.
They and the skrimshankers at the front, of whom
there were thousands more, reduced the battle strength
of the fighting troops, especially of the infantry, to
which most of them belonged, to a vital degree. If
these men had been got hold of, the recruiting difficulty
would not have been so great. More recruits could
have been raised if only the fighting spirit had been
stronger at home. It was on this spirit that the
ultimate decision depended—but it failed.

War consumes men; that is its nature. The modern
defensive battle is more costly than the attack, one
reason more in favor of the latter. The months of
August, September, and October 1918 cost us far
more than March, April, and May of the same year.
In the earlier months our losses consisted mainly of
slightly wounded men who came back. The prisoners
we lost in the defense had to be struck off as lost for
good. That the large masses which were led into battle
would suffer heavy casualties, in spite of all tactical
counter-measures, was unfortunately a matter of course.

The recruiting difficulties were not removed by
March 1918, although a few hundred thousand more
men were available. They continued to be an uncertain factor in the tremendous contest. England and
France had similar difficulties to contend with. In the
autumn of 1917 the English divisions still had twelve

battalions; now they were reduced to nine. Since the Aisne-Champagne battle, France had disbanded far more than one hundred battalions, as well as territorial and territorial reserve formations. The new American formations, which could not have much fighting value, had not yet arrived. The submarine war had continued to be effective; we could not estimate the amount of tonnage the Entente would set aside for transport work.

The army had thrown off the depressing effects of the previous year's fighting in the knowledge that it was passing from the defense to the attack. Its morale appeared completely restored, but in March 1918 it could not be denied that secret agitation was making progress here and there. When the 1919 class reached the recruit depots, we began to receive complaints about its general quality and spirit. Moreover, many recruits seemed to have a great deal of money, which must have greatly embittered the older men, who had been a long time in the field.

Nothing had been done to strengthen the warlike spirit at home. The abuses in the various departments of war administration had become more flagrant than ever. The generally improved spirit of the army had a temporary influence on that at home and blinded us to a good deal. But the large mass of the people was unaffected, caught in the toils of enemy propaganda, wrapped up in its own interests and cares, and utterly unconcerned about the doubtful issue of the war. The nation could no longer brace the nerves of the army; it was already devouring its marrow. How far the secret agitation of the Independent Socialists had extended we were unable to determine. The strikes at the end of January 1918 had thrown another lurid light upon their activities. The party was continually gaining adherents, and was firmly controlled by its leaders, whereas the unions were losing influence.

The Government itself, although taking energetic action against the strikes, failed to see the signs of the times in them, as it had in the naval mutiny in the autumn of 1917.   Everything turned more and more on maintaining order in Germany by energetic action, even at the risk of a temporary falling off in the manufacture of the stores of war.   Otherwise it was to be feared that the revolutionary movement would do even more harm.   The Imperial Government was acquainted with this view of General Headquarters.   During those days the revolution was decisively advanced in Germany.   It was at that time, as I have just heard, that the first German Soldiers' and Workers' Council was formed at Reinickendorf.   Thus a further element of weakness had developed in our own body while we were in the midst of a struggle for our very existence.   At that time I did not attach vital significance to these symptoms.   My belief in the German people as a whole was then still unshaken.

The commanders and troops in the line shared with General Headquarters the feeling that they would prove equal to the demands that would be made on them in the coming struggle.   We hoped for success, even though they were no longer the troops of 1914, but only a kind of militia with much experience of war. The enemy was no better.   Wherever we had attacked with similar troops, who were not so well trained for the offensive, we had won.   What we would achieve, whether we should break through and start a war of movement or whether our effort would remain a sortie on a large scale, was uncertain—like everything in war.

In my audience with the Emperor at Hamburg on February 13 I had expressed my view of the forthcoming event to him and the Imperial Chancellor in the following terms:

"The battle in the West is the greatest military task

that has ever been imposed upon an army, and one which England and France have been trying for two years to compass. Yesterday I spoke with the commander of the Seventh Army; he told me that the more he thought about this task the more impressed he was with its magnitude. That is how all responsible men in the West think. I believe, too, that I, who have to furnish the Field-Marshal with the foundation on which he bases his request for His Majesty's decision, am more than any one impressed by the immensity of the undertaking. It can be successfully accomplished only if the authorities who conduct the war are relieved of all intolerable shackles, if the very last man is employed in the decisive conflict, and is animated, not only by love for his Emperor and his native land, but by confidence in the strength of the military leadership and the greatness of our country. These spiritual forces cannot be underestimated; they are the foundation of the greatest deeds. They must be strengthened by the energy of our action in the East.

"The army in the West is waiting for the opportunity to act.

"We must not imagine that this offensive will be like those in Galicia or Italy; it will be an immense struggle that will begin at one point, continue at another, and take a long time; it is difficult, but it will be victorious. . . ."

The crown of success was an operation in which we could bring to bear the whole of our superiority. It was our great object. If we did not succeed at the first attack, we should have to do so at the next; by then, indeed, the situation would have become less favorable—how much less favorable would depend upon the rate of arrival and value of the Americans and on the losses which both sides sustained. Everything was based on the assumption that we should do well in this respect, and although, of course, I expected our own army to be weakened, I hoped it would be less so than that of the enemy. By continuing to attack we should still retain the initiative. More I could not aim at.

I reported to the Emperor that the army was assembled and well prepared to undertake the "biggest task in its history."

# THE OFFENSIVE IN THE WEST, 1918

The Plan of Attack—The Great Battle in France—The Battle of
Armentières and Around Kemmel—New Plans in Contemplation
—The Situation on Other Fronts—The Campaign in Finland—The
Battle of Soissons and Rheims and the Austro-Hungarian Offensive
in Italy—The Decline of the War Spirit—Our Political Policy in
the East—The Offensive on the Marne and in Champagne—Foch's
Counter-attack South of Soissons.

(Map XII)

I

IT was difficult to decide where to attack, but it was
necessary to do so early. It took weeks, and required considerable foresight and the most detailed
preliminary work, to concentrate the troops in a confined area, bring up by rail the tremendous quantities
of ammunition and other stores of all kinds, carry out
the work allotted to the troops themselves, such as
preparing battery positions, screening roads, con-
structing anti-aircraft shelters, and preparing gear for
crossing the trenches, and finally to deploy for battle.

Of course all this increased the danger of discovery.
It was therefore necessary to commence dummy works
on the fronts remote from the attack, which, as a
matter of fact, served as the basis of attack later on.
But most of the available labor troops were required
on the front of attack at an early date. The preparations on other fronts could not be extensive, but there
was some chance of misleading the enemy, and the
deception was to be completed by skilfully conducted
defensive measures.

I discussed the selection of the front of attack with the chiefs of staff of the army groups, and with the officers of my staff, and heard their opinions. Three sectors were considered—Flanders between Ypres and Lens, between Arras and St.-Quentin or La Fère, and on both sides of Verdun, leaving out the fortress. As is always the case, there was a great deal to be said for and against each proposal.

The enemy was in great strength about Ypres and Arras, in front of the Ailette position, and farther to the east, as far as Verdun; the weakest part was on both sides of St.-Quentin; north of that town the enemy line had been denser since the battles of Cambrai.

In the north the ground was difficult. The condition of the Lys valley, west of Lille, across which the main force of the attack would pass, depended to an extraordinary degree upon the season and the weather; before the middle of April its passability away from the roads was doubtful. That was very late, in view of the Americans.

In the center the ground itself caused no difficulties, but further progress would be hampered by the crater-areas of the Somme battle.

The attack at Verdun would lead us into very hilly country.

These two attacks could take place at any time of year.

Tactical conditions, therefore, favored the center sector; here the attack would strike the enemy's weakest point, the ground offered no difficulties, and it was feasible at all seasons.

Strategically the northern attack had the advantage of a great, though limited, objective. It might enable us to shorten our front if we succeeded in capturing Calais and Boulogne. The attack on Verdun might also lead to an improvement in our front, though more of a tactical nature. The center attack seemed to lack any definite limit. This could be remedied by directing the main effort on the area between Arras and Péronne, toward the coast. If this blow succeeded the strategic result might indeed be enormous, as we should cut the bulk of the English Army from the French, and crowd it up with its back to the sea.

I favored the center attack; but I was influenced by the time factor and by tactical considerations, first among them being the weakness of the enemy. Whether this weakness would continue I could not know. Tactics had to be considered before purely strategical objects, which it is futile to pursue unless tactical success is possible. A strategical plan which ignores the tactical factor is foredoomed to failure. Of this the Entente's attacks during the first three years of the war afford numerous examples.

After determining the divisions and other forces available for the attack, it was decided to strike between Croisilles, southeast of Arras, and Moeuvres, and, omitting the Cambrai re-entrant, between Villers-Guislain and the Oise, south of St.-Quentin. It was to be supported on its left by a subsidiary attack from La Fère.

The preliminary work and the conduct of the attack made it necessary to interpolate two army headquarters, and new lines-of-communication inspectorates. The Seventeenth Army, formerly the Fourteenth in Italy, under Gen. Otto von Below, Chief of Staff Gen. Krafft von Delmensingen, was put in between the Sixth and Second opposite Arras, and the Eighteenth, formerly Von Woyrsch's group headquarters, now commanded by General von Hutier, Chief of Staff General von Sauberzweig, between the Second and Seventh Armies, opposite St.-Quentin and La Fère. The boundary between the Seventeenth and

Sixth was about half-way between Lens and Arras that between the Seventeenth and Second approxi mately at Moeuvres. The boundary between the Second and Eighteenth Armies was formed, roughly by the Omignon brook, that between the Eighteenth and Seventh was just south of La Fère.

The Seventeenth Army, therefore, had to make the attack on the line Croisilles-Moeuvres, the Second and Eighteenth that between Villers-Guislain and La Fère In this operation the Seventeenth and Second were to take the weight off each other in turn, and with their inner wings cut off the enemy holding the Cambra re-entrant, afterward pushing through between Croi silles and Péronne. This advance was to be protected on the south flank by the Eighteenth Army, in com bination with the extreme left wing of the Second. The strength and equipment of these armies were adapted to their tasks.

For the decisive operation the Seventeenth and Second Armies were to remain under the orders of the army group of Crown Prince Rupprecht. The Eigh teenth Army joined that of the German Crown Prince Remembering the November campaign in Poland in 1914, I meant to exercise a far-reaching influence on the course of the battle. That was difficult if it was to be conducted by one group only; every intervention was only too apt to become mere interference from above. It was desirable to make the fullest possible use of the resources of the group of the German Crown Prince, and this was facilitated by the organization adopted.

Moreover, it was a personal satisfaction to the Field-Marshal and myself, since the strategical situation required it, that His Imperial Highness the Crown Prince would take part in the first great offensive battle in the West. Dynastic interests did not influence me

Though profoundly loyal to my King, I am an independent man and no courtier.

The possibility of broadening the attack on the north toward Arras, and on the south toward the left bank of the Oise, was anticipated.

Feints and preparations for further attack were made:

Between Ypres and Lens, by the group of Crown Prince Rupprecht.

By the German Crown Prince's group, particularly between Rheims and the Argonne.

By the newly formed group of Von Gallwitz, on the old battle-fields of Verdun.

By the group of Duke Albrecht, between Saarburg in Lorraine and Ste.-Marie-aux-Mines, and also in the Sundgau.

The group of General von Gallwitz was formed because that of the German Crown Prince had now been extended toward St.-Quentin, and could no longer properly attend to affairs at Verdun as well. General von Gallwitz was in immediate command of his own Third Army, as well as Army Detachment "C."

The Headquarters of the German Southern Army in Galicia, under General von Bothmer, joined the army group of Duke Albrecht, and was put in the line in Lorraine as the Nineteenth Army Headquarters; the Chief of the Staff was Colonel von Hemmer, who had already greatly distinguished himself in a similar position in the East. "A" Army Headquarters took over the sector Saarburg-Ste.-Marie-aux-Mines.

All fronts maintained their defensive arrangements in case the enemy should himself attack. In some places it was intended to retire in that case.

Work had been carried on along these lines according to program and with the greatest devotion from the middle of January. By the beginning of February the attack was fixed to commence on March 21, although the situation in the East was still quite obscure. The military situation, however, made a decision imperative. Later on we could always make changes, but we would be unable to make a fresh start.

The work of the army headquarters, the Quartermaster-General, the Intendant-General, the Director of Railways and the officers of my immediate staff all fitted in admirably. I was able to satisfy myself of that when I visited the front. On these occasions I discussed all relevant questions, adjusted difficulties, and helped. The chiefs of staff at the army and group headquarters gave me short verbal reports on the ground, the distribution of the troops, the artillery combat, and the state of the preparations. In my remarks I laid the greatest stress on co-operation between the inner wings of the Seventeenth and Second Armies of Crown Prince Rupprecht's group, so as to insure the Cambrai re-entrant being cut off, as so much dopondod upon it, and it seemed to me that the Seventeenth Army was beginning to look to the west a little too soon. We discussed the co-operation of the two army groups on the boundary between the Second and Eighteenth Armies. The preparations were carried out as intended. Work was carried on everywhere with confidence and without losing sight of the object. All arrangements fitted in like clockwork. It was certain that the armies would be ready for battle on the day.

I considered it necessary to take advantage of such successes as we might obtain in order to strengthen the enemy's inclination to peace by means of propaganda. Colonel von Haeften had drawn up a memorandum on the subject, which I sent to the Imperial Chancellor, who apparently passed it to the Foreign Office. Nothing of importance was done.

The Imperial Chancellor was perfectly acquainted with our intention of attacking in the West. It was the reason why we insisted on the diplomatic negotiations in the East being accelerated, and why we had decided to denounce the armistice with Russia. He knew the enormous importance we attached to this offensive. Further, I had him informed of the date it was to begin. Germany could make the enemy inclined to peace only by fighting. It was first of all necessary to shake the position of Lloyd George and Clemenceau by a military victory. Before that was done peace was not to be thought of. All the world, including the Entente, knew we were going to attack in the West. Clemenceau declared himself decisively, I think on March 6, in favor of continuing the war, in spite of events in the East and in spite of our imminent attack.

At that moment I could not possibly believe in a just peace. Up till now the enemy had invariably rejected a peace by understanding. Should we, in the actual situation, have offered him Alsace-Lorraine, parts of the province of Posen, and an indemnity?

Nor did the Imperial Government mention the possibility of peace. Secretary of State von Kühlmann, who was supposed to be conducting the whole of our foreign policy, was first at Brest and then at Bucharest. Neither he nor the Imperial Chancellor had been able to open up any negotiations which might have led to peace without further fighting. They probably continued their endeavors in that direction, in spite of the Entente's refusal of the invitation to Brest. It was their duty to spare the people and army further fighting if possible. Count von Hertling's declaration of February 25, in which he took his stand on President Wilson's four [sic] points of February 11, had met with no response from the Entente.

Colonel von Haeften had just been visiting foreign countries in order to discuss questions relating to propaganda. Without my knowledge he established communication with a subject of one of the enemy countries, who was acquainted with the objects and intentions of the authorities in London and Washington, and made me a verbal report on the subject. The terms then demanded of us were so severe that only a defeated Germany could have acceded to them. The Colonel further informed me that Conrad Hauszmann, then Reichstag Deputy, who has since confirmed this statement, and Herr Max Warburg-Hamburg had also tried to negotiate peace, but without success. The Government never informed me of these events, though it must have known of them. I am all the more surprised that it did not contradict the rumor that a peace would have been arranged in March if I had not insisted on attacking. I personally requested the Imperial Chancellor and the Vice-Chancellor to do so. Both of them refrained, without ever giving me any reason for it.

II

Early in March General Headquarters left Kreuznach, where it had been for more than a year.

The new headquarters had in the mean time been established at Spa. We got very good accommodation there. The offices were in the Hôtel Britannique, in which I had been billeted before, during our invasion of Belgium in the autumn of 1914. Spa was much nearer the front, and with Verviers could accommodate the whole of General Headquarters. For directing the battle, for operations, it was still too far back. I had therefore proposed to take Avesnes as the quarters of the augmented Operations Branch. From there we could easily reach all parts of the front by car. I intended to see a great deal for myself, and to send my staff-officers to the scenes of important events, in order to obtain impressions at first hand.

On March 18 the Field-Marshal and I went to Avesnes with the augmented Operations Branch. Our offices there were not good; everything was very cramped, but it had to do. We had chosen the place because the Eighteenth Army Headquarters had been there and the telephone communications needed only slight additions.

Our mess was at first very unpleasant; later on we found more agreeable rooms. We rationed the owners and fitted the place up with furniture from Spa. To stay in those rooms and have our meals there was a relaxation we all needed.

His Majesty came the next day. He lived in his court train, which was side-tracked in a neighboring station.

On March 20, along the whole front of the attack, the guns and trench-mortars, with their ammunition, were in position behind the foremost trenches, and in places even in front of the trenches. It was a remarkable achievement, and at the same time a marvel that the enemy had neither seen anything nor heard any movement at night. At times our batteries were subjected to harassing fire, and ammunition-dumps went up here and there. All this must have attracted the enemy's attention. But he observed it all along the front, and could therefore obtain no certain indication.

The divisions had at first been distributed behind the front of attack, but were now crowded together in anti-aircraft shelters behind the jumping-off places in our foremost lines. This concentration of forty or fifty divisions had not been observed by the enemy, nor had it been reported to him by his highly developed secret service. The marches took place at night, but

the troops sang as they passed through the villages.
Such masses cannot be concealed. But no more did
the airmen discover the railway transportation that had
been taking place behind the front of attack since
February. It was heavy behind the whole front, but
the bulk of it was unmistakably going on behind the
line Arras-La Fère, as was reported by German airmen
up to report.

Nor did the enemy discover anything by other means.
I must assume this, otherwise his defensive measures
would have been more effective and his reserves would
have arrived more quickly. In spite of all efforts to the
contrary, the essence of war is uncertainty; that is our
experience, and the enemy's, too.

On March 18 or 19 two men deserted from a trench-
mortar company. According to notes found by us, or
according to prisoners' statements, they are alleged
to have given information of the impending attack.

On the other fronts, particularly near Lille and
Verdun, artillery activity had increased.

At noon on the 20th General Headquarters had to
face the great decision whether the attack was to
commence on the 21st or be put off.

Every delay must have increased the difficulties of
troops crowded together close up to the enemy. Already the tension was very hard to bear. The spiritual
pressure of the mass was urging them forward.

And yet our artillery relied on gas for its effect, and
that was dependent on the direction and strength of the
wind. I had to rely on the forecast submitted to me
at 11 A.M. by my meteorologist, Lieutenant Doctor
Schmaus. Up till the morning of the 20th strength
and direction were by no means very favorable; indeed,
it seemed almost necessary to put off the attack. That
would have been very hard to do. So I was very
anxious to see what sort of report I should get. It

was not strikingly favorable, but it did indicate that the attack was possible. At 12 noon the army groups were told that the program would be carried out. Now it could no longer be stopped. Everything must run its course. General Headquarters, senior commanders, and troops had all done their duty. The rest was in the hands of fate; unfavorable wind diminished the effectiveness of the gas, fog impeded and retarded our movements and prevented our superior training and leadership from reaping its full reward. This was the predominant opinion about the fog, but a few thought it an advantage.

On the 21st, just before 4 A.M., the battle began with a tremendous crash on a front of forty-five miles, between Croisilles and La Fère. As regards the Second and Eighteenth Armies, the hours had been fixed by higher authority for the main operations; the Seventeenth Army, which was fighting by itself, was left more latitude. Within these limits matters were left to the groups.

For about two hours the whole of our artillery engaged the enemy's batteries; then most of it was switched on to trench bombardment, in which the trench-mortars also took part. A little before 9 A.M. most of our fire —only a portion being left on hostile batteries and special points—was concentrated to form a barrage. Our infantry advanced to the assault.

The Seventeenth Army, which had the strongest enemy in front of it, reached only his second line; the barrage had gone far ahead; the infantry had lost touch with it. It remained in this position, lying down, with no artillery support.

During the Second Army's attack, the co-operation between the infantry and the artillery was better. The infantry penetrated into the enemy's second position

EXPLANATION

━━━ German line before beginning
the attack March 21, 1918.
••••• German line reached the even-
ing of March 21.
×××× German line reached March 23
ooooo German line reached March 25
•••• German line reached March 27
━ ━ German line reached March 30
•+•+• German line reached by attack
on April 6.
▨▨▨ Result of German attack, April
24.

**FIG. 31. THE GREAT BATTLE IN FRANCE, 1918**

With the Eighteenth Army everything proceeded as
intended. It was making good progress.

On March 22 there was little change on the Seventeenth Army front, but, the Second being firmly in
hand and led with energy, defeated the enemy and

pressed on. The Eighteenth gained a considerable amount of ground. The Seventeenth appeared to give its various tactical groups too much latitude; but for this the action of the different formations was too interdependent. General Headquarters took steps to get the general direction of the fighting taken more firmly in hand.

The result of the situation on the Seventeenth Army front was that the enemy in the Cambrai re-entrant was not cut off, nor could the opposition to the Second Army be indirectly reduced. The latter had been obliged to rely on its own unaided efforts, and had, therefore, not got ahead so fast as was desirable from the point of view of assisting the Seventeenth. And so again Crown Prince Rupprecht's group could not gain ground between Croisilles and Péronne to the extent that had been originally intended.

On March 25 the Seventeenth and Second Armies had passed far beyond the line Bapaume-Combles, fighting hard all the way; the Eighteenth Army had taken Nesle and met with but little resistance. The Seventeenth Army was already exhausted; it had lost too heavily on the 21st and 22d, apparently because it had fought in too dense formation. The Second Army was fresher, but was already complaining of the old shell-holes. It could get no farther than Albert. Its left wing had been more delayed by having to cross the Somme than by the enemy. The Eighteenth Army was still full of fight and confidence; on the 27th it took Montdidier. Soon the enemy formed a new front north of the Somme, which was sure to be difficult to overcome. In the direction of Amiens the enemy's resistance seemed weaker.

The original idea of the battle had to be modified, and the main weight of the attack vigorously directed at that point. I still hoped we should get through to open warfare, and kept it in view in my instructions to the armies. But the Seventeenth Army could not get on; the Second and Eighteenth were still gaining ground. I continued my efforts toward reinforcing the left wing of the Second Army, and to direct it and the Eighteenth on Amiens.

The enemy's line was now becoming denser, and in places they were even attacking themselves, while our armies were no longer strong enough to overcome them unaided. The ammunition was not sufficient and supply became difficult. The repair of roads and railways was taking too long, in spite of all our preparations.

After thoroughly replenishing ammunition the Eighteenth Army attacked between Montdidier and Noyon on March 30. On April 4 the Second Army and the right wing of the Eighteenth attacked at Albert and south of the Somme toward Amiens. These actions were indecisive. It was an established fact that the enemy's resistance was beyond our strength. We must not get drawn into a battle of exhaustion. This would accord neither with the strategical nor the tactical situation. In agreement with the commanders concerned, General Headquarters had to make an extremely difficult decision in abandoning the attack on Amiens for good.

The Entente now attacked at Albert and southeast of Amiens in a disconnected sort of way and achieved nothing. On April 24, after careful preparation, the Second Army made another attempt, with the aid of tanks, to improve its position at Villers-Bretonneux; it got ahead well, but was unable to hold what it gained.

The front between Albert and Montdidier settled down only gradually. From time to time fighting broke out again, and the situation remained permanently doubtful. The other parts of the new front, toward Arras and Noyon, became quiet much more quickly.

The battle was over by April 4. It was a brilliant feat, and will ever be so regarded in history. What the English and French had not succeeded in doing we had accomplished, and that in the fourth year of the war.

Strategically we had not achieved what the events of the 23d, 24th, and 25th had encouraged us to hope for. That we had also failed to take Amiens, which would have rendered communication between the enemy's forces astride the Somme exceedingly difficult, was specially disappointing. Long-range bombardment of the railway establishments of Amiens was by no means an equivalent. However, our troops had beaten the French and English and had proved themselves superior. That they did not achieve all the success that was possible was due, not only to their reduced fighting value, but, above all, to their not being in all cases under the firm control of their officers. They had been checked by finding provisions, and valuable time had thus been lost.

Generally speaking, our tactics had proved sound. What had happened in the Seventeenth Army did not necessitate any fundamental changes, although some lessons needed more drastic application. Above all, the infantry must be more extended. At many places machine gun posts had given us an undue amount of trouble and so caused delay. The infantry groups had often been lacking in initiative, and their co-operation with the companion arms had often failed. The troops had found special difficulty in reorganizing themselves for defense at the conclusion of the attack, and particularly in recognizing when no further success was to be gained by continuing the attack. All troops, especially mounted troops, had suffered heavily from bombing by hostile airmen.

It was as yet too early to give a final opinion on the strategical situation; in itself it was by no means favorable. How General Headquarters was to deal with it later on could not yet be determined, as we were still in the first stages of the operations. The Avre bridge-head was a special difficulty in the tactical sense. The advisability of giving it up was discussed. But as this would have shown the enemy that we had given up any further attack on Amiens we kept it.

The new front had now to be fortified. Some of the played-out divisions were relieved by fresh ones from quiet fronts, the less tired ones were left in the line. Everywhere the greatest attention and care were bestowed on completing the communications in rear. For the main operations it was, however, of the highest importance to take back troops that were no longer required in the new line for rest, training, and improving their discipline. We had to collect reserves for further operations and to repel possible counter-attacks, which could, however, for the present be only of a local character.

The troops of the Second Army were particularly handicapped by having stuck fast in the western edge of the Somme battle-field. They could find real rest only to the east of our starting line, although in the country they had traversed numerous English hut camps had fallen into our hands undamaged.

Our losses were not inconsiderable; we had been fighting with large numbers for a long time. The percentage in the Seventeenth Army was too high; the losses in officers had been heavy throughout. But, besides rich booty, we had taken some 90,000 unwounded prisoners, and in addition the enemy's battle casualties had been heavy. We could expect to get back many of the slightly wounded within a reasonable time. We had been attacking and had come off well, even in the matter of casualties.

The arrangements for dealing with the wounded had

not sufficed at all points, although they had been carefully examined by the Director of Medical Services before the battle.  The numerous slightly wounded made things more difficult by the stupid and displeasing way in which they hurried to the rear.

The battle cost me a great deal also.  My wife's youngest son fell on the 23d.  He was a flying officer, and was at first reported missing.  On the battle-field we found a grave with the English inscription, "Here rest two German flying officers."  I had the sad task of identifying my son.  Now he rests in German soil.  The war has spared me nothing.

My journey to the battle-field had taken me through the two trench systems in which the opponents had faced each other for so long.  The impression it made was deep; a strip, many miles in width, bleak and devastated, stretches through France, the mark of the war conjured up by the Entente.

On the enemy the defeat produced an overwhelming impression.  In spite of my request, we did nothing in the diplomatic sense to utilize it.  France trembled.  It wanted to be sure of the military support of England and America.  Clemenceau appealed to the Allies.  In England tens of thousands of miners and munition workers were enrolled in the army, and yet some ten divisions could not for the time being be brought up to establishment.  They disappeared from the front, and most of them did not come in again until the autumn.  The term of service was prolonged, but the British Government did not yet dare to think of enforcing compulsory service in Ireland.  In other respects Lloyd George shrank from nothing.  As may be seen by his speeches after the conclusion of the armistice, he urgently demanded help from Wilson and sent all available shipping—regardless of whether England would suffer or not—to America to fetch the new formations. What did we do? Did we give all? It is well to draw comparisons, so that the lessons of this war may later be taken to heart by the German people. Only the greater energy is any good in war.

For the sake of victory England and the United States violated the neutral European countries by political and economic pressure, and requisitioned their tonnage in order to reduce the strain on their own. In the long run the submarine war had proved unpleasantly effective, after all, and produced a severe transport crisis on land and sea. "In April the German submarines were so successful that England would have been ruined in nine months if the sinking had continued at the same rate." This was the declaration made by an English statesman in the House of Commons in November 1918. England utilized the shipping taken from neutrals, and whatever else it could make available, for bringing over the American masses, crammed tight in the transports, to France. The men carried only their personal equipment. What they needed in Europe they were given by England and France, but also by the neutral countries, especially Spain. The whole operation was a *tour de force*, uncommonly effective for a short time, but impossible to maintain for a long period. Had the war lasted longer a reaction must have followed.

According to *The New York World* of May 8, 1918, the president of the Tonnage Committee of the United States Chamber of Commerce, Edward A. Filene, expressed the following opinion: "At the request of the Allies we are now sending men to France in absolutely senseless numbers. We are sending them without having tonnage enough to keep them supplied. We are literally risking the life of our boys on the assumption that America will be able to provide the minimum tonnage required for their maintenance."

Ruthlessness and energy once again brought success.

During the battle we had commenced bombarding Paris from near Laon with a gun having a range of seventy-five miles. This gun was a marvelous product of technical skill and science, a masterpiece of the firm of Krupp and its director, Rausenberger. The bombardment made a great impression on Paris and on all France. Part of the population left the capital and so increased the alarm caused by our successes.

The same effect was intended to be produced by the great activity displayed by our airmen.

### III

The operations designed to broaden the front of our attack and improve our strategical position were carried out at the end of March and early in April.

On April 6 the Seventh Army attacked on the left bank of the Oise from Chauny and La Fère in the direction of Coucy la Ville, and also farther south. It pushed the French back across the Oise-Aisne Canal, and so gave more security to the long south flank of the Eighteenth Army.

The Seventeenth Army had already attacked in the last days of March in the direction of Arras, making its principal effort on the north bank of the Scarpe. It was to capture the decisive heights east and north of Arras; the next day the Sixth Army was to prolong the attack from about Lens and carry the high ground in that area. I attached the greatest importance to both these attacks. To have the high ground in our possession was bound to be decisive in any fighting in the plain of the Lys.

In spite of employing extraordinary masses of artillery and ammunition, the attack of the Seventeenth Army on both banks of the Scarpe was a failure; it fought under an unlucky star. Only the 12th Division, under General Lequis, made good progress south of the stream; but this was not enough to influence the whole operation. Apparently the artillery had not been sufficiently effective. General Headquarters now abandoned the attack by the south wing of the Sixth Army. It decided to strike in the plain of the Lys between Armentières and La Bassée, as had been proposed by Crown Prince Rupprecht for the main operation. The weather had been dry, and the English had greatly reduced their numbers in the plain of the Lys, as well as in front of Ypres.

The attack was very carefully planned by the Sixth Army. General von Quest and his Chief of Staff, Lieutenant-Colonel Lentz, were untiring, and had arranged everything in the same manner as had been done for March 21. In spite of having but few men available for work, everything had progressed so well that the attack could be arranged to begin on April 9. I was glad of this. The sooner it took place the more likely was it to surprise the Portuguese in the plain of the Lys.

I myself visited the 55th Corps Headquarters in the Sixth Army as late as April 7, and received the impression that we could keep to the time proposed. In order to go over all the preliminary artillery work, Colonel Bruchmüller had been sent to the Sixth Army. As early as July 1917 he had arranged the employment of the artillery in the break-through in East Galicia, and at the time of the attack in March he was Artillery General at the Eighteenth Army Headquarters. His great knowledge and capacity, his devotion to his profession and his artillery, and his military enthusiasm marked him out as one of the most prominent soldiers of this war. His suggestions had already formed the groundwork for the employment of the artillery on

March 21.  The artillery of the Eighteenth Army was
completely imbued with his spirit.  This, added to the
fact that it struck the weakest point in the enemy's
line, contributed greatly to the fine success of that
army.  The Seventeenth Army, which, moreover, had
the strongest part in front of it, worked on similar
principles, but the vitalizing energy which emanated
from Colonel Bruchmüller was lacking.  This is another
instance of the decisive influence of personality on the
course of events in war, as in life generally.  General
Headquarters had not only to reckon with the enemy,
but also with the personal qualities of the men who
were striving for the same object with the same devotion.

Colonel Bruchmüller inspected the preliminary arrangements and reported that all was in order.  On the
morning of April 9 the attack at first went ahead very
well.  The reports which came in up till noon were
favorable.  This was a different birthday from the one
I had passed the year before, the day of the heavy
defeat at Arras.  His Majesty listened to the report
on the military situation at Avesnes and stayed to
lunch.  He remembered me in a few words, and also
my two dead sons, and presented me with an iron
statuette of himself by Betzner.  There were many
things which formed a barrier between His Majesty
and myself; our characters were too different.  He was
my Imperial Lord and I served him, and my country
in his person, with the most loyal devotion.  The
statuette will remain a sacred memento of my Emperor
and Supreme Commander, who loved his soldiers,
desired only the best for his country and his people,
and whose whole inmost nature was averse to war—
of a man whose nature was typical of the German of
post-Bismarckian times.  The monarch on whom such
enormous responsibility lay did not, like his Imperial

grandfather, find men who were, like Roon and Bismarck, in the time of the constitutional struggle, resolved to demand from the country everything needed for the prosecution of the war. That is what proved fatal to the Emperor and the country in this war.

In the afternoon the attack seemed to progress more slowly. The ground was still soft in places and this made it very difficult to bridge the enemy's trench system. The direction of the roads was not favorable to that of our attack, and the detachments of tanks we had employed had proved a hindrance. It took a long time to get up guns and ammunition. The country was close, and this enabled the enemy's machine gun posts to delay our infantry considerably. In the evening we were advancing toward Armentières, had reached the Lys, and were approaching the Lawe. In the direction of Béthune we made little progress. On the left, at Givenchy and Festubert, we were held up. The result was not satisfactory.

On April 10 the attack continued, but it gained sufficient ground only toward Armentières and across the Lys immediately above Armentières. Toward Estaires we did not penetrate far enough, but stuck fast in the Lys position; toward the Lawe, also, our progress was but slight.

The enemy's machine guns continued to give our infantry much trouble; it should have grappled with them more vigorously, as a General Staff Officer told me who had been sent up. But often it wasted time looking for food. The divisions fighting on this front were not "attack divisions" in the same sense as those that had gone into action on March 21. But on other battle-fields the trench divisions did as good work as the so-called attack divisions.

On April 11 we took Armentières. Toward Bailleul the rate of advance was better; Merville also fell. The

EXPLANATION
━━━ German line before April 9.
●●●● German line on evening of April 9.
✕✕✕✕ German line on April 11.
╍╍╍ German line reached through the attack.
➤ Direction of German attack.

FIG. 32. THE BATTLE OF ARMENTIÈRES AND KEMMEL, 1918

day before the left wing of the Fourth Army had started and retaken Messines, which had been lost on June 7 the year before.

The objective of the further attack by the Fourth and Sixth Armies of Crown Prince Rupprecht's group was the high ground which bounds the Lys valley on the north. Unfortunately, we had been unable to hold on to it in the autumn of 1914. It begins at Mount Kemmel, which affords a distant view to the east, and ends at Cassel. The possession of these heights would bring about the evacuation of the Yser position to the north.

After April 12 the driving force of the Sixth Army began to fall off, while the Fourth gradually captured more and more ground. The capture of Mount Kemmel on the 25th marked the climax of the fighting. More and more French divisions arrived in front of the Fourth Army. Further attacks promised no success.

As the attack on Mount Kemmel progressed the English, who were east of Ypres, were gradually drawn back toward the town. A blow by the Fourth Army in the direction of Langemarck was too late.

South of Mount Kemmel, Bailleul had also fallen into our hands, but farther south the Sixth Army had made no more progress.

The results of the battle of March 21 had caused General Foch to be appointed Commander-in-chief of the Entente. In order to hold up the first great penetration, the English reserves were concentrated in front of our Seventeenth and Second Armies, while French divisions from the Aisne-Verdun front opposed the Eighteenth Army. The attacks by the Fourth and Sixth Armies caused General Foch to move his reserves still farther to the north. His attempts to recapture Mount Kemmel were unsuccessful. In view of the enemy's strength, General Headquarters now checked the attack.

As is the case whenever the front becomes rigid during the actual progress of fighting, the situation of the Fourth and Sixth Armies was difficult. The same care was bestowed on strengthening the front line, completing communications with the rear, withdrawal into rest of all troops that could be spared, perfecting training and discipline, as had been done at the end of the great battle between Croisilles and La Fère.

<h2 style="text-align:center">IV</h2>

By the end of April the offensive begun on March 21 had come to an end. Local attempts at improving our positions and counter-attacks by the enemy prolonged the fighting into May. The main centers were Mount Kemmel and Bailleul, Albert, and the country south of the Somme as far as the Luce.

We had achieved successes; that we must not allow later events to make us forget. We had defeated the English Army. Only a few British divisions were still intact. Of the fifty-nine English divisions, fifty-three had been engaged, twenty-five of them several times. The French had been obliged to engage nearly half their divisions. The enemy had lost large quantities of stores. Italian troops appeared in the Argonne, while the English and French troops that went to Italy the previous autumn stayed there. In Macedonia, English troops were relieved by Greeks.

How many Americans had got across by April we did not know. In the middle of the month, between St.-Mihiel and the Moselle, the first more important engagements took place against United States troops, who had already been a long time in France. The individual American fought well, but our success had, nevertheless, been easy.

The effect of the submarine war had ceased, but

enterprises by the English navy against the submarine
bases of Ostend and Zeebrugge proved how painful it
had been.    It was uncommonly difficult to estimate its
probable influence on the food-supply of England and
on the transport of the Americans to France.    From
our previous experience of the submarine war, I expected
strong forces of Americans to come.    But the rapidity
with which they actually did arrive proved surprising.
General von Cramon, the German Military Plenipotentiary with the Imperial and Royal Headquarters,
often called me up and asked me to assist on the
sinking of American troop-ships; public opinion in
Austria-Hungary demanded it.    Admiral von Holtzendorff could only reply that everything was being
done to reduce enemy tonnage and to sink troop-ships.
It was not possible to direct the submarines against
troop-ships exclusively.    They could approach the
coasts of Europe anywhere between the north of England and Gibraltar, a front of some fourteen hundred
nautical miles.    It was impossible effectively to close
this area by means of submarines.    One could have
concentrated them only on certain routes; but whether
the troop-ships would choose the same routes at the
same time was the question.    As soon as the enemy
heard of submarines anywhere, he could always send
the ships new orders by wireless and unload at another
port.    It was, therefore, not certain that by this method
we should meet with a sufficient number of troop-ships.
The destruction of the enemy's freight tonnage would
then have been undertaken only spasmodically, and
would have been set back in an undesirable manner;
and in that way the submarine war would have become
diverted from its original object.    The submarine war
against commerce was therefore continued with all
the vigor possible. According to the information
available, the enemy's remaining tonnage and his food-

supply were so reduced that the hope of attaining our object by this means was justified. The shortage of cargo space, at any rate, was established.

The suspension of our offensive had, of course, the most far-reaching results. The enemy grew stronger at the same time that we did. Owing to lack of drafts, our losses made themselves unpleasantly felt. In April I again approached the War Ministry with the request that the withdrawal of reclaimed men from munition-work might be carried out more strictly.

The only increase in drafts that I received in the future was furnished by prisoners of war returned from Russia. General Headquarters now fell back on its own reserves of men and prepared its own drafts from the troops in the Eastern Army and Rumania, as well as from among the technical branches and lines-of-communication troops. But these could not suffice unless the Government released the reclaimed men and took energetic action against deserters and skrimshankers.

Our troops had fought well; but the fact that certain divisions had obviously failed to show any inclination to attack in the plain of the Lys provided food for thought. However, in that low-lying, intersected country it had been so difficult to arrange proper artillery support that this phenomenon did not cause grave anxiety. On the other hand, the way in which the troops stopped round captured supplies, while individuals stayed behind to search houses and farms for food, were serious matters. This impaired success and showed poor discipline. But it was equally serious that our young company commanders, as well as senior officers, did not feel strong enough to take disciplinary action and to seize sufficient authority to enable them to lead their men forward without delay. The absence of our old peace-trained corps of officers was most severely felt. They had been the repository of the moral strength of the army. In addition, during the first half of the war the Reichstag had made the penal laws more lenient. The commanders responsible for maintaining discipline were deprived of their most effective punishment, in that a sentence of "severe arrest" no longer involved being tied up to a fixed object. No doubt this punishment was extraordinarily severe, and its execution should not be left to the juvenile and inexperienced company commanders, but to abolish it altogether was fatal. The alleviation may have been justifiable at the time, but now it proved disastrous. The frequent declarations of amnesty also had a bad influence on the men. The Entente no doubt achieved more than we did with its considerably more severe punishments. This historic truth is well established.

Other evils in connection with the administration of justice were also due to the long war. The judges had come to regard military offenses with a leniency which was often incomprehensible. A contributory cause of this was that the cases which had occurred at the front were not dealt with immediately by the unit, but farther in the rear in quite different circumstances and after a certain time had elapsed. It should always have been remembered that there were many men in the army who deserved no mercy whatever; of this the numerous deserters and skrimshankers are a melancholy proof. These people required severe punishment; that was demanded by the distress of our country, but also by consideration for those who were well conducted and brave. Thank God, the latter were always in the vast majority. If one of these men forgot himself, the confirming officer always had it in his power, by delaying punishment, to make sufficient allowance for a special case. Many offenses were committed in order to escape regimental duty and

ighting by undergoing punishment. We eventually
ook to forming punishment companies, which were
mployed on work in the front trenches. That is a
ad chapter. I talked it over with the War Minister.
Ie is responsible for the administration of justice in
he army; General Headquarters had nothing to do
vith it. Even in dealing with the army commanders,
ll I could do was to point out and emphasize that the
naintenance of discipline was the first essential. The
ommanding officers had to be instructed as to the
owers and means of dispensing justice at their dis-
osal. All army commanders were convinced of the
ron necessity of exerting their influence, accordingly.
With that, all that could be done from outside was
lone; it now became the duty of the troops to display
he strength required to keep their discipline unim-
aired. Here again all depended upon the officer.
And if the discipline in units became slack, the com-
nanders were not without fault.

During this time, on the occasion of exercises, I had
nany conversations with officers of all ranks, and they
ll complained of the tired and discontented spirit
vhich was being brought into the army from home.
The leave men had been exposed to the influence of
gitators, and the new drafts had a bad influence on
liscipline. All this was lowering the fighting value
of the army. Among a number of drafts very serious
rregularities had occurred, particularly among those
rom Bavaria and the East. There were also strong
complaints about the spirit of the men trained at the
Belgian training-camp of Beverloo. The units attached
all the more importance to getting back to the greatest
possible extent men who had already served in their
ranks and who belonged to them territorially. As far
as possible I met their wishes, but could not always get
it done. Afterward I heard that somebody in an

office at home had been systematically opposing these measures. There were those who were working to undermine the army.

I repeatedly spoke with the authorities concerned about the spirit of the people at home. In these days I was for the first time met with the reply that men were also returning from the army discontented and tired of the war. They seemed surprised at this; but at some time or other the army was bound to echo back what was so constantly being shouted into it from home; every part of the army at the front was bearing heavy burdens, heavier by far than ever the people at home were. The man who joined the army after being embittered and worked upon by agitators at home, and then had to suffer great hardships, could not help causing more ill-feeling when he got home again. But, in spite of these disintegrating influences, and in spite of the decay of discipline, the mass of the army was enthusiastically confident of victory. It has always been an article of my creed that army and people have but one body and one soul and that the army cannot remain sound forever if the people is diseased. Really grave symptoms in the field army still came to my knowledge only occasionally, as before. As a whole, it was still orderly and disciplined, and, after all, it had beaten the enemy. I hoped that the sense of duty and determination of the army were still strong enough to overcome the numerous adverse influences. The loss of many officers of senior and medium rank during the last actions was bound to make matters worse, as the very young new officers suffered from their natural defects. It was much the same as regards experienced non-commissioned officers. We had reached such a pitch that before an action units detailed a reserve of leaders, who did not take part in the fighting, in order that there might be some leaders left at the end of it.

It was necessary to instruct the troops according to the tactical lessons gained in the latest fighting. These were more extended formations for infantry, greater importance to be attached to "soft-spot" tactics (*Stosztruppentaktik*), better co-operation between groups and companion branches, and between infantry and artillery.

The 28th Division and detachments of the 3d Jäger Battalion, troops that had had a particularly thorough tactical training, were moved to the neighborhood of Avesnes. The details were discussed and practised with them, and then demonstrated to a large number of senior officers, including most of the army commanders and many corps commanders. In this way recent experience was quickly placed within reach of the whole army.

On all occasions I emphasized the need of not forgetting the necessary formations for defense, and of recognizing the moment when the attack must be stopped and the defense resumed. This must be felt by the systematic hardening of the enemy's resistance.

In arranging for further operations there was no time to lose. The initiative which we had seized on the Western front must be kept, and the first great blow must as soon as possible be followed by a second.

The movement of the prodigious means of attack, the supply and storage of ammunition, the concentration of the divisions, and, not least, the utilization of the experience gained in the last attack, all these things and many others took time. That was a disadvantage, but, with the forces actually available, it could not be altered.

The most favorable operation in itself was to continue the attack on the English Army at Ypres and Bailleul; but on that front the enemy was now so strong in numbers that it was impossible, even with rested troops. Before we could attack here again the enemy must become weaker, and our communications must be supplemented. Farther south conditions were similar. Besides, the Somme area afforded too little cover for the necessary preliminary work. In front of the Seventh and First Armies the enemy was weak. Troops had been sent from here to Ypres and replaced by tired English divisions. The strong positions on the hills certainly looked difficult to attack. But if our own artillery did its work well, only the difficulties of the ground would remain to be dealt with. They undoubtedly were considerable, but easier to overcome than those we surmounted on the Italian frontier on October 24, 1917. Early in April the group of the German Crown Prince was directed to submit a plan for an attack between Pinon and Rheims.

At the same time, General Headquarters had to determine what troops were to make this attack. It would be necessary to employ troops that had already taken part in the March attack, but had since then been rested and trained. Before the end of May these divisions would not be fresh and fit to attack, that was obvious. But the preparations would take as long as that. We dare not risk failure, which would have resulted in huge losses by undue haste. I could not act according to my wishes and hopes, but must simply deal with the facts as they actually were. It was obvious that all unnecessary loss of time was to be avoided.

During the discussions with the group of the German Crown Prince and the Eighteenth, Seventh, and First Armies the following operations were decided upon and their feasibility was established:

1. Attack by the Seventh and First Armies from the line Anizy (southwest of Laon) south of Berry-au-Bac, in the direction of Soissons-Fismes-Rheims.

2. Prolongation of the attacks, to the right across the Ailette toward the Oise, and to the left as far as Rheims.

3. Attack by the Eighteenth Army west of the Oise, with its principal efforts toward Compiègne.

A simultaneous attack on so broad a front was impossible, as a part of the artillery employed in the attack on March 21 had to remain for defense with the group of Crown Prince Rupprecht.

How far the attack would take us could not be foretold. I hoped it would lead to such an expenditure of force on the part of the enemy as would enable us to resume the attack in Flanders.

The group of Crown Prince Rupprecht was to remain purely on the defensive, although it was also to make preparations for a real attack in Flanders, and, by way of a feint, along its whole front. It was to be expected that in the coming period of rest its divisions, which had suffered and become reduced in the fighting in March and April, would recover and increase again by getting back men who had been wounded, and by the arrival of something in the shape of reinforcements. Should the enemy be obliged to employ considerable force against the group of the German Crown Prince, then a continuation of the offensive in Flanders would be the proper operations.

On other parts of the Western front also, where it was not intended to attack, preparations were to be continued.

It was obvious that all troops who now found themselves in new positions must first of all prepare them for defense.

All armies were specially instructed to devote particular care to men and horses in rest. Troops in the line could, of course, not be so spared as I should have wished. Those in the new positions had a hard time;

but the enemy was no better off, although in many places, particularly as regards our troops on the old Somme battle-field, his billets were better than ours. That was unavoidable. But we tried to make up for it by bombarding many places with long-range guns and bombing. On the quiet fronts, from the Seventh Army to the Swiss frontier, our formations recovered in their positions and found time to carry out battalion and regimental (*i.e.*, brigade) training in the infantry, and battery training in the artillery. In addition to improvement in discipline, much attention was paid to vigorous training in rear of the whole army and in many parts of the actual front.

The equipment of the troops was completed. Each infantry company, which had hitherto had four light machine guns, now received a fifth, as well as improved rifle grenades. Machine guns were issued to supply columns and transport, as a protection against aircraft, and the equipment of the artillery with them was gradually completed.

The first anti-tank rifles came in; they were effective, but unfortunately very heavy, and took two men to work them; so that meant the loss of one rifleman.

The men's rations were sufficient, but very inferior to those of the enemy. Grazing turned out to be favorable; the horses found enough to eat and gained strength, but there was not much corn. Health had so far been good. The first cases of influenza appeared, but the medical officers classified them as slight.

### V

During the great events in the West, quiet had been maintained on the Italian and Macedonian fronts. They were merely a prolongation of the Western front, and formed the protection of our flanks, the Macedonian fronts at the same time protecting the flank of Austria-Hungary. The assistance we received from the Austro-Hungarian artillery in the West was, owing to its meager supply of ammunition, insignificant. It went back after it had fired off the ammunition.

The situation of the Austro-Hungarian Army in Italy had improved, inasmuch as several hundred thousand prisoners of war had rejoined it from Russia. The army had thus been strengthened, and felt equal to making an attack on the Italians. General von Arz had sent officers to witness our attacks, and was kept informed of our tactical experiences. He intended to assume the offensive in the first half of June—that is to say, soon after our attack on the Chemin des Dames. Thus, at the end of May and in the beginning of June there was to be a great combined effort against the Entente.

It would now have been possible to reinforce the German Army in the West by a few Austro-Hungarian divisions, if the attack in Italy had been given up. But their fighting capacity could not be considered sufficient for employment on the Western front, and, as long as the Austro-Hungarian General Headquarters at Baden was honestly working for an offensive in Italy, it could not be better engaged. A victory in Italy would relieve us just as much as it had done in the autumn of 1917; at the best it would draw off a part of the new American formations. This would be of more service than a mere reinforcement of the Western front by divisions of poor quality. If the attack in Italy should prove unsuccessful, it would still be possible to send a direct reinforcement to the West.

The food situation of Austria and the Austro-Hungarian Army was uncommonly serious. It had received its share of the Rumanian supply in advance and used it up, and was now extracting all it could get hold of from the occupied portions of the Ukraine, needless to say, without any consideration. But even this did not suffice, and early in May Austria, being in great need, seized grain belonging to Germany, which was being forwarded us from Rumania, while it was in transit through the Dual Monarchy. As we had already given help in February, this high-handed action therefore aroused considerable astonishment and indignation. But indignation was no use; we had to give again, which was the more annoying, as the horses on the Western front depended for their meager corn rations on the Rumanian supply.

The Macedonian front continued quiet. The Bulgarian Army had time for rest and training. But it could not be denied that since about March its spirit had visibly deteriorated, owing to bad food and clothing. The irritation against Germany was cleverly fomented by hostile propaganda and by Bulgarians who favored the Entente. The Peace of Bucharest and the withdrawal of a few German formations to the West added fresh fuel to it. Cases of mutiny showed how far the process of corrosion had gone. General Headquarters and the Group Headquarters of General von Scholtz did all they could to help and to influence the Bulgarians. We gave them food, and the Prussian War Minister provided clothing. We also complied with the wishes of Crown Prince Boris, who had visited the Western front, and had asked that the removal of several batteries be delayed.

We impressed upon the Bulgarian Headquarters the need for preparing reserves. It had put too many troops in the front line and kept back too few complete formations. Gradually General Jekoff decided to follow our advice. This was facilitated by transferring the troops in the Dobrudja to the Macedonian front, which, however, proceeded very slowly. On the enemy's side there now appeared Royal Greek troops, in addition to the Venizelists.

In Palestine the English had in March attacked across the Jordan, just north of the Red Sea, with the obvious intention of working round the left wing of the Turkish Army group posted there and of driving it off the Damascus Railway. The English attack gained ground at first, but ended in defeat, and they were driven back to the west bank of the Jordan. Unfortunately, General von Liman, who had in the mean time taken over in Palestine from General von Falkenhayn, had not enough troops to follow up. At the end of April the English repeated their attack, with the same result. At the end of the hot weather, which was now beginning, its continuation was to be expected, but by that time I hoped that the reinforcement of the Palestine front, promised by Enver, would have been effected. In Mesopotamia English troops were pushing on toward Mosul, and obtaining a firm footing in North Persia, replacing the Russians, who had dispersed.

In Armenia the Turks had begun their advance at the end of February. By the end of March they had cleared the Russians out of their territory, and by the end of April they had occupied the territory of Kars and Batum, allotted to them in the Peace of Brest. But this was not the limit of their ambition; they contemplated extending their influence in the Caucasus. For this purpose they developed active propaganda among the Mohammedan population of Azerbijan, where Enver's brother, Nouri, also appeared, in order to raise new formations. At the same time Turkey opened negotiations with the Russian Republics of Georgia, Azerbijan, and Armenia, which were in process of formation on the south side of the Caucasus. By order of the German Imperial Government General von

Lossow went from Constantinople to attend these negotiations.

In themselves I was able to assent to Turkish measures, which were of service to the general scheme of the war. But they must not be allowed to divert Turkey

FIG. 33. TURKISH ADVANCE IN ARMENIA, 1918

from its proper military rôle nor impede our supply of raw materials from the Caucasus, from which we anticipated very considerable alleviation. Enver's task was to fight England in the first place on the Palestine front, as I pointed out to him repeatedly in clearly worded telegrams. And now there was an opportunity of striking the English in North Persia. This was made more favorable by the railway line from Batum *via* Tiflis to Tabriz. In North Persia it was possible for the Turks to oppose the English with superior numbers. It would have been a real service to have raised the inhabitants of Azerbijan against the English, and I should gladly have supported every effort directed to that end. But Enver and the Turkish Government thought less of fighting England than of their Pan-Islamic aims in the Caucasus. And with these they combined a very material object—namely, the lucrative exploitation of the raw materials to be obtained there. That this would not suit Germany's war industry every one knew who was acquainted with Turkish business methods. In this way we came into conflict with Turkish policy.

During the negotiations at Batum the representatives of the Georgian Republic had approached General von Lossow with a request for the protection of the German Empire. In 1915 and 1916 we had employed Georgian irregulars in Armenia, though without success, on military questions, and in so doing had come into contact with influential Georgians. I could only welcome this connection, as I did also Georgia's request for the protection of the German Empire. We thus acquired a means of getting at the raw materials of the Caucasus independently of Turkey and of getting a hold on the working of the Tiflis Railway. The latter was of decisive importance in any fighting in North Persia and would give better results under a management influenced by us than under one in which the Turks shared. Finally, we must endeavor to strengthen ourselves by raising Georgian troops who might be used against England. Besides, we could never tell what difficulties we might have to meet from the volunteer army commanded by General Alexeieff on the north of the Caucasus. I therefore requested that the Imperial

Chancellor should take Georgia's application in
consideration.

For other reasons also the Government was incline
to a policy of encouraging Georgia. It was afraid
difficulties that might arise out of Turkey's attitu
toward Bolshevist Russia. The Imperial Chancell
strongly condemned the violent measures adopted
the Turks against the Christian Armenians. The
were indeed a grave blunder, and nothing could justi
them. So, when the Georgian representatives came
Berlin with General von Lossow in June, the Gover
ment did not give them an uncompromising refusal.

In the Ukraine, the German troops had, after takir
Kiev on March 1, continued their advance mo
slowly. Odessa had fallen on the 12th, after a sligl
resistance. In this operation German troops, who ha
advanced through Moldavia after the conclusion
the preliminary peace with Rumania on March 7, ha
co-operated. In the succeeding period General Head
quarters had to bear in mind the objects for which th
occupation of the Ukraine had been undertaken, an
to carry the advance no farther than those object
necessitated.

The Ukraine had asked for help. We ourselves, an
even more so Austria and its army, needed corn; th
country could not, therefore, be allowed to become
prey, and a source of strength, to Bolshevism. We ha
to strengthen it sufficiently to enable it to be useful to u

The principal grain district we had occupied afte
the capture of Charkoff on April 8. The Commande
in-chief in the East now found that the railways coul
not be worked without the coal of the Donetz Basir
So, willy-nilly, we had to agree to occupy this part c
the Ukraine as well, and to advance our lines as far a
Rostoff, which was reached at the beginning of May
In spite of this we were obliged at first to send ver

nsiderable quantities of coal from Germany to the
kraine; this import, however, decreased when more
al was procurable locally.

Besides the railway, we also needed secure water-
ansport from the Black Sea ports to Braila.    The
ussian Black Sea Fleet had caused us difficulties
Odessa, Nicolaieff, and Cherson.    Which Govern-
ent it was under was doubtful; in any event, it did
ot carry out the conditions of the Peace of Brest.    In
ebastopol it would always be a danger to navigation,
at the end of April we occupied the Crimea.    Part
the Russian fleet escaped to Novorossisk.    It was
tended to make use of the ships captured in Sebastopol
far as we could provide crews for them.

The occupation of this extensive territory had led
fresh conflicts with Bolshevist bands and troops.
most cases they were driven off without trouble.
fter the advance was stopped, the Commander-in-
ief in the East had agreed upon a line of demarcation
ith the Soviet Government.    It was significant of
is Government that it often accused our troops of not
especting this line, while we had reports from our
ommander-in-chief that Bolshevist bands had raided
e territory which our troops were to protect.    Un-
rtunately, the Foreign Office appeared to believe
olshevist lies sooner than our statements.

After a good deal of discussion with the Austrian
eadquarters at Baden, our respective spheres of
terest in the Ukraine were settled.    On this, the
uartermaster-General effected an agreement with
ustria-Hungary and the exploitation of the supplies
as regulated.    Afterward, however, in view of the
ay Austria-Hungary had been seizing our supplies,
is agreement had to be modified, so that we under-
ok the collecting of supplies in the whole of the
kraine as well as their distribution.    This was only an

expedient, unfortunately a necessary one, in order to
establish a practical working system.

The German military and civil authorities found
ample scope for their activities.  I followed everything
with great attention, since General Headquarters was
principally interested in the result.  Field-Marshal
von Eichhorn had taken over the army group at Kiev
the Government was represented by Ambassador von
Mumm.  The collection of supplies was in the hands
of the Imperial Economic Office (*Reichswirtschaftsamt*)
A more confused and many-headed organization it
was impossible to imagine, and it was all due to Berlin's
unfortunate attitude toward "militarism," as well as
its own "bureaucratism" and hidebound methods

As was to be expected, the new Government of the
Ukraine had proved incapable either of settling the
unrest in the country or of delivering grain to us.  This
Government disappeared from the scene, and Hetman
Skropadsky assumed control.

While at the end of April and early in May I was
occupied with important work connected with the
operations in the West, I received through the Emperor's Military Cabinet a telegram from the Imperial
Chancellor to the Emperor, complaining in strong
terms of the "militarist" attitude of the group headquarters at Kiev and requesting His Majesty to remedy
it   The Military Cabinet had informed the Imperial
Chancellor that His Majesty proposed that in the first
instance the whole episode should be investigated by
means of a joint inquiry by the authorities concerned
I looked forward to this with satisfaction, for I was
firmly convinced that by probing the matter to the
bottom, and eliminating all gossip and prejudice, we
should once more find there was nothing in the whole
affair.  In this case we did not even reach the conference stage, for it was soon made clear that the

ield-Marshal and the ambassador had personally
worked well together. So, it happened, "militarism"
ad had nothing to do with it. What actually occurred
was that during the course of events a general had dealt
somewhat harshly with a former member of the Government, whose conduct had betrayed a highly doubtful
attitude toward German interests. But the whole
business left a bitter taste behind. I mention this
incident only because it was characteristic of the feeling
in Berlin. They were always ready there to go against,
instead of with, us. It was thought more important
to consider certain political interests than practical
requirements, even though the latter, like Field-Marshal
von Eichhorn's care for agriculture, was of the greatest
consequence to our subsistence. It was particularly
regretable that, without hearing the other side, the
War Minister had sided with the Government.

Hetman Skropadsky turned out to be a man with
whom it was possible to work well. He was determined
to maintain order in the country and to meet us as far as
possible. I made his acquaintance later and formed a
very good impression of him. He was never superficial,
but penetrated to the bottom of everything.

General Headquarters could not be otherwise than
satisfied with the change of Government at Kiev,
as it was favorable to the prosecution of the war. I
anticipated being able to increase our armies and our
food-supply; and the raising of new Ukrainian formations was actually commenced. This, of course, required time and brought us no immediate relief. The
German troops that were in the Ukraine were urgently
needed by the group for protection against the Bolshevists and securing the economic exploitation of the
country. Whenever we wanted to reduce the troops
the Ukraine complained that they were not strong
enough to stand a reduction in numbers.

The Imperial Economic Office pursued a peace-tim
policy in the Ukraine which anticipated a state
affairs that did not yet exist; to that no one coul
object, provided that with the more limited econom
policy the purely military motive, for which I pleade
was not thereby excluded. In its need, Austri
Hungary had taken drastic measures and, althoug
it did not get anything like what Count Czernin, earl
in February, had stated to be necessary, the suppli
it drew from the Ukraine, combined with our assistanc
undoubtedly saved Austria and its army from starva
tion. Only the most urgent needs, however, wer
satisfied, and even then we did not receive the bread
corn and forage so urgently required to revive th
strength of our people at home. Still, the Ukraine di
help Germany. In the summer of 1918 it supplied u
with meat, and thus the scanty meat ration we had wa
made possible without encroaching upon our own live
stock reserves and those of the occupied territorie
The army was also able to get horses in great numbers
without them warfare would have been altogether im
possible, for if Germany had been obliged to raise thes
horses our own agriculture would have been hard hi
We also obtained from the Ukraine raw materials of a
kinds.

The hope that the corn of the Ukraine would prov
to be an economic weapon which would improve ou
position in regard to the neutrals, and would bring u
that further economic alleviation which was so im
portant for maintaining our warlike capacity, had soo
to be abandoned.

By occupying the Ukraine we had considerabl
weakened the military policy of the Soviet Governmen
We also established connection with many representa
tives of nationalistic tendencies of Great Russia, an
with the Don Cossacks, whom we could have made us

to combat Bolshevism if the Government had agreed
do so.

On the Great Russian front of the Commander-in-
ief in the East, from the Pripet to the Gulf of Fin-
ad, no change had occurred since March 3.

Finland had risen, and urgently required immediate
lp. Arms alone were not enough. The Soviet
overnment made no preparations to withdraw its

FIG. 34. CAMPAIGN IN FINLAND, 1918

oops from Finland. The moment when that country
uld receive assistance from England was approaching.
In order to prevent the formation of another Eastern
nt, and to increase our military strength, we com-
ed with Finland's request for troops. General von
annerheim also supported the despatch of German
oops. He did not want them too soon nor in too
eat strength, so that his Finns might have some
hting to do, and thereby gain confidence. Those
re sound military ideas.

With the consent of the Imperial Government, of

which we continued to assure ourselves, we first e
tablished an advanced base in the Aaland Islands, be
cause at that time it appeared necessary to land i
the Gulf of Bothnia. As a short time before, Swede
had also landed troops on the islands, we had to ente
into special negotiations with that country, which pre
ceeded without difficulty. Later on, Sweden withdre
her troops; and we ourselves abandoned the island
soon after General Headquarters had decided to lan
the expedition at Hangö.

Liaison with General von Mannerheim was mair
tained by Major Crantz, whom I had sent to the Fir
nish Headquarters, where he settled how the Germa
troops were to be employed. Co-operation with Ger
eral von Mannerheim was always satisfactory an
marked by mutual confidence.

The Baltic Division had been formed at Danzig unde
General Count von der Goltz; it consisted of three ba
talions of Jägers, three regiments of Mounted Rifle
(*Kavallerie-Schützen*), and a few batteries. It landed a
Hangö early in April, while General von Mannerhei
with the Finnish White Guards, who had been partl
armed by us, was northwest of Tammerfors with h
back to Wasa. The Finnish Jäger battalion had bee
sent to him. Being composed of picked men, it forme
an excellent training-school for the new Finnish officer

While General von Mannerheim advanced *via* Tan
merfors, the Baltic Division moved northeast towar
Tavastehus. In co-operation with the fleet, it occt
pied Helsingfors on April 13, with a weak force; th
Commander-in-chief in the East landed a weak detach
ment under Colonel von Brandenstein at Lovisa an
Kotka, east of Helsingfors. This detachment marche
north in order to block the retreat of the Red Guard
who were near Tavastehus, at Lahti. In a concentr
attack they were completely surrounded after heav

ghting at the end of April and forced to surrender.
inland was thus liberated.

In the mean time Viborg had been occupied from the
orth by the White Guards; strategically this was a
ood move; what its actual result would have been,
the decision had not taken place farther west, could
ot be foreseen, owing to the uncertain fighting value
 the opposing forces and the support of the Bol-
evists from Russia. The tactical victory and the
ompt liberation of Finland were achieved on the
ld of Lahti-Tavastehus by the splendid collaboration
 German and Finnish troops. This concluded
erations.

We now held positions at Viborg and Narva which
ould at any time enable us to advance on Petrograd,
 order to overthrow the Bolshevist Government or
event the English from reaching there from Mur-
ansk. From Finland, moreover, the Murmansk
ailway was flanked along its whole length, so that
ngland could not undertake any serious attempt on
etrograd. The English expedition which had occu-
ed the Murman coast was firmly held there. The
version of the weak Baltic Division, of which the
ree Jäger battalions returned to Germany in August,
as well worth while. The Finnish Government at
ice set about organizing the Finnish Army, assisted
 German instructors. That we did not achieve more
 Finland is mainly owing to our ever vacillating policy.
eneral Count von der Goltz had won universal con-
ence, even that of the leading politicians, which the
presentative of the German Government was not so
ccessful in doing. The want of decision in our
reign policy was unfortunately made evident in this
here also. The Foreign Office adopted no definite
an, and so became nobody's friend in Finland, but
ly offended Germany's faithful adherents.

The many proofs of warm sympathy which I receive
from Finland after my resignation prove that gratitud
still exists in the world. This sympathy touched m
all the more because it was not Finnish, but purel
German interests that took us there. When in Febru
ary 1919 the Swedish Government, for no reason
that I could understand, made objection to my sta
ing there, a Finnish delegate suddenly appeared a
Hessleholmsgard to offer me an asylum in Finland.
was pleased, but of course refused, as I wanted
return to Germany.

Amid the tremendous overwhelming events of th
world-wide war the Ukraine and Finland seem me
incidents. Still, I hope that permanent good ma
result. Both countries will always afford typic
examples of the way in which our Government misu
derstood the nature of this war up to the end, an
treated every problem merely according to the dictat
of party politics. In the military sense both cou
tries afforded us for the time being what we expecte
of them. The formation of a new Eastern front w
prevented, or at least almost indefinitely postpone
We had broken the blockade in the East, and it seeme
as if we might regain our strength in that way. Th
position of the Soviet Government was severely shake
its continued existence seriously threatened.

When at the end of May the German attack in tl
West was continued, to be followed in the first half
June by an Austro-Hungarian one in Italy, the situ
tion on all fronts was satisfactory. Special dang
seemed to exist only in Palestine.

## VI

The second great German attack in France and t
attack of the Imperial and Royal Army in Italy we
in their main features carried out as intended.

In the middle of May we commenced to concentrate
the troops who were to break through over the Chemin
les Dames. The preliminary work was completed up
o time. The artillery was brought into action accord-
ig to Colonel Bruchmüller's proposals, which were also
dopted as regards the preparatory artillery fire.

I frequently visited the army commanders concerned and was most favorably impressed.

On May 27 the attack began between Vauxaillon and Lapigneul. Once more it proved a brilliant success. I had thought we should succeed in reaching only the neighborhood of Soissons and Fismes. By the second and third days these objectives had in place been left far behind. We had gained ground especially beyond Fismes, not so much beyond Soissons. It was most regretable that one headquarters did not perceive the favorable situation at Soissons and that we did not push ahead with the same energy as at Fismes although it would have been possible. Otherwise our situation would have been considerably better, not only at Soissons, but on the whole front of the attack. It would have been more than doubtful whether the French would have held their positions between the Oise and the Aisne any longer. This was another case where in a few moments, much might have been achieved which was left undone. The Commander-in-chief sit and thinks and can make all preparations, but the execution of his plans is no longer in his hands. On the battle-field he must make the best of the *fait accompli*.

The center of the Seventh Army advanced to the south as far as the Marne. Its left wing and the right of the First Army, which had, as intended, prolonged the attack on the left toward Rheims, pushed ahead between the Marne and the Vesle toward the wooded heights of Rheims, where they soon encountered resistance too stiff to be overcome. The right wing of the Seventh Army gained ground between the Aisne and the Marne, southwest of Soissons and as far as the eastern edge of the forest of Villers-Cotterets, and captured Château-Thierry. General Foch concentrated strong reserves southwest of Rheims and near Soissons with which he made fruitless counter-attacks which subsequently extended as far as Château-Thierry.

Early in June we stopped our advance. General Headquarters did not intend to attack further except between the Aisne and the forest of Villers-Cotterets, southwest of Soissons. We wanted to gain more ground to the westward, on account of the railway which leads from the Aisne valley east of Soissons into that of the Vesle, and afforded tactical support to the attack of the Eighteenth Army on the line Montdidier-Noyon.

In spite of a few unavoidable temporary crises, our troops remained masters of the situation both in attack and in defense. They proved themselves superior to both the English and the French, even when their opponents were assisted by tanks. At Château-Thierry, Americans who had been a long time in France had bravely attacked our thinly held fronts, but they were unskilfully led, attacked in dense masses, and failed. Here, too, our men felt themselves superior. Our tactics had proved sound in every way, our losses, compared with those of the enemy and the large number of prisoners, though in themselves distressing, had been very slight. Again, the cessation of the attack did not take place early enough at all points. Here and there it was continued where defense was already indicated. With a few exceptions, the troops had everywhere displayed good conduct and endurance.

On the whole the impression had been very favorable. The group of the German Crown Prince had gained a great tactical victory in the offensive. The enemy had been forced to put in more of his reserves than the troops we had expended. Paris once more received the impression of defeat, and many inhabitants left the city. In the session of the Chamber early in June, which I awaited with interest, there appeared, indeed, no sign of weakness. Clemenceau's words were full of pride and exemplary strength: "We are now giving ground, but we shall never surrender." "We shall be victorious if the public authorities are equal to their task." "I fight before Paris, I shall fight in Paris, I shall fight behind Paris." "Remember the fate of Thiers and Gambetta; I do not long for the difficult and thankless task of Thiers."

Even after this second great defeat in one year the Entente was not yet ready for peace.

It was a strategical disadvantage to us that we had been unable to take Rheims and push our armies farther forward in this area into the mountain country. The supply of the center of the Seventh Army was thereby restricted to the broad-gage railway which leads from the valley of the Aisne, east of Soissons, into that of the Vesle. In order to handle the traffic without accidents, the construction of a second curve to connect the two valleys farther to the eastward was ordered. It was not possible to put in other broad-gage sections south of the Aisne, as the country was so irregular. From Laon a broad-gage line ran direct to Soissons *via* Anizy. The tunnel north of the town, between the Aisne and the Ailette, had been blown up and had to be repaired. One meter-gage line and sundry light railways (*Feldbahnen*) led toward the left wing of the Seventh Army and the right wing of the First, and they afforded great relief; but they had first to be extended across the two trench systems before they could be connected up to those already in our possession. The unfavorable railway communications threw a great strain on our mechanical transportation, which again made the fuel situation serious.

On June 1, as intended, our attack had already been extended to the west as far as the junction of the Ailette and the Aisne. The transfer of the necessary artillery had been carried out smoothly. The fighting

took us forward in the trench system which we had
abandoned in March 1917.

It was intended that the Eighteenth Army should
attack on June 7 between Montdidier and Noyon, the
Seventh to attack at the same time southwest of Soissons.   At a conference early in June at the Eighteenth
Army  Headquarters  I  became  convinced  that  its
preliminary artillery work would not be done in time.
The arrival of the reinforcing artillery from the Seventh
Army had been delayed.   The attack was, therefore,
postponed to June 9.   This was a drawback, since it
thus lost much of its tactical connection with the great
action between the Aisne and the Marne, for which a
local operation southwest of Soissons could form no
complete substitute.   The enemy would find the transfer of his reserves facilitated.   In spite of these objections I decided for the later date because thorough preparation was essential to success and to keep down
casualties.

The attack of the Eighteenth Army began on the
9th, and was directed on the right toward Méry, on
the left against very strong positions on the high
ground just west of the Oise.   This time the enemy
was prepared, but our infantry got through his whole
trench system and beyond it, in some places as far
as the Aronde.

On the 11th the enemy directed very heavy counter-
attacks, particularly against our right on Méry, which
gained some ground.   They continued throughout the
12th and 13th without result.   In consequence of the
great accumulation of enemy troops General Headquarters directed the Eighteenth Army to stop the
attack on the 11th, in order to avoid casualties.   It
was quite evident that the attack commenced in the
mean time by the Seventh Army southwest of Soissons
would not get through.

The action of the Eighteenth Army had not altered the strategical situation brought about by the attack of the Seventh Army, nor had it provided any fresh tactical data.

In the middle of June nearly the whole of the new front of the German Crown Prince's group became quiet. Only between the Aisne and the forest of Villers-Cotterets some tension remained, which occa-

EXPLANATION

▬▬ Extreme German position at the time of the attack, June 9, 1918.
➡ Direction of German attack.
▬ ▬ German line reached through the attack.

1 : 500000

FIG. 36. BATTLE BEFORE NOYON, 1918

sionally broke out into local actions. On both banks of the Ardre, between Rheims and the Marne, matters also remained somewhat unsettled. The captured territory provided us with plentiful resources and eased our food-supply.

The attack of the Austro-Hungarian Army in Italy was originally fixed for June 11. Owing to the backward state of the preparations it was put off till the 15th. It was to commence with an advance at the Adamello on the West Tyrol front, so as to distract the attention of the Italian Headquarters in that direction. General von Arz intended to make the main attack between Asiago and the sea in several groups directed on the Brenta, the Montello, and farther down the Piave. In spite of local successes, the attack produced no gain, and after a few days General von Arz had to make up his mind to withdraw the troops that had pushed across the Piave under General Goiginger. According to the reports I received

FIG. 37. AUSTRIAN DRIVE IN ITALY, 1918

from Baden, the Austro-Hungarian troops had fought well. What causes prevented their success I do not know. I have no means of judging whether it is correct that the attack was made on too broad a front, as it is stated to have been.

The manner in which the failure on the Piave was discussed shortly afterward in Austria-Hungary, especially in the Hungarian Parliament, was most deplorable. Under very similar circumstances after the

Aisne-Champagne battle in 1916, and now in far more
difficult ones, the French had maintained a great and
dignified demeanor. From Budapest we heard unpleasant speeches, which could only make every one
more depressed. Nobody asked the Hungarian Parliament by what right it pronounced this criticism. Had
it really done everything to make victory possible?
If so, it might criticize, but to do so in public and at that
time was a mistake. The impression produced by
the failure on the Piave was further deepened by events
in the Dual Monarchy.

This unsuccessful attack was extremely painful to
me. I could no longer hope that relief on the Western
front might be gained in Italy itself. However, in
other respects the military situation there remained as
before. For the time being the opposing forces balanced each other. A further reinforcement of the
Entente front in France by Italians was not to be
feared. General von Arz considered the possibility of
renewing the attack in the autumn.

I at once proposed to the allied headquarters that it
should send all its available troops to the Western front.
General von Arz agreed. In this matter he probably
had a struggle with his Imperial Master, who disliked
sending troops away. After a good deal of pressure
the whole reinforcement provided by Austria-Hungary
amounted to four divisions. In the first instance,
only two arrived in July. They were supposed to be
known as good troops, but their condition, particularly
as regards ammunition-supply, was wretched. They
required several weeks' training before they were fit
to put in the line in trench warfare on the Western
front. Late in August and early in September the
other two arrived. In the middle of September General
von Arz was going to send two more, but they had to
go to Serbia, as the defection of Bulgaria threatened

to lay open Austria's flank, and therefore ours, to the Entente.

Accordingly, the German Army had to continue the battle without material help, but with only such resources as General Headquarters could get together and the home country provide.

On the other portions of the allied fronts in Europe there had been no particular activity; only west of Ochrida Lake the Austrian troops had been pushed back in June and July, as far north as Berat.

We now had better hopes of the Bulgarian Army, as its spirit had distinctly improved with the first arrivals of clothing and supplies of food. General von Scholtz fully realized the gravity of the situation, and was always complaining that the army, ever more deeply involved in party politics, was being played off against Radoslavoff. He would have been glad of more German troops, but as they were needed on the Western front he had to do without them in Macedonia. In the event of attack by the enemy, General Headquarters and the Group Headquarters anticipated local retreats. The Bulgarian reserves that had been formed in the mean time were some guaranty against any serious piercing of our line.

In Palestine local English attacks had failed, and in Mesopotamia those English detachments that had been pushed up to Mosul were again withdrawn, but, on the other hand, the English appeared to be stronger in northern Persia and on the southern shore of the Caspian Sea. The Turks were still round Tabriz and close up to Baku.

On the Eastern front the situation was unchanged, and everything was in suspense.

The contingent that the United States sent to France in April, May, and June was, according to the information obtainable, estimated at fifteen divisions. At the moment there might be twenty American divisions in all in France, more than I had believed possible, and not only had our March superiority in the number of the divisions been canceled, but even the difference in gross numbers was now to our disadvantage, for an American division consists of twelve strong battalions. In those parts of the line where we had hitherto been fighting with divisions which had already been in France some time, we had remained masters of the situation, in spite of our inferiority in numbers.

It was not to be expected that the new formations, which had been hastily brought up and received less training, would fight better than the old divisions. No enemy should be despised, but neither should he be overestimated. How otherwise should we have been able to attack and overcome the Russians in 1914? As long as our troops maintained their morale they would be able to cope with any enemy, even with the strong American divisions, whose nerves were less shaken than those of our men who had been in action continuously for a long time. But the fact that these new American reinforcements could release English and French divisions on quiet sectors weighed heavily in the balance against us. This was of the greatest importance and helps to explain the influence exerted by the American contingent on the issue of the conflict. It was for this reason that America became the deciding factor in the war.

On June 15 General Foch had largely spent his reserves and there was no doubt that no more could be asked of the French Army. From the early summer of 1918 until now France had disbanded very few battalions. She now drew more heavily on the great reserves of man-power in her colonies than she had done in previous years. It was quite clear that the

French would make use of the approaching lull in hostilities to gather up all their strength.

Since the middle of May the English Army had been more or less inactive, and its reconstruction must have made great progress, although there is no reason to suppose that it recovered more quickly, even taking the better living conditions into account, than the army group of Crown Prince Rupprecht. But the fact that the Entente armies were far better fed than ours must by no means be left out of account.

Our pro-Flemish propaganda had begun to influence the Belgian Army. Deserters continually came over to us, from whose reports it was clear that, thanks to the Flemish movement, the Belgian Army was becoming more friendly toward us.

Our army had suffered. Influenza was rampant, and the army group of Crown Prince Rupprecht was particularly afflicted. It was a grievous business having to listen every morning to the chiefs of staffs' recital of the number of influenza cases, and their complaints about the weakness of their troops if the English attacked again. However, the English were not ready yet. The number of influenza cases diminished, although it often left a greater weakness in its wake than the doctors realized.

The long rest gradually improved the condition of the troops. The battalions of the Crown Prince Rupprecht's group reached a fairly satisfactory level of strength, not much below the English standard. Only a few divisions remained below strength. The army group of the German Crown Prince had, of course, been heavily taxed in the constant fighting; but there were sufficient reserves at hand to make me hopeful that during the lull the battalions might, with few exceptions, be brought up to the French standard.

The battalion strength had been reduced, but was

still high enough to allow us to strike one more blow that should make the enemy ready for peace. There was no other way.

Again and again our thoughts returned to the idea of an offensive in Flanders. Strong English reserves were still assembled here, even after the French divisions had been withdrawn under pressure of the battles with the army group of the German Crown Prince. But an offensive at this point still presented too difficult a problem. We had to postpone it.

The bulk of the enemy reserves was the arc described by the Eighteenth and Seventh Armies in the direction of Paris, while the line from Château-Thierry-Verdun was only weakly held. General Headquarters again decided to attack the enemy at his weak point. Accordingly, an attack on both sides of Rheims was planned for the middle of July, whereby the rear communications of the Seventh Army between the Aisne and the Marne would be incidentally greatly improved. Immediately following this operation we meant to concentrate artillery, trench-mortars, and flying squadrons on the Flanders front, and possibly attack that a fortnight later. There were hopes that, if the offensive at Rheims succeeded, there would be a very decisive weakening of the enemy in Flanders.

In order to reduce transportation movements to a minimum and accumulate enough artillery for the two offensives, the fifth and sixth guns were in many places reissued to the field artillery from the reserve of guns. For a short time this increased number of guns had to be served by the batteries, although their personnel was not increased for the purpose. Batteries were also transferred from the East.

General Headquarters was in a very difficult position as regards fixing a time for the offensive. By the middle of July the movement of troops and other preparations for the attack on both sides of Rheims would have been completed, but for the sake of the troops I should like to have waited a little longer.   At a pinch, however, it would do, and postponement would have been of advantage to the enemy also.   So we decided to stand by our schedule, and keep the first days of August in view for the Flanders offensive.   The concentration of troops for this purpose necessitated a certain weakening of other fronts, with the result that the Eighteenth Army and the right wing of the Ninth, between the Oise and the Aisne, were at times in some danger, while the whole of Crown Prince Rupprecht's group and the Seventh Army, south of the Aisne, were always well supported.

Strong reserves, which had been resting for some time, were behind the army group of Crown Prince Rupprecht, while the army group of the German Crown Prince was compelled to build up its reserves by withdrawing divisions of the Eighteenth and Seventh Armies, which were already very tired.   The army groups of Von Gallwitz and Duke Albrecht had to give up rested divisions in exchange for tired ones.   It was once more our business to build up the army and prepare it for the coming offensive.   We lived the same life both at and behind the front as we had lived before the offensive of May 27.

## VII

The attack on Rheims was based on sound military principles, and we undertook the operation with the firm conviction that it would succeed.   In the recent battles the men of the German Crown Prince's group fought as well as their militia character led us to expect they would.   In all essentials the men had shown themselves superior to the enemy so long as they were handled carefully and with an eye to their peculiarities

and temperament. I gave serious thought to the
question whether, in view of the spirit of the army and
the condition of our reserves, it would not be advisable
to adopt the defensive. But I finally decided against
this policy, because, quite apart from the bad influence
it would have on our allies, I was afraid that the army
would find defensive battles an even greater strain
than an offensive, because such a policy would make it
easy for the enemy to concentrate his vast resources
in war material on any given battle-field. Of the two
an offensive makes less demand on the men, and involves
no higher losses. The offensive had the incalculable
moral advantage that it could not voluntarily be
broken off. Further, all weaknesses in any army
become much more prominent in the defensive.

Reports from the army about the evil influence of
the mood prevailing at home and reports from home
about the low morale of the army became more frequent. The army also complained of the effect of
enemy propaganda, which was bound to be great,
as the men came under its influence even at home.
The Fourth Army quoted the following instance: The
enemy propaganda had obtained possession of Prince
Lichnowsky's pamphlet, which, in a manner entirely
inexplicable to me, put the whole blame for the outbreak of war on Germany, although His Majesty and
the Imperial Chancellor always maintained that the
Entente was alone responsible. The Kaiser's words
were compared with the corresponding passages of the
pamphlet, and denounced as falsehoods. In order to
heighten this impression the opinion expressed in a
Social Democratic newspaper was appended. That
opinion almost coincided with Prince Lichnowsky's
and could be published, to the great injury of the
nation, without fear of the consequences. It was no
wonder that the man in the trenches did not know

what to think, since Prince Lichnowsky was still at large and such views were printed with impunity. I had already begged the Imperial Chancellor, Doctor Michaelis, to take proceedings against Prince Lichnowsky. On the military side Captain von Beerfelde was called to account for disseminating the pamphlet. But as the author remained unmolested, Captain von Beerfelde could not possibly be punished, so I again approached the Imperial Chancellor, and explained to him that legal measures against the Prince had become a matter of military necessity for the sake of our men, who had to be ready to fight, and, if need be, to die for our good cause. I reported in the same sense to His Majesty, but nothing was done. Prince Lichnowsky shares the gruesome distinction of having undermined the discipline of the army with the Bolshevists and many others.

It was just about this time that Clemenceau spoke the words, "We shall achieve victory if the public authorities are equal to their task."

In France they were equal to it, but how was it with us? I have given one instance of enemy propaganda, which could never have been so effective if public men in our own country had realized the iron necessities of this war.

The army was literally swamped by enemy propaganda, the serious danger of which was clearly recognized. General Headquarters gave rewards for the surrender of such pamphlets, but this could not prevent them from poisoning the minds of our soldiers before the pamphlets were gathered up. Unfortunately, the enemy propaganda could not be really effectively fought without the help of the Government. Patriotic instruction alone was insufficient.

It was certainly discouraging that our two great attacks had not forced a decision. That they had been victories was obvious. Disillusionment had come; it was impossible in this World War to gloss that over The reason for the falling off in our morale was not to be found in that. It lay very much deeper. The evil effect of the disillusionment was doubled by the fact that we could not overcome it in our then state of mind. For the rest a belief in a favorable issue of the war still prevailed in every quarter.

A decided deterioration in the army's morale resulted from the re-enrollment, after long leave, of soldiers returned from captivity in Russia. They introduced a spirit of general insubordination, showing itself particularly in definite refusal to return to the front, thinking that, like the prisoners of war exchanged from England and France, they were under no obligation to fight any longer. In Graudenz it came to very serious disorders.

In Beverloo it was discovered that some hundreds of Alsatians had formed a plot to escape to Holland. The continual drifting of troops from the East compelled me to send the Alsace-Lorrainers back to the West, where they were by no means welcome. Moreover, the greater part of the reserves who were transferred from the special branches showed themselves unwilling to join the infantry. In this many saw themselves confronted with dangers which had been avoided hitherto.

Meanwhile there were very many things affecting the spirit of the troops in the West, already weakened by influenza and depressed by the uniform diet. Stores, captured in our offensives, made it possible for the moment to vary the food rations, but now potatoes began to fail, despite the fact that the preceding year's harvest in Germany had been particularly good.

Among the Bavarian troops the separatist spirit was becoming ever more dominant. The influence of efforts in this direction, tacitly permitted by the Bavarian Government, made itself felt and thus increased the success of enemy propaganda.   The agitation against the Kaiser and the Crown Prince, and also against the Bavarian royal house, bore its natural fruit.   The Bavarian troops gradually came to regard the war as a purely Prussian affair.   The commands were no longer so eager to employ them as in the earlier years of the war.   Only a few divisions fought as well as before.

The homeland itself was completely under the influence of hostile propaganda and of speeches made by enemy statesmen which were directly leveled at us. We still failed to realize the mental attitude of our enemies.   All parties represented in the Reichstag Majority, with the exception of the right wing of the Center, persistently echoed the catchwords of hostile propaganda, and, just as before, rushed forward their proposals for universal reconciliation, understanding, and disarmament.

The Secretary of State for Foreign Affairs, who was the very personification of this idea of universal understanding, expressed his opinion that the war could not be decided on the battle-field.   He was quite right, if he meant that it should be waged against the enemy home front, and that the conduct of the war should be supported by an active war - policy.   But he was wrong if he placed his faith in reconciliation and understanding, as was really the case.

The Secretary of State was repeating only what was in the minds of the majority.   And this was the doctrine that was preached everywhere, in the Reichstag, in the press, to our worn and weary people, and to our soldiers, whom the High Command was asking to offer their lives on the battle-field for the sake of the Fatherland.

Was that the kind of influence calculated to restore

flagging spirits? Was it to be expected that neglected youths, who during these past years had been growing up without paternal guidance, amid party strife and general unrest, who had been earning high wages and were now drafted into the ranks after a short period of training, or that men disposed to unruliness because they were no longer exempt, would make soldiers who would fight devotedly for king and country? Would it not be far more probable that all of them would think only of preserving their own lives? Was it not to be expected that such ideas must have a pernicious influence on less stable characters, especially in times of stress, when human weaknesses tend to assert themselves? Was not all this bound to have its reaction at home?

In addition there was ever-increasing evidence of the creeping growth of Bolshevism, only too gladly accepted and disseminated by the Independent Social Democrats, and which had all this time been allowed to establish itself officially in Berlin. We had protested against Joffe being allowed to go to Berlin, and, prompted by the Commander-in-chief in the East, had proposed to negotiate further with him in any town in occupied territory. We were soon familiar with the working methods of Bolshevism. Warnings innumerable were given. Members of the General Staff sent ample data to the responsible authorities in Berlin regarding Bolshevist activity in Germany. Unfortunately, further conduct of the affair was out of their hands.

Meanwhile the army command in the Marches and myself repeatedly drew the attention of the Imperial Chancellor, the War Ministry, and Foreign Office, and also the Home Office, to the revolutionary intrigues of the Russian embassy in Berlin, with its very large staff and its association with the Independent Social

Democrats, as well as to the revolutionary activity of the latter. But it was all in vain. When once more I called the attention of the Foreign Office to Joffe's work and to the danger of his presence in Berlin, I was told that it was better that he should be in Berlin than anywhere else. There they had him under their eyes. Unfortunately, those eyes were blind. Joffe, while Bolshevism showed itself officially compliant toward Germany, was able to undermine the fighting power of the German people in a way that the Entente alone, despite blockade and propaganda, could never have done.

For this purpose he placed ample means at the disposal of the destructive elements in the country, though, of course, the full extent of his revolutionary activities was revealed only at a later date. At Magdeburg, later, the leader of the Independent Socialists announced:

"We have been preparing systematically for this upheaval since January 25, 1918. We encouraged our people who went to the front to desert the colors. We organized these deserters, furnished them with false papers, and supplied them with money and unsigned pamphlets. We despatched these men in all directions, but chiefly back to the front, to get at the men there, and so undermine the front itself. These men incited the soldiers to desert, and thus, slowly but surely, the collapse was brought about."

In conjunction with this, revolutionary and Bolshevist influence was brought to bear on the men on leave. The most extensive propaganda was carried on in railway trains. Soldiers going home on leave were urged to refuse to return to the front; those returning to the front were incited either to offer passive resistance, to desert, or to mutiny. Much that was still imperceptible during the end of June and the beginning of July was, nevertheless, in a state of silent, unceasing development.

Whether Radical, Socialist, or Bolshevist, the effort to subvert authority was common to all and had already been in operation for decades. Now, in the State's hour of need, it emerged into the light.

I have no wish to refer now to those ambitious members of the Reichstag who deprived the enfeebled Government of all remaining respect, nor to the efforts exerted on all sides to undermine my position and the confidence reposed in me, just because they saw in me the prop of authority. It is my purpose to deal only with the systematic campaign against the officer.

That was a crime for which the Democratic and Majority Socialist parties were responsible; indeed, in the words of Talleyrand, it was worse than that, it was a blunder. A blunder so short-sighted and productive of such endless calamity that it can never be excused. Instead of seeing in the officer the pillar of law and order of the State, many regarded him only as the representative of militarism, without being at all clear as to exactly what the officer had to do with the grievances which they felt called upon to bring forward.

It was all so senseless. In Germany the Corps of Officers has never taken part in politics; during the war it had long lost that exclusiveness, antagonism to which was considered a duty in pre-war days. The corps was recruited from all social circles and from all parties —anybody could become an officer. In many respects, unfortunately, it was no longer the old Corps of Officers. Improprieties were due to foreign elements, to the decline of public morality, and to the inexperience of many officers, who were commissioned so quickly only because the losses among officers on the battle-fields had been so extraordinarily high.

At some future date the eyes of the credulous German people will be opened to these facts, and in that hour they will realize their ingratitude and their own criminal guilt against the officers, the army, the Fatherland, and themselves. Let us hope that the real culprits will then be discovered.

Complaints against the officers followed one another as if by order.

The officers, it was implied, lived much better than the men, although while in the field or in the trenches they had their meals from the same field kitchen. In billets behind the lines, one officer was always served from the field kitchen, while the others messed together. The non-commissioned officers and men were represented on the mess committee, so why were no complaints heard from them?

The cultivation of *esprit de corps*, the authority of the commanding officer, the influence of the older men upon the younger—were these things less important for the officer? Where could they operate to better effect than in the common life of the regiment? The hours of duty alone did not suffice, even during the war, to hand over the tradition of the German Corps of Officers to the younger generation. The officer had to live with his men, and he did so. It was not possible to do otherwise in battle or while in the trenches. Finally, he had to keep up the dignity of his position, which must be clearly defined, and he had to maintain his authority, for how else would it have been possible for him to exert any decisive influence over the troops in all emergencies? All this demanded, among many other requisites, an attitude of authoritative exclusiveness, for otherwise the officer would lose respect.

Were the reasons forgotten which in peace-time prompted the removal of the non-commissioned officers from the men's quarters into separate quarters of their own? But there was no inclination to think of such things; people were anxious only to undermine authority, to shatter the foundations of the State in order the more easily to further their own wretched interests.

Life in the Corps of Officers was governed by regard for the men, the officer himself, and, lastly, the whole structure of municipal and imperial order which stands and falls with the status of the officer.

The way of life of the higher staff-officers was also sharply criticized. Yet is there a man who does not know of the nerve-racking work and colossal burden they bear unceasingly? The troops were relieved, but the staff remained on duty day and night. For four years I endured this state of tension without rest or relief. In such circumstances I could not live on field-kitchen rations. Nevertheless, in October 1918 I declared to the new War Cabinet of Prince Max that Headquarters was willing to live on the fare provided by the field kitchens if the various Secretaries of State and the whole of Berlin would undertake to do likewise, but until then we should live in such a way as was considered best for the men and ourselves. The Imperial Chancellor, Prince Max, declined to eat field-kitchen fare, and so long as I remained in the field we messed simply, but as before.

The other higher staffs were in a similar position. They lived much in the same way as we did. I have never countenanced excesses, and if they have occurred I disclaim all responsibility. So long as we have any social order at all, authority must exist and there must be social distinctions. There must still be, as before, a corps of officers, in which the individual officer must keep himself distinct from the soldier while continuing to be his true friend.

Then came complaints that the officers were living at the expense of the men—a shameful calumny spread by enemy and home propaganda. Many men of undoubted honesty and intelligence came to me bleating out such general accusations, instead of vigorously assailing them. They had already lost all regard for the morality of the Corps of Officers, so inextricably had they fallen into the snare spread by the circulators of these reports.

It was said that officers of the regular army hid in their quarters. This was the reward of a grateful people to the regular officer for his sacrifice and devotion! There were only a few of them left. The remainder had fallen or had been hopelessly disabled. The Corps of Officers had lost from 80 to 90 per cent. of its full strength. Could they not understand that to fill certain posts on the staffs, on which the fate of the troops depended, officers of exceptional experience and initiative were required? It is obvious that for such duties the regular officer was more fitted than an officer of the reserve, and that eventually it would be impossible to replace the former.

I begged the Military Cabinet to investigate these charges. This exposed their falsity all along the line.

Notwithstanding this, I persistently issued reminders that officers fit for service should be sent from home and from the various staffs to the front, to be replaced by officers fit only for garrison duty. The staffs during the summer of 1918 were so composed that several divisional commanders complained to me that they had too few fit officers on their staffs to cope with all demands.

I was always opposed to the presence of father and son on the same staff. When I had direct command, as well as when I was Chief of Staff in the East, I set my face against this. Now all I could do was to draw the attention of the Military Cabinet to it.

I heard unfavorable reports concerning the working of

canteens.   Here, also, the officers were said to be acting
to the detriment of the men.   I went into the matter.
Everything was in order.   The canteen commissions,
on which the soldiers were represented, controlled the
working and the distribution of profits.   The sale of
goods in the canteens was strictly rationed for officers
and men alike at so much per head.   Each man might
buy only as much as was allowed on the carefully
calculated distribution schedule.

The higher staffs, having no canteens of their own,
drew on the central stores at the same prices as the
canteens did.   As these supplied officers and men at a
fixed rate and a certain profit, the higher staffs—both
officers and men, of course—bought their goods somewhat cheaper than the regiments.   This I also stopped.

Then it was asserted that the canteen moneys were
unfairly administered.   This accusation was as false
as the others.   It was only the soldier who derived any
benefit from the profits, mainly, of course, in kind.

But it was in the lines of communication that the
officers were supposed to live in special luxury.   There
I have seen an enormous amount of loyal work, from
which the army derived incalculable benefit.   It was
obvious that in these lines officers, as well as men, lived
more quietly and comfortably than was the case with
the troops who were only in the communication areas
on their way to and from the line.   Naturally, also,
the men felt this, although everything possible was
done for them.

Was it such a crime for an officer to buy something
in Belgium, or anywhere else, to send it home to his
family, in order to brighten their life a little?   Was it
not the families of officers, who are rarely men of means,
who suffered most severely from the increased cost of
living at home?   When I was with the Commander-
in-chief in the East in July 1916 I arranged similar

facilities for the men, these facilities being, later, still further developed. From the West and from Rumania parcels were sent home in large numbers by the men.

Any special case of irregularity on the part of an officer which was brought to my notice, even anonymously, was subjected to most searching investigation. The status and way of life of the officers were frequently discussed by the higher staffs. Under the pressure of the continual complaints the Field-Marshal issued an appeal to all officers.

The Corps of Officers has emerged triumphant from this attack on its honor. The man who infringed the code was an exception and was not one of us. No measures adopted against him could be too severe. The officer who did not emerge from this war with clean hands as an honorable man, who retained property which was not his, even if only to save it from destruction, besmirched the Fatherland, the army, the Corps of Officers, and himself.

The Corps of Officers, as a whole, may be proud of itself, not least because, despite all the work of agitation going on in its rear, it held the army together for four years, led it so often to victory, and was still able, in co-operation with loyal non-commissioned officers and men, to lead it back over the Rhine—a stupendous achievement, among the greatest deeds of the war.

Enemy propaganda did not concern itself with the non-commissioned officers. It was considered that their authority was already impaired, and it was not deemed necessary to pay any particular attention to them. But antagonism between commissioned and non-commissioned officers, which had not existed in the army in peace-time, was ingeniously created.

Many signs of disease had been progressively showing themselves in the German people and army. The symptoms of disorder were no longer to be ignored;

indeed, their presence was recognized by many. The German Crown Prince, who frequently visited me at Avesnes, referred to the matter with increasing anxiety, and also sent in a report to the Kaiser on the subject. I could only acquiesce in this. In cases of mental disease it is exceedingly difficult to know exactly what to do during the initial stages. The existence of the malady is felt. It is only later, however, when the disease comes to a head, that the significance of the preliminary manifestations can be fully realized.

The process of disintegration at work in many parts of the army, with all its serious consequences, was as incomprehensible to me as the disintegration of the nation, which revealed itself in such a surprising fashion on November 9, was to millions of Germans.

I communicated my anxiety again and again to those gentlemen who, with me, were called upon to diagnose these symptoms and provide a remedy. But I spoke to deaf ears. The German nation, itself not without guilt, has now to pay the penalty with its very life.

The question of reserves was a constant anxiety to us. I had the opportunity of impressing upon His Majesty the gravity of the situation. The desire had been expressed that the so-called Asiatic contingent should be reinforced, so that Jerusalem might be re-taken, whereas, taking into consideration the question of our reserves, I had agreed with Enver upon a reduction of German troops and had prevented the despatch of more men to Palestine

The Supreme Command had again approached the Imperial Chancellor with those old demands of the autumns of 1916 and 1917 for an increase of the quota of recruits. I sent Colonel Bauer to the meetings called in Berlin to consider the matter. But we found that we were without the necessary support of the War Ministry. At the end of June discussions on all

the above-mentioned questions were resumed at Spa
between the Imperial Chancellor, the Field-Marshal,
the War Ministers, and myself.   I referred to the conferences in Berlin with Colonel Bauer, and once more
emphasized as gravely as I could the necessity of
obtaining adequate reserves, of adopting the most
severe measures against shirkers and deserters in the
homeland, and, above all, of encouraging in the people
a determination to fight, with regard to which I again
drew attention to the dangerous influence of a section
of our press, enemy propaganda, and Bolshevism.

I spoke my mind on these points far more often than
I have recorded in these pages.   Once more I was
promised a great deal.   The situation, however, remained unchanged.   I do not know whether those
gentlemen thought that my reports were exaggerated
or that they were merely the fruit of my "militarism."
Neither would the War Office accede to my request for
a general conference of employers and employees, to
come to an understanding with regard to the necessity
of drawing upon the exempted men.

Meanwhile I tried again to exploit our successes in
order to further the peace movement in enemy countries.   Another memorandum on this subject was sent
to the Imperial Chancellor.   On June 19 he sent for
Colonel von Haeften.   After long consultation the essentials of such propaganda were decided on.   Vice-
Chancellor von Payer, in particular, showed a lively
interest in these questions.   During the discussions at
Spa I again begged the Imperial Chancellor to appoint
a Minister for propaganda.   Beyond this we did not
refer to the prospects of peace.

In view of Clemenceau's speeches we were compelled,
in my opinion, to continue the war or submit to humiliation.   I must assume that the responsible statesmen held the same view, for, even though I always

hoped for success, they could have had no doubt of the gravity of my view of the situation.

In May and June Colonel von Haeften, quite in accord with my views, urged the Foreign Office to make a conciliatory declaration concerning Belgium. Secretary of State von Kühlmann, however, declined to take any initiative in the matter. He was well aware of the impossibility of any exchange of ideas with the enemy Governments. So much he frankly and openly stated.

On June 24, basing his remarks on a speech of Mr. Asquith's on May 16, in favor of peace. he spoke in the Reichstag to the following effect:

"As long as every opening is accepted by the other side as a peace offensive, as a trap, as untrustworthy, as calculated to sow dissension between the Allies, and so long as every advance is violently denounced by the opponents of a *rapprochement*, it is impossible to foresee how any exchange of ideas that might lead up to peace is to be brought about."

The Imperial Chancellor adopted the same attitude in his speech of July 12. He gave expression to our constant readiness for peace, but so long as the enemy's will to destruction persisted we must continue; though as soon as the enemy evinced any serious inclination to pave the way to peace we should at once prepare to meet him.

"I may also tell you that this point of view is not confined to myself, but is shared by the leaders of the army, for they are not carrying on the war for its own sake, but told me, 'So soon as an earnest desire for peace shows itself on the other side, we must not be behindhand.'"

The Imperial Chancellor has accurately represented the view of the Field-Marshal and myself.

When I now reflect on the possibility and prospect

of a peace move, had it been undertaken by the Government, I am firmly convinced that we should have been granted an armistice and peace only on the conditions that we are now compelled to accept. We should not have taken upon ourselves this responsibility, as indeed in October we ought not to have done, despite the gravity of our situation.

Whether I was right or wrong in my view of the conditions then existing, only Clemenceau, Wilson, and Lloyd George can decide. England and the United States wished for our economic destruction; England, in addition, wanted to render us powerless, and France to bleed us white. Common to all our antagonists was the desire to inflict the deepest humiliation on their hated enemy before the world, and to impede the development of the German people for all time.

The Entente pursued ideals for the betterment of the world only in so far as they were compatible with a strong national policy. This was the motive of all its actions; all else was but a means to the same end. It was the very reverse with us; our first ideal was universal happiness, our second the security of the Fatherland. The war once begun, its conclusion did not rest with us alone.

At the beginning of July, Secretary of State von Kühlmann retired from office. His attitude in the Reichstag, and particularly his assertion that the war could hardly be ended by a purely military decision, was going too far for the Imperial Chancellor. We also had felt it our duty to express our opinions. But what finally turned the scale in our favor of the resignation of the Secretary of State von Kühlmann was his personal attitude during these days.

I was in Avesnes and had neither the time nor the inclination to interfere in the proceedings at Spa. Secretary of State von Kühlmann was the typical German diplomatist of post-Bismarckian times. His name will always be associated with the entry of the Bolshevists into Berlin, and the tacit acquiescence in the propaganda work of the Russian embassy.

I was glad to see Secretary of State von Hintze appointed his successor, as I considered him a strong man. I discussed with him my hope of even yet making the Entente ready for peace, pointed out to him the danger of Bolshevism, and also drew his attention to the revolutionary activities of Herr Joffe. He pursued the same course as regards Bolshevism as his predecessor, partly because of his own views on the Russian situation and partly, also, because he was not really strong enough to master the old tendencies of the Foreign Office.

## VIII

In Russia events had developed along lines of their own, illustrative of the lying propensities of the Soviet Government. With the consent of this Government the Entente had formed Czecho-Slovak units out of Austro-Hungarian prisoners. These were intended to be used against us, and were therefore to be conveyed to France by the Siberian Railway. All this was sanctioned by a Government with whom we were at peace, and we actually took it lying down! At the beginning of June I wrote to the Imperial Chancellor specially on the subject and pointed out the dangers which threatened us from the Soviet Government.

The weapon forged against us was now to be turned against the Soviet Government itself, for the Entente, realizing that it could not work with a Government which looked for support to Germany, took action against Bolshevism and, instead of sending these troops to France, held them up along the Siberian Railway or the frontier between Russia and Siberia, in order to fight against the Government in Moscow. They gradually pushed forward to the middle Volga, in the direction of Kazan and Samara. In addition to this, by garrisoning the railway, the Entente prevented the return of our prisoners of war from Siberia. This was unquestionably a serious loss for us.

If the Soviet Government had been really honest in its professions of peaceful intention, the trains which took away the Czecho-Slovaks could have brought back German prisoners of war. But it was not honest. Bolshevism did us all the damage it could.

The situation in Siberia, behind the Czecho-Slovaks, was so confused that the Entente could find no support there. For that reason it was without importance for us also. From the point of view of the war, the only serious thing was that the Siberian Railway was in the Entente's possession. The relations between Japan, England, and the United States were without interest except in so far as they showed signs of approaching differences between these countries.

The new Entente front in Russia began with the Czecho-Slovaks on the middle Volga.

It was continued north by the Entente troops which were feeling their way forward from the White Sea, up the Dvina, and south from the Murman coast along the railway of the same name.

On the Dvina they were advancing slowly, but not surely. As the White Sea freezes in winter, nothing of importance could be undertaken here. The Murman Railway was torn up by the Bolshevists. The Finnish patrols, on reaching the railway, found nothing more to be done. The united German and Finnish troops were now so strong that the Entente gave up its advance.

Up the Volga, and west of its lower course, which was still entirely in Bolshevist hands, the Don Cossacks held the lower Don as far as our own positions. Their Hetman, General Krasnow, was decidedly anti-Bolshevist, and was opposing the Soviet troops. He had, however, neither arms nor ammunition. I had got into touch with him in order to prevent his joining the Entente. The situation was complicated by the fact that I could not put difficulties in the way of the Home Government's pro-Bolshevist policy, which I, of course, was propagating, and Krasnow regarded the Soviet Government, and not the Entente, as his enemy.

At all events, I succeeded in holding him back from openly siding with the Entente and, to a certain extent, in making an ally of him. If we had decided to attack Moscow he would openly have thrown in his lot with us.

In the wide, fertile steppes of the Kuban region between the Don Cossacks and the Caucasus General Alexeieff, with his Volunteer Army, was, as I have already stated, fighting the Bolshevist troops. He was acting under English influence. I think, however, he was too good a Russian not to have joined us if we had been opposing the Soviet Government. Alexeieff's military position was at the moment unfavorable; he had neither arms nor ammunition. The Bolshevists, for the time being, had the upper hand. Although the Government in Moscow was prepared to go to any length in its assurance of peace, at the end of July it sent several thousand men from the region southwest of Azov, across the Sea of Azov, and landed them at Taganrog. Here they were very soon annihilated by German troops. From about the beginning of August the position of the Volunteer Army in the Kuban region became more secure. In Novorossisk lay what was left of the Russian ships that had escaped from Sebastopol. It was certainly our military right and a law of necessity to demand or compel their return. Here, again, the Foreign Office prolonged the negotiations out of regard for the Soviet Government, although no better proof of its hostile attitude, or, at any rate, of its inability to prevent hostile conduct by its troops, could possibly have been furnished than the landing at Taganrog. At last the Soviet Government consented to the return of the ships to Sebastopol. Only a part of them arrived, the majority being sunk in the harbor by the Bolshevists in an outburst of what was, after all, patriotism. We had stipulated with the Soviet Government that during the war we were to make as much use of the ships as the military situation demanded. We had no need to take advantage of this.

As on the lower Volga, the Bolshevists were in June also masters of the Caspian Sea. To the Soviet Government this was still of great importance in connection with the oil-supply of Great Russia, which had already lost the coal of the Donetz basin and the corn of the Ukraine and the Don and Kuban districts.

The Turks were before Baku. They had also firmly established themselves in northern Persia, without, however, making any definite progress in that region. English troops were at Enseli, on the southern shore of the Caspian Sea, in touch with the Kuban district.

This position, coupled with the situation in Finland and the Ukraine, formed the basis of our whole policy in the East. As regards Great Russia, this policy, as carried out by *Ministerialdirektor* Krieg, worked directly in favor of the Bolshevists. There is no doubt that right through the summer it prevented us from forming a new military front. This I recognized. On general grounds I held such a policy to be short-sighted, as it was bound in the long run to strengthen the whole Bolshevist movement. That could only do us harm; and I regarded it as the duty of our Government to guard against such an eventuality, not only on military grounds, but also, and indeed more urgently, from the purely political point of view. Doctor Helfferich regarded this as quite possible. The position of the Government was certainly difficult, but it had only itself to thank. The authorities assured me that their policy reflected public opinion in Germany. Here, again, I was compelled to believe that consideration for tendencies of internal politics was impeding the effective prosecution of the war. As for our military position, we could easily have made a rapid attack on Petrograd with the troops we had in the East. With the help of the Don Cossacks we could also have attacked in the direction of Moscow. This would have been far better than merely defending a long line, which absorbed more troops than would have been required for a short advance, besides unnerving the troops, whose morale would have been maintained by active operations. We could have deposed the Soviet Government, which was thoroughly hostile to us, and given help to other authorities in Russia, which were not working against us, but indeed anxious to co-operate with us. This would have been a success of great importance to the general conduct of the war. If some other government were established in Russia, it would almost certainly have been possible to come to some compromise with it over the Peace of Brest-Litovsk, whereas, in dealing with the Bolshevists, a simple abandonment of the treaty, without any idea as to how matters would develop, would have been the same kind of "payment in advance" policy as were all the ideas about a peace of "understanding," so long as the enemy would accept no such peace.

The Berlin authorities remained wholly ignorant of the underground activities of the Bolshevists, whom they regarded, or wished to regard, as honest. They entered into further negotiations with them over those points of the treaty which had not been cleared up. Nothing, not even the unavenged murder of our ambassador at Moscow, shook their faith. They walked straight into the trap set by the Bolshevists, while simultaneously showing distrust of all other tendencies in Russia. The Bolshevist Government was very accommodating; it granted the German demands with regard to Esthonia and Livonia, conceded the independence of Georgia, agreed to pay an indemnity by instalments, and held out prospects of the delivery of raw materials, including oil, from Baku. What we had to give in return was relatively little. Coal from the Donetz basin, the transport of corn from the Kuban district by means of the railway running northward from Rostoff on the Don (which, I must admit, was hardly feasible, in view of the attitude of the Don Cossacks), and finally the exercise of our influence in persuading Turkey not to take Baku. We further agreed to evacuate, *pari passu* with the payment of the instalments of the indemnity, the Great Russian territory which we had occupied in February on the Beresina and Dvina. Later on, the first instalments were actually paid as agreed, rather to my surprise.

Our Government's confidence in the Bolshevists went so far that the authorities actually wanted to supply arms and ammunition to Herr Joffe. The gentleman who brought from the Foreign Office the document dealing with the matter remarked to me, "This material remains in Germany, and Joffe will use it against us here."

At the conference in Spa, when our Georgian policy was being discussed, the Imperial Chancellor agreed to send Colonel von Kresz, who had returned to Germany from the Palestine front, to Tiflis as his representative, with an escort of one or two companies.

It had become essential for us to show a stronger hand in this district—not merely because we hoped to secure some military assistance from that quarter, but also in order to obtain raw materials. That we could not rely on Turkey in the matter had been once again demonstrated by her conduct in Batum, where she claimed the right to retain all the stocks for herself. We could expect to get oil from Baku only if we helped ourselves. The shortage of fuel at home, and the difficulties of our winter lighting, with all their attendant inconveniences, were only too firmly impressed on my memory. After the attack of the Seventh Army, the army's reserves of fuel had also run out, and we felt the shortage keenly. Oil was needed for the Ukraine railways also. The production of oil in Rumania had increased to the limit, but this could not make good the whole shortage. It now seemed possible to supplement it from trans-Caucasian sources, and in particular from Baku, if transport facilities could be provided.

The Director of Railways had to solve the problem of tank ships. I was highly disgusted when the Bolshevists, simply in order to injure us, sank the *Elburz*, the largest tank steamer in the Black Sea, at Novorossisk. The Batum-Tiflis-Baku Railway, which was well supplied with oil-trucks, was to be taken in hand by Colonel von Kresz in co-operation with the Turks. The crucial question, of course, was how we were to get to Baku. Here, again, consideration for the Soviet Government prevented us from acting firmly or rapidly, and the first event of importance was that the English from Enseli crossed the Caspian Sea at the beginning of August and took possession of the town.

Their occupation of Baku, which was rendered possible only by the complete inactivity of the Turks in North Persia, was a serious blow for us. By this move the English also came into closer touch with the Volunteer Army in the Kuban district, but, on the other hand, at Baku they were within our reach. An attack upon them, involving only a small force, seemed possible. General Headquarters set about preparing a blow against them, with the co-operation of Nouri's troops, and sent a brigade of cavalry and a few battalions to Tiflis. The question of the transportation of troops had not yet been settled when Nouri took possession of Baku, and immediately afterward the situation in Bulgaria compelled us to send the troops to Rumania.

The position in North Persia was not destined to undergo any change. We supplied arms from the Ukraine for the tribes there who wished to join the Turks, but the latter remained absolutely inactive, although they had ample forces round Batum and Kars.

In the East I went only so far as in my view was absolutely demanded by our military position and economic needs. I had no Napoleonic dreams of world conquest. The anxious struggle in which I was so deeply engaged left me no time to pursue fantastic schemes. I wanted no territory in the Ukraine or Caucasus; my only object was to procure the supplies that were so urgently needed for our bare maintenance and the prosecution of the war. I hoped, also, now that we had succeeded in breaking the blockade at this point, to improve our economic position and thus to raise our physical strength and morale. I wished to make what use was possible of the man-power of these districts, partly by direct recruiting, but on a larger scale, and with greater prospect of success, through enlisting labor for employment in Germany, so as to release men for the front. I pursued this course in all parts of the East and had hopes even of obtaining direct recruits from the German population there.

We did not, however, work quickly enough. The Eighth Army, at Riga, complained that the Ministry of War, in spite of all my persistence, had failed to give any instructions in the matter.

It was only to protect and foster German *Kultur* that I went beyond immediate military requirements and thought of the future. That did not involve any expenditure of military strength. I wanted to strengthen and consolidate German national spirit, and thus increase its influence. Some of my acquaintances had placed a substantial sum of money at my disposal for this end. I used it to support the German national press in Austria. I steadily furthered my pet scheme of settling the isolated Germans scattered throughout Russia, side by side with our soldiers, in the Eastern districts. In this matter I made myself the advocate of Germanism against the Government. I rejected as fantastic, however, such proposals as the foundation of a German colonial state on the Black Sea.

With regard to the districts lying within the administrative area of the Commander-in-chief in the East, I asked the Government, on several occasions in the course of the summer, to give a clear definition of its policy, in order that my actions here should be consistent with the views of the highest authority. Esthonia and Livonia were, with Courland, united into one military governmental district, the "Baltic Littoral." Lithuania had retained its former frontiers. I proposed to extend to Livonia and Esthonia the policy which had hitherto been employed in Courland. The civilization of the Esthonians and Livonians was German, and I aimed at uniting them in one state under German influence without obliterating their racial distinctions. Immediately after the liberation of these countries in February much could have been done, but our Government let valuable time slip by. It even asked me to lay down our policy in Esthonia and Livonia, though nothing could be expected from that unless we were really supported by Berlin. However, all Berlin did was to press for the establishment of the university at Dorpat. In filling the chairs there the Esthonians were ignored for some wholly incomprehensible reason, and the whole point of the measure was thus lost.

In Lithuania, too, we made no progress, the negotiations with the National Council coming to a complete standstill. The Poles were becoming more and more active; the Government was still unable to see the danger from that quarter, and failed to use its influence in Rome in favor of the appointment of a cleric of Lithuanian sympathies to the vacant see of Vilna, an appointment the Lithuanians earnestly desired, and which I did my best to secure. It is possible, however, that the Government did what it could without meeting with any encouragement from the Vatican.

No progress had been made with the solution of the Polish problem. The Emperor Charles's attitude varied from time to time. Baron Burian, the successor of Count Czernin, adhered to the Austro-Polish solution. Our Government was still in the position of not knowing its own mind. It was as uncertain on this point as in the rest of its Eastern policy. A good opportunity to dispose of the Austro-Polish question once and for all was not taken. The Emperor Charles had written the Parma letters. Under pressure from Vienna he had to decide in May to make his "Canossa" pilgrimage to Spa. The position was one of which anything might have been made. The Field-Marshal and myself urged Count von Hertling and Secretary of State von Kühlmann to use this favorable opportunity to get matters put on a clear footing. They, however, lacked the necessary resolution. With great solemnity, some document or another was drawn up and signed, not merely by the leading statesmen, but also by the two monarchs personally. This agreement, however, laid no obligations whatever on Austria-Hungary, and was utterly worthless. Our diplomacy had failed, and the Dual Monarchy had won. Everything had turned out as we soldiers had prophesied. Baron Burian felt himself, and with good reason, not bound by anything. He continued to aim at the Austro-Polish solution with the persistence which was at once so prominent a feature of his character and so annoying to our diplomats.

### IX

The preparations for the third great offensive in the West were carried out on exactly the same lines as were those for the battles of March 21 and May 27. Colonel Bruchmüller again acted as artillery adviser to the army group of the German Crown Prince.

The Seventh Army was to effect a crossing of the Marne east of Château-Thierry and then advance on both sides of the river in the direction of Epernay, while the First and Third attacked from the east of Rheims to Tahure. These armies were to bring their right wing past the Forêt de la Montagne de Rheims to Epernay, and make Châlons-sur-Marne their principal objective. The offensive of this army group left untouched the enemy line approximately from the Ardre to the east of Rheims, and thereby gained a considerable breadth that seemed to favor its chances of success. The junction of the two attacking groups in the direction of Epernay might produce great results. The attack was to be made chiefly by those divisions that had carried out the advance across the Chemin des Dames. This made great demands upon our troops, but in our position there was no other course possible, and it allowed the divisions of the army group of Crown Prince Rupprecht all the more rest before the work that lay in front of them, the offensive in Flanders.

In order to relieve the Seventh Army Headquarters, the Ninth Army Headquarters from Rumania was pushed into the line on both banks of the Aisne, between the Oise and the Ourcq.

In the attack on Rheims we reckoned on an enemy counter-offensive between the Aisne and the Marne, with Soissons as its principal objective, and we organized the Ninth Army and the right wing of the Seventh accordingly.

Originally the attack of the army group of the German Crown Prince was to be carried out on July 12, but, in order to make thorough preparations possible, it had unfortunately to be postponed until the 15th. On the 11th or 12th, while the preparations were in full swing, a deserter brought news that a big tank offensive from the forest of Villers-Cotterets was imminent, and this report gave us additional reason to re-examine and perfect our defensive measures. At the most critical point, southwest of Soissons, we had placed a division that had fought with special success in the East, and which had always met the demands made upon it in the West. This division had not taken part in the May battles, and was therefore as much rested as could be allowed to any division. In this respect, at any rate, we were no worse off than the enemy. Farther south, two divisions, not fully rested, and whose battalion strength was not up to the standard required, held that space along the front that was usually allotted to one division only. The other divisions were good trench divisions, and held normal divisional fronts; a few were kept behind the lines as reserves. The fortification of our positions was, of course, not far advanced; high corn obstructed the view in front of and still more within them. Influenza was prevalent, but not more so here than anywhere else along the front. The attack that had been announced never took place, and I hoped that the news would have thoroughly aroused the men.

The army group of the German Crown Prince emphasized the necessity of the organization in depth of all our defensive fronts.

I was always in touch with the headquarters of the armies detailed for the attack. Above all, I was

EXPLANATION

Position until German attack on July 15, 1918.
Direction of German attack.
German line reached by the attack.
Army frontier.

FIG. 38. BATTLE DURING THE DRIVE ON THE MARNE AND IN CHAMPAGNE, 1918

anxious to know if in their opinion, or in that of the troops, the enemy had any knowledge of our preparations. They thought not, and only on the Marne was the artillery fire more lively.

I had especially pointed out that no reconnoitering was to be carried out on the southern bank of the Marne, but in spite of my warning a pioneer officer swam over and was captured. As we found out after the battle, he gave away much information to the enemy. Acting officers of the heavy artillery, who fell into the hands of the enemy on the Ardre, acted in the same way. In some places the Entente made raids and took prisoners, but I do not know what information was gained in this way.

It is also a fact that an attack on Rheims was discussed in the most irresponsible way throughout Germany, and to my great regret it was only later that I received many letters from home on the subject. Wireless messages sent out by the enemy after the battle also plainly indicated that he had had early information of our plan. Within the army itself it was very difficult to keep the secret, as the very concentration of heavy artillery and trench-mortars, which took part in every attack, revealed our intentions.

In spite of long consideration, we had been unable to think of any other way. We clearly realized how cumbrous was the method of attack, and made all efforts to deceive the enemy as to our intentions; everything possible was done in this direction. Postal prohibitions were useless; there were so many channels connecting us with home, and I could not stop leave, which was, after all, the only concession the army could make to the men. Leave had to be stopped for a considerable period on account of the railway transport conditions in February and March, and at that time many army commanders urgently desired it to be resumed. While the commanders were doing their utmost to keep these secrets, the love of talking and boasting that is inborn in Germans betrayed to the world and to our enemies things of the greatest weight and significance.

We attacked early on the 15th. Our crossing of the Marne was a remarkable achievement, which succeeded, although the enemy were fully prepared for it. The Seventh Army, between the Marne and the Ardre, also penetrated the most obstinately defended positions. The Italian divisions stationed there suffered particularly.

About five kilometers south of the Marne the attacking troops came upon an enemy force so strong that it could be overcome only by bringing a large number of batteries over the river, and so the attack at this point came to a standstill. On the 16th, by hard fighting, we slowly gained ground up the Marne and toward the Ardre.

According to plan, the enemy had withdrawn in front of the First and Third Armies, to their second position, and held us firmly all along the line.

By noon of the 16th General Headquarters had given orders for the suspension of the offensive of the First and Third Armies, and for their organization for defense by withdrawing certain divisions for this purpose. A continuation of the offensive would have cost us too much. We had to content ourselves with the improvement in our position brought about by regaining possession of the heights we had lost in the spring of 1917, and we had even secured a deep forward zone. The troops that had been withdrawn were at the disposal of the group of the German Crown Prince or of General Headquarters as reserves. I considered it of the greatest importance that they should be available as soon as possible.

Once the difficult decision to suspend the offensive of the First and Third Armies had been made it was useless to attempt to advance farther across the Marne or to leave our troops on the southern bank. It seemed out of the question to withdraw the troops immediately, as the few bridges were under incessant artillery fire, and were constantly bombed or machine-gunned by enemy 'planes. We had to make arrangements for crossing before the retreat could even begin. On the 17th the retreat was fixed for the night between the 20th and 21st. The troops on the Marne had lived through days of severe trial and behaved like heroes.

General Headquarters thought that only north of the Marne could the offensive be continued up the Ardre valley in order to surround Rheims still more closely, and possibly even to take it. By the 16th the army group of the German Crown Prince had received the necessary instructions. On the afternoon of the 17th I was in Rethel at First Army Headquarters to discuss the continuance of the attack on Rheims. I urged the necessity for speedy action, so that we might retain the initiative on this battle-field also. From the report of the Chief of Staff I gathered that many days would be needed for the preparations to continue even this purely local attack. I was therefore obliged to resign myself, but I begged the German Crown Prince to build up reserves as quickly as possible, and pointed out the probable immediate necessity of strengthening the Eighteenth Army and the right wing of the Ninth.

The other fronts were, in my opinion, sound. For the moment General Headquarters still clung to the idea of an attack in Flanders, under the army group of Crown Prince Rupprecht, although the hoped-for weakening of the enemy had not come about. The railway transportation of artillery, trench-mortars, and 'planes from the Rheims district had begun according to plan on the 16th.

In the night of the 17th I myself went to the headquarters of the army group of Crown Prince Rupprecht, to reinspect the state of their preparations. The attack was intended as a continuation of the one that had been suspended at the end of April. It was to be made by the Fourth and Sixth Armies north of the Lys, its objectives being the possession of the commanding heights between Poperinghe and Bailleul, as well as to the high ground round Hazebrouck. During the discussion with the army group of Crown Prince Rupprecht on the morning of the 18th I received the first news that, by means of an unexpected tank offensive, the French had pierced the line southwest of Soissons. At the same time the army group of the German Crown Prince announced that it had sent to the battle-field, partly by motor transport, those divisions (in the first instance the 20th Infantry Division) which had been intended for the continuation of the offensive up the Ardre.

I immediately ordered the 5th Infantry Division to proceed by rail, via Laon, to the district just northeast of Soissons, where the tunnel was already complete. This division, which had been held at the disposal of General Headquarters, was quartered northeast of St.-Quentin, and all arrangements had been made for its rapid movement by rail to any point.

I concluded the conference at the army group of Crown Prince Rupprecht (naturally in a state of greatest nervous tension) and then returned to Avesnes. I saw the Crown Prince Rupprecht for the last time on that day, and our relations then, as ever, were cordial.

I reached Avesnes at 2 P.M. and was met at the station by the Field-Marshal. We immediately retired to the office. The position of the left wing of the Ninth Army and the right of the Seventh had become serious.

By the 17th General Foch had attacked without success on the battle-field of Champagne, in the Forêt de la Montague de Rheims, between the Ardre and the Marne, and also south of the Marne, and had continued the offensive southwest of Rheims and south of the Marne on the 18th, with the same results, but between the Ourcq and the Aisne he had won considerable ground.

After a short and sharp artillery preparation and a smoke screen, he attacked with massed infantry and a stronger force of tanks than had ever before been concentrated in one place. For the first time small, low, fast tanks that allowed the use of machine guns above the corn were used; our machine guns were hindered by it except when they were mounted on special tripods. Here again the effect of the fire from the tanks was insignificant. Tanks were also observed which were used solely for the transport of men. These passed through our lines, put down their passengers with machine guns behind them, to form machine gun nests, and then promptly returned for reinforcements.

Our infantry had not stood firm at all points, and in particular the division southwest of Soissons, that had been considered so reliable, had given way. The gap rapidly widened, especially toward Soissons. Farther south there were other deep dents in the line. The three divisions in reserve here, although not fresh and thrown into action piecemeal, were able to hold the enemy upon the heights southwest of Soissons and to the west of Parcy-Tigny, as well as at the Savières bottom. Between the Ourcq and the Marne the attacks were repulsed. The situation north of the Ourcq made a withdrawal of the troops fighting on the south bank necessary. They were closely followed up by the enemy.

This was the condition of affairs that was revealed to me in the early hours of the afternoon in Avesnes.

We now had to deal with the heavy counter-offensive by General Foch against our sharp salient between Soissons and Rheims. English divisions were also taking part. The enemy offensive was mainly directed on Soissons and southwest of Rheims down the Ardre. Foch's intention was clearly to cut off this salient. On the Ardre the attack was repulsed, but toward Soissons it made considerable progress. All counter-measures that could be adopted were already under

way.   At the moment General Headquarters was unable
to give any further help.

The 5th Infantry Division was being transported
northeast of Soissons, but as enemy artillery soon
began to shell the railway stations in that area, the
troops were compelled to detrain in the Ailette valley.
Their arrival was therefore postponed, which was most
inconvenient.

The 20th Infantry Division could be concentrated
at its destination by the evening of the 19th.   Only the
infantry could be brought up by lorries, without any
horses or vehicles.   Everything else was forced to
march, and so the division was completely broken up,
the infantry being left with no regular supplies.   In
the use of these divisions this point had always to be
borne in mind.   The divisions despatched by the army
group of the German Crown Prince could not arrive
till later.   They, too, arrived in lorries.

For the rest we could only await the further development of the situation.   The troops on the south bank
of the Marne could not be bundled back at a moment's
notice.   The order to retreat to the north bank on
the night of July 20 was not canceled, to avoid confusion.   It would not do for the troops to be unsettled.
For this reason we had to prolong our occupation of
the sector west of Château-Thierry for a considerable
time, in fact, until we had evacuated the south bank
of the Marne.

A stand southwest of Soissons and on the Ardre was
a necessary consequence.   A crisis lay before us for
the next few days, and until it was over no great
strategical decisions could be taken.

The army group of Prince Rupprecht continued its
preparations for attack.   It had to arrange to relin-
quish certain divisions, but even then an offensive was
still possible.

FIG. 39.   DEFENSIVE BATTLE BETWEEN SOISSONS AND RHEIMS, JULY 1918

For the time being I shelved my anxiety concerning the Eighteenth Army and the right wing of the Ninth. The enemy could not attack everywhere.

July 19 was again a critical day, but it passed quite satisfactorily.

In the neighborhood of Soissons the enemy made no appreciable progress. Farther south, it is true, he crossed the Soissons-Hartennes road, but toward evening he was thrown back by a mighty massed attack of the 20th Infantry Division. This saved the situation there. Southwest of Hartennes the enemy gained more ground, but was unable to achieve anything decisive. American attacks in the south, in the direction of Château-Thierry, broke down, as on the previous day. Enemy attacks south of the Marne, between the Marne and the Ardre, collapsed again and again. Local fighting took place in Champagne also.

On the whole the situation was much more favorable. Even the remnants of the troops who had allowed themselves to be surprised on the 18th had, generally speaking, recovered and fought well on the 19th.

On the 20th the Fifth Infantry Division would be available southwest of Soissons and new divisions in line on the Ourcq.

I inquired into the reasons for our failure of the 18th. The men no longer believed in the possibility of an attack. A divisional commander with whom I was acquainted told me that he had been to the front lines on the 17th, and had seen not the slightest sign of activity on the part of the enemy. As a matter of fact, the French troops received the order to attack only a few hours before they came up. Information which was coming through to our lines until immediately before the battle began no longer reached us. The rapid movement of the numerous fast tanks in the high corn increased the effect of the surprise. To all this must be added the diminished strength of the divisions, the result partly of influenza and partly of the monotonous diet. In the sector into which the two weak divisions had been put there had been somewhat of a lull after the earlier battles. All these things helped to heighten the effect of the enemy surprise. When it had worn off on the 19th the troops held well.

The fact that particular divisions had not yet distributed their artillery in depth was of the greatest significance. Once more they were too intent on following up the attack. This was very laudable in its way, but tactically unsound in the point of position.

The result of the surprise had been an over-hasty throwing in of reserves.

The battle between the Aisne and the Marne demanded unity of command, so the left wing of the Ninth Army, south of the Aisne, was again put under the command of the Seventh.

At the points of greatest pressure, south of Soissons and southwest of Rheims, we were, on the whole, successful in repulsing, on the 20th and 21st, strong enemy massed attacks, in which tanks were again employed in large numbers.

The withdrawal of the troops south of the Marne to the northern bank took place during the night of the 20th, and was effected in exemplary order. The fact that the French had not attacked here on the 20th helped considerably. Their thrust early in the 21st found everything already evacuated.

Following the withdrawal of the German troops from the south to the north bank of the Marne, we straightened our lines between the Ourcq and the Marne, and between the Marne and the Ardre, to secure local improvements in our positions.

On the 22d there was a lull in the fighting. The enemy thrust was definitely held up. The crisis had terminated in our favor. General Headquarters was at this time faced with momentous decisions. The situation of the Seventh Army in the Marne salient was grave, not only on account of the unfavorable shape of the front, but also because of its communications. Transport movement between the Aisne and the Vesle valleys had been rendered unsafe. The railway curve east of Soissons was exposed to the effective fire of long-range guns. The line in course of construction at high pressure farther to the east was not yet ready, and was in any case only a makeshift. The other means of communication were useless for moving troops. Reinforcements for the Seventh Army had therefore to be detrained in the Aisne valley or farther north, and so were tired even before they reached the front. The necessity for continual relief was as obvious as it had been in the case of the Flanders and Somme battles. We had, in addition to other supplies, to send up immense quantities of ammunition and other war materials. The railway communications behind the lines could not cope with all this. Motor transportation and rolling-stock that would have made good this deficiency were not available.

We should have continued to be very seriously handicapped in our struggle with an enemy who had the best imaginable communications at his disposal.

That our strategic position in this salient was a critical one went without saying. Every enemy success at Soissons or on the Ardre would have the most far-reaching consequences. It would not be possible to hold the salient permanently, and a new attack on Rheims seemed hopeless.

I sent officers, among them General von Loszberg, to the fighting front, to report on the position. The commanders and troops at Soissons were obviously under the impression of the battles of the 18th, and the feeding of the troops was everywhere described as very difficult. From a tactical point of view the forward zone system had not proved a success in these battles involving retreats, for its evacuation too easily caused disorder in the main line of resistance immediately behind it.

The descriptions given to General Headquarters confirmed us in our resolution, to which we had come in

EXPLANATION

▬▬▬ German line previous to the French attack on July 18, 1918.
●●●●●● German line on the morning of July 20.
xxxxx German line on the morning of July 27.
▬ ▬ ▬ German line at the beginning of August.

FIG. 40. DEFENSIVE BATTLE BETWEEN SOISSONS AND RHEIMS, JULY 1918

the evening of the 22d, to withdraw the troops on the night of July 26 from the Marne to the Fère-en-Tardenois—Ville-en-Tardenois line. With that end in view I was naturally in constant touch with the army group of the German Crown Prince and the Seventh Army. Only a short stand was to be made on the line indicated. The enemy would renew his massed attacks. We had to make them very expensive for him. We had in view a withdrawal behind the Vesle of a straight line between Soissons and Rheims in the beginning of August, but before this could be carried out the salient south of the Vesle, and especially the Vesle valley itself, had first to be cleared. The masses of stores accumulated there were absolutely vital to us. Our front contracted as our retreat proceeded. We thereby accumulated reserves, but so did our enemy, who could use them for attacks elsewhere.

The serious weakening of the Eighteenth Army and of the right wing of the Ninth could now no longer be justified. It had to be made good by reinforcements. These could be drawn only from the army group of Crown Prince Rupprecht.

The offensive in Flanders could not bring a rapid and decisive success. According to all indications, the enemy was ready for it. If he avoided the attack, as he had done east of Rheims, we should be unable to force a decision. If he stood firm, his numerous reserves were in a position to hold us up, as they had done on June 11 and 12 in the direction of Compiègne. General Headquarters therefore decided to abandon this offensive. The Rupprecht army group was to stand on the defensive and to surrender reserves to reinforce the Eighteenth, Ninth, and Seventh Armies; this it was quite capable of doing. The necessary orders were issued. I had as yet no idea how, if at all, we should be able to recover the initiative after taking up the Vesle position. The army group of Duke Albrecht was instructed to submit plans for an attack on its front. General Headquarters suspended its instructions as regards the use of the forward zone on the front of the Seventh and Eighteenth Armies, and also for any future retirements.

On the 23d there was again an extremely vigorous attack, which, on the whole, was successfully repulsed

ong the whole front.  During the next few days there
ere only local attacks which failed everywhere.

In the night of the 26th the withdrawal of the front
orth of the Marne was accomplished according to
an and in perfect order.  In the next few days
eneral Foch made further violent but unsuccessful
tacks, which cost us the loss of some small strips of
gh ground northwest of Fère-en-Tardenois.  Accord-
g to reports from the troops, the enemy had suffered
oody losses.  Of course, very heavy demands were
ade on us, too.  As had been the case in previous
fensive battles, constant relief by new divisions was
ntinually necessary.

The evacuation of the salient went on steadily, thanks
the splendid organization of the army group of the
erman Crown Prince and of the First and Seventh
mies.  The second railway line was now completed
d made the work considerably easier.

In the night of August 1 the front was withdrawn
hind the Vesle, where troops in hastily prepared
sitions were ready for the enemy.  The enemy fol-
wed close on our heels and made a sharp attack
the line of the Vesle.  He was everywhere repulsed.
ir defensive battle of movement between the Marne
d the Vesle was at an end.

The battle was a brilliant achievement on the part
the leaders and men concerned.  The shadow cast
the events of July 18 had passed.  After that day,
spite of the heavy demands made upon him, the
erman soldier had fought well, and felt himself a
tter man than his enemy.  In some divisions there
d certainly been unpleasant revelations.  Among
her things I subsequently received a report which
rew a very grave light on the spirit of one of these
visions; I sent it to the Seventh Army for further
quiry.

As in every other engagement, the losses we h
suffered since July 15 had been very heavy. July
and the defensive battles arising with it had in partic
lar been very expensive, although we got our wound
back and did not lose any considerable number
prisoners.

The losses through the battle had been so hea
that we were compelled to break up about ten divisic
and use their infantry as reserves for others. T
other branches, generally speaking, were not brok
up. Those divisions that had been withdrawn fr
the battle, and other troops, were distributed behi
the whole Western front. This was the beginning o
vast railway transportation movement. It opened at t
end of July and increased considerably at the beg
ning of August, and from that time onward hardly ev
diminished. The troops, who were very much
hausted, had to be brought up to establishment, rest
and given time to recuperate.

I had not succeeded in getting any clear idea of t
enemy's losses since July 15, but, considering t
massed tactics of the Entente, they must have be
high, and in no way less heavy than ours.

The armies of the Entente had also suffered; the bat
had cost the enemy as much as it had cost us. T
French had sent into action a remarkably large numl
of Senegalese and Moroccans, and had endeavored
spare their own people. The six American divisic
that had taken part in the battle had suffer
most severely without achieving any successes. C
division appears to have been broken up in orc
to bring them up to establishment. Notwithstandi
the gallantry of the individual American soldier, t
inferior quality of the American troops is proved
the fact that two brave German divisions were able
withstand the main attack made by very super

merican forces for several weeks; and these two divi-
ns, the 4th Ersatz and the 201st, I had up till then
nsidered no better than the average.

The losses sustained by the English and Italian
visions were also heavy.

In the mean time the group of Crown Prince Rup-
echt had prepared for the defensive, by relieving
visions that had been in position for a long period
others that had been intended for attack. Their
ttalions were fairly strong. Many divisions had not
en in action since April. The Eighteenth Army and
e right wing of the Ninth had also become stronger.
an earlier date the Eighteenth Army had fought in
e Arve bridge-head without success. One of the
visions there, which was holding a wide front, had
en driven back on the river.

The attempt to make the nations of the Entente
clined to peace before the arrival of the American
nforcements by means of German victories had
led. The energy of the army had not sufficed to
al the enemy a decisive blow before the Americans
re on the spot in considerable force. It was quite
ar to me that our general situation had thus become
ry serious.

By the beginning of August we had stopped our
tack, and had reverted to the defensive on the whole
ont. When the divisions that had taken part in the
st attack had been rested, we should be able to make
w plans. A pause in the operations was nothing
traordinary; it had occurred after the cessation of
e great offensive of March 21, and again after that
May 27. The fighting since July 15 had been no
s costly than had those attacks. The desire for rest
us as legitimate now as it had been then. Whether
e enemy would let us have it was the question.

I considered that the enemy might either continue

his attack on the Vesle, toward which he was exerti
an ever-increasing pressure, or that he might exte
it to the area between the Aisne and the Oise, whe
in expectation of an attack on our part, he h
got together large forces. I also thought he mig
possibly make advances between the Oise and t
Somme, perhaps also near Albert and in the plain
the Lys, and, finally, in the Sundgau (Upper Alsac
But I further assumed that these operations wo
take the form of only isolated local attacks, for t
enemy was also tired, and, on the whole, not less
than ourselves. And attacks did take place; that th
subsequently developed into a great battle on t
whole front was mainly due to the considerable su
cesses gained by the enemy on August 8 and 20. Th
must have demonstrated that our troops were no long
what they had been and invited him to continue t
fight.

Early in August I decidedly hoped that we shou
be able to defeat the imminent attacks and to deliv
counter-strokes, though on a smaller scale than her
tofore. Even in extremely critical situations we h
hitherto always succeeded in discovering a strategic
remedy, and I had no reason to suppose we shou
not do so again.

In anticipation of these battles a new Group Hea
quarters was put in the line to take over the Secon
Eighteenth, and Ninth Armies; its commander w
General von Boehn; Chief of Staff General von Lo
berg. This organization was to come into force betwe
August 10 and 15. As late as the first days of Augu
I was able to tell General von Boehn that I hoped
hand him over a well-established line. Unfortunate
I was wrong.

If our line held we would have to co-operate with t
Imperial Chancellor, who was kept regularly inform

events at the front, in framing decisive plans for the
ure.    That I should in so doing be obliged to bury
ny hopes was a fact I could not conceal from myself.
was in this sense that I discussed matters with my
ff; and while still occupied with these thoughts the
w of August 8 fell upon me.

# THE LAST PHASE, SUMMER AND AUTUMN 1918

### (Maps X and XIII)

I

AUGUST 8 was the black day of the German Arn
in the history of this war. This was the wor
experience that I had to go through, except for t
events that, from September 15 onward, took pla
on the Bulgarian front and sealed the fate of t
Quadruple Alliance.

Knowing that the next measures must be pure
defensive, General Headquarters had early in Augu
ordered a gradual withdrawal of our lines in the pla
of the Lys, and the evacuation of the bridge-hea
on the Ancre and Avre. They were evacuated
August 3 and 4.

At my special request General von Kuhl proceed
to the Second Army, in order to discuss once again t
defensive measures on the line Albert-Moreuil.

s area two divisions that had been a long time in
:ition, and seemed specially tired, were relieved by
:h ones. In this storm-center the divisional fronts
·e narrow, the artillery powerful, and the organiza-
ı deep. All experience gained on July 18 had been
ed upon. Only as regards the construction of
·ks, the Second Army had not done so much as, for
mple, the Eighteenth, which had captured its posi-
ıs at a later date.

:arly on August 8, in a dense fog, rendered still
:ker by artificial means, the English, mainly with
:tralian and Canadian divisions, and the French
ıcked between Albert and Moreuil with strong
adrons of tanks, but otherwise in no great superior-

Between the Somme and the Luce they penetrated
p into our positions. The divisions in line at that
ıt allowed themselves to be completely overwhelmed.
·isional staffs were surprised in their headquarters
enemy tanks. The breach very soon extended
ɔss the Luce stream; the troops that were still
antly resisting at Moreuil were rolled up. To the
:hward the Somme imposed a halt. Our troops
ıction north of the river had successfully parried a
ilar assault. The exhausted divisions that had
ı relieved a few days earlier, and that were lying
he region southwest of Péronne, were immediately
med and set in motion by the commander of the
ɔnd Army. At the same time he brought forward
ard the breach all other available troops. The
ɔprecht army group despatched reserves thither by
ı. The Eighteenth Army threw its own reserves
ctly into the battle from the southeast and pushed
ɔr forces forward in the region northwest of Roye.
an order from me, the Ninth Army, too, although
f in danger, had to contribute. Days, of course,
sed before the troops from more distant areas

could reach the spot. For their conveyance the m
extensive use was made of motor-lorries.

By the early hours of the forenoon of August 8
had already gained a complete impression of the sit
tion. It was a very gloomy one. I immediately
spatched a General Staff officer to the battle-field,
order to obtain an idea of the condition of the troo

The reserves of the Second Army were able to st
the enemy's advance on Péronne at a point south
Bray. In the direction of Roye the enemy had ab
reached Arvillers; south of the Avre our front had
be bent back from Montdidier onward.

Six or seven divisions that were quite fairly to
described as effective had been completely brok
Three or four others, together with the remnants
the battered divisions, were available for closing
broad gap between Bray and Roye.

The situation was uncommonly serious. If
enemy continued to attack with even ordinary vi
we should no longer be able to maintain ourselves w
of the Somme. But the Second Army would have
hold on here, while the Eighteenth Army, with its
wing standing fast on the heights along the Ma
swung its right back as far as Roye. This movem
was fixed for the night of August 9; should it fai
great enemy victory was possible.

On August 9 the enemy, whose attack, fortunat
for us, was not pressed with sufficient vigor, gai
ground between the Somme and the Avre. North
the Somme, too, the Second Army had to fall bac
little. South of the river, it succeeded in formin
continuous, if thin, line. These troops fought c
siderably better than the divisions between the Som
and the Luce had done the previous day. The g
behavior of the divisions which had been relie
shortly before the battle on account of exhaustion

EXPLANATION

EXPLANATION

German line at the beginning of the attack on the morning of Aug. 8.

Direction of English and French attack on Aug. 8.

German line on the morning of Aug. 9.

French attack on Aug. 9.

German line on the morning of Aug. 10.

Direction of French attack on Aug. 10.

German line on Aug. 18.

Position after falling back.

Army frontier.

FIG. 41. DEFENSIVE BATTLE BETWEEN THE SOMME AND THE OISE, 1918

particularly notable. Northwest of Roye the line held
The Eighteenth Army was able to carry out its difficul
maneuver on the night of the 10th. On the followin
morning the French vigorously attacked the origina
positions of that army, which were then evacuated b
the rear-guards according to plan. Of course, it ha
to leave a lot of material behind.

The stand made by the Second Army and the with
drawal of its line by the Eighteenth on the night of th
10th had improved the situation between the Somm
and Roye. Reserves, too, had arrived and strengthene
the front of the Second Army.

On the 10th and 11th severe but successful fightin
took place on our positions south of Albert and betwee
the Somme and the Avre, while between the Avre an
the Oise the enemy followed up closely and attacke
vigorously. Local attacks occurred all along the lin
during the next few days. Once more our troops stoo
their ground, but the Second Army was thoroughl
disorganized, whereas the powers of resistance of th
Eighteenth were in no way impaired.

The losses of the Second Army had been very heavy
Heavy demands had also been made upon its reserve
to fill up the gaps. The infantry of some division
had had to go into action straight off the lorries, whil
their artillery had been sent to some other part of th
line. Units were badly mixed up. It could be fore
seen that a number of additional divisions would be
come necessary in order to strengthen the Second Army
even if the enemy continued the offensive, and that wa
not certain. Besides, our losses in prisoners had bee
so heavy that General Headquarters was again face
with the necessity of breaking up more divisions t
form reserves. Our reserves dwindled. The losses c
the enemy, on the other hand, had been extraordinaril
small. The balance of numbers had moved heavil

against us; it was bound to become increasingly unfavorable as more American troops came in. There was no hope of materially improving our position by a counter-attack. Our only course, therefore, was to hold on.

We had to resign ourselves now to the prospect of a continuation of the enemy's offensive. Their success had been too easily gained. Their wireless was jubilant, and announced—and with truth—that the morale of the German Army was no longer what it had been. The enemy had also captured many documents of inestimable value to them. The Entente must have gained a clear idea of our difficulty in finding reserves, a further reason why it should pursue the offensive without respite.

The report of the staff-officer I had sent to the battle-field as to the condition of those divisions which had met the first shock of the attack on the 8th perturbed me deeply. I summoned divisional commanders and officers from the line to Avesnes to discuss events with them in detail. I was told of deeds of glorious valor, but also of behavior which, I openly confess, I should not have thought possible in the German Army; whole bodies of our men had surrendered to single troopers or isolated squadrons. Retiring troops, meeting a fresh division going bravely into action, had shouted out things like "Black-leg" and "You're prolonging the war"—expressions that were to be heard again later. The officers in many places had lost their influence and allowed themselves to be swept along with the rest. At a meeting of Prince Max's War Cabinet in October, Secretary Scheidemann called my attention to a divisional report on the occurrences of August 8, which contained similar unhappy stories. I was not acquainted with this report, but was able to verify it from my own knowledge. A battalion commander from the front, who came out with a draft from home shortly before August 8, attributed this to the spirit of insubordination and the atmosphere which the men brought back with them from home. Everything I had feared, and of which I had so often given warning, had here, in one place, become a reality. Our war machine was no longer efficient. Our fighting power had suffered, even though the great majority of divisions still fought heroically.

August 8 put the decline of that fighting power beyond all doubt, and in such a situation, as regards reserves, I had no hope of finding a strategic expedient whereby to turn the situation to our advantage. On the contrary, I became convinced that we were now without that safe foundation for the plans of General Headquarters, on which I had hitherto been able to build, at least, so far as this is possible in war. Leadership now assumed, as I then stated, the character of an irresponsible game of chance, a thing I have always considered fatal. The fate of the German people was to me too high a stake. The war must be ended.

August 8 also opened the eyes of the staff on both sides; mine were certainly opened, and so, according to his statement in *The Daily Mail*, were those of General Foch. The Entente began the great offensive, the final battle of the World War, and carried it through with increasing vigor, as our decline became more apparent.

I considered it possible that the occurrences since July 15 might have shaken the confidence of His Majesty and the Field-Marshal in me. Possibly, also, a fresh mind might be able to judge the situation from an unprejudiced point of view. I therefore earnestly requested the Field-Marshal, as I have previously mentioned, to replace me if he no longer had full confidence in me, or if he considered it advisable for other reasons. He refused. I also discussed my replacement with the

Chief of the Military Cabinet, in case it had anything against me personally. The Emperor gave me quite special proofs of his confidence in those days. I was deeply moved, but remained anxious as to whether His Majesty really read the whole situation aright. I have since been reassured. The Emperor told me later that, after the failure of the July offensive and after August 8, he knew the war could no longer be won. The official report of the evening of the 8th announced briefly that the enemy had penetrated our line south of the Somme on a wide front. The following morning General von Cramon rang me up at once from Baden. He informed me that my report had caused great alarm in Vienna. I could not leave him in any doubt as to the serious view I took of the situation. Nevertheless, he begged me to remember how detrimentally the blunt admission of a defeat must affect our allies, who placed all their hopes upon Germany. This occurred again on September 2.

The impression made on our allies by the failure on the Western front was great. The Emperor Charles announced his intention of coming to Spa in the middle of August.

Nothing was to be expected from Bulgaria. There the Radoslavoff Cabinet, under the influence of events on the Western front and the Treaty of Bucharest, not to mention personal reasons, had been succeeded by Malinoff. Malinoff was no friend of the Alliance; some of his ministers were openly against it and favorable to the Entente. When later the Entente occupied Bulgaria, although Malinoff was dismissed, they remained in office. The Imperial Chancellor had to pass over the behavior of Malinoff's Ministry and invoke the assistance of the King to prevent a fresh orientation of policy. The visit of a few Bulgarians to Switzerland also gave food for thought. That, too, we permitted. It was quite obvious that Bulgaria was intent on peace. It was also significant that the Bulgarian Military Representative, General Gantschew, very seldom visited our General Headquarters.

As soon as I had obtained a grasp of the whole situation brought about by the events of August 8, I decided to arrange conferences as soon as possible with the Imperial Chancellor and the Secretary of State for Foreign Affairs. These took place on August 13 and 14 at Spa.

On the 13th there was a discussion between the Chancellor, the Field-Marshal, Secretary of State von Hintze, and myself, in the Field-Marshal's room at the Hôtel Britannique. I reviewed the military situation, the condition of the army, and the position of our allies, and explained that it was no longer possible by an offensive to force the enemy to sue for peace. Defense alone could hardly achieve this object, and so the termination of the war would have to be brought about by diplomacy. At the moment our line on the Western front was holding, though, in view of the element of uncertainty which the insubordination of some of the troops had introduced into our calculations, circumstances might necessitate a withdrawal of the front. I sincerely hoped, however, that the army in France would stand fast. The state of affairs on the Western front was naturally bound to make an unfavorable impression on our allies. In this connection, the morale of our army and people became a matter of even greater importance than before. I laid special emphasis on this. I drew their attention in particular to the damage done by Prince Lichnowsky. I again emphasized the necessity for speeches by our ministers calculated to make an impression abroad, and the importance of even now inaugurating a propaganda department for educating public opinion.

The Field-Marshal said nothing about the state of feeling at home; he took a more optimistic view of the military situation than I did. Secretary of State von Hintze drew, from what he had heard, the logical conclusion that peace negotiations were essential, and that we should have to bring ourselves to take up a very conciliatory attitude.

The Chancellor spoke briefly of the state of public opinion at home without saying anything worthy of notice. He was very reserved about Prince Lichnowsky's case, and referred us to the Supreme Court of Justice.

The following morning there was a conference presided over by His Majesty. The first matter to be discussed was the state of public feeling at home. The Chancellor made a few introductory remarks. I repeated my statement of the previous day about moral endurance. His Majesty then called on Secretary of State von Hintze. Von Hintze offered no opinion about affairs at home, but went straight to the military and political situation, adopting the view I had given the previous day, drawing the same conclusion; he was manifestly moved; tears stood in his eyes. The Emperor was very calm. He agreed with Secretary of State von Hintze, and instructed him to open up peace negotiations, if possible, through the medium of the Queen of the Netherlands. He also pointed out the desirability of enlightening the people, and the necessity for a united and firm government policy. The Chancellor emphasized the need for upholding authority at home. Diplomatic negotiations must be opened at the right moment. The conference then closed; deeply moved, I shook hands with Secretary of State von Hintze.

Meanwhile the Emperor Charles had arrived in Spa with Baron Burian and General von Arz. The statesmen are said to have discussed peace questions, as demanded by the situation; in particular, the step taken by Baron Burian. I was not informed of this at the time, but learned it later from a remark made by Von Hintze. Further, the Polish question also came under discussion. Baron Burian adhered to his own conception. We had missed a good opportunity of coming to a definite agreement with Austria. His Majesty, meanwhile, supported by the Chancellor, was inclined to favor a solution by which Poland was to have a prince of her own choosing, while retaining her economic dependence on Germany. With such divergent views, an agreement with Austria-Hungary was impossible. His Majesty's proposal seemed to me really practical, and indeed corresponded to my personal convictions. I must expressly state here that the Emperor was always against the idea of a personal union with Poland.

The general military situation which had developed was discussed with General von Arz, and also the necessity of reinforcing the Western front with more Austrian divisions; so far only two had arrived. General von Arz had not abandoned the idea of an offensive in Italy, but was now of opinion that the Austro-Hungarian Army was no longer in a condition to hold out through the coming winter; that was my last interview with this general, whom I held in the highest esteem both as a man and a soldier.

After the Emperor Charles had left for Vienna the Field-Marshal and I immediately returned to Avesnes. I had thought that the Chancellor would leave Spa as well, in order to acquaint the Secretaries of State and the Reichstag with the situation, in the light of our conference. The education of public opinion was one of his functions. He remained in Spa, however, and left it to Vice-Chancellor von Payer and Secretary of State von Hintze to talk to the party leaders, Ebert, Groeber, Stresemann, Count von Westarp, and Wiemer. They were requested to attend at the Ministry of the Interior on the 21st. At the conference there, Secretary of State von Hintze explained the military and political situation, and arrived at the same conclusion as had been reached at Spa, that the war must be brought to a close as speedily as possible. He announced his intention of taking all steps to procure peace. Gentlemen who were present at this conference told me how they had been very gravely impressed by our military situation. Of course, military considerations and the proposed peace negotiations imposed the necessity for extreme reticence on Secretary of State von Hintze; it was bound to injure both seriously if, as happened later, our intentions were to be advertised broadcast. With an enemy such as we had to deal with this could mean only the continuation of the war, and the peace offer that would completely destroy us. For similar reasons to those which must have actuated Secretary of State von Hintze, I was not in a position to give my views on the peace question to the world in general. I discussed it with a few of the members of my immediate circle. General von Bartenwerffer knew about the conference of August 14 through a note from the Secretary of State.

In addition, I discussed the situation with various ministers. Secretary of State Solf came about this time to Avesnes. A private letter from Weimar informed me of the impressions he had received here. It was said there, by people standing in close touch with Solf's family, that, in Solf's opinion, I no longer believed in a victorious issue of the war, whereas the Field-Marshal still had hopes that with God's help it was not beyond attainment.

Vice-Chancellor von Payer came, too, and in the

Chancellor's name placed before me a proposal with regard to the Belgian question which corresponded to the unfavorable turn in the military situation. I accepted it. I thought it was to serve as a foundation for the negotiations of the Secretary of State for Foreign Affairs. Instead of this, Vice-Chancellor von Payer made use of it in September in a speech delivered at Stuttgart; it caused a sensation because of its attitude toward Belgium.

II

Days of great anxiety were to follow our return to Headquarters. Our position on the Western front became more serious. When, on the 14th, His Majesty ordered peace negotiations to be opened, the front was still holding, though it gave us cause for anxiety. After August 8, General von Boehn took over command of his army group—the Second, Eighteenth, and Ninth Armies—a few days earlier than had originally been intended. He and his Chief of Staff, General von Loszbcrg, did all they could to increase the resisting power of their sector.

The fighting between the Somme and the Oise was still continuing in the middle of August; the center of gravity of the enemy's attack lay on both sides of Roye, which was held through severe fighting. A reserve position in the rear, which meant that the left wing of the Seventeenth Army would have to swing back, was prepared and consolidated on a line running through Bapaume, west of Péronne, along the Somme, west of Ham, the hills northeast of Noyon. Where possible, old trench systems were incorporated. Rupprecht's army group had withdrawn the front line of the Sixth Army in the Lys plain a few kilometers. A further straightening out of the salient, entailing the evacuation of Kemmel Hill, was in preparation. Here, too, reserve lines were established and our former lines evacuated. There was no fighting of any importance. Nothing beyond occasional enemy raids disturbed our peace. About the middle of the month an English attack seemed probable.

The position of the Seventeenth Army was similar. Here, after the 15th, there were indications of an offensive between Arras and the Ancre, especially toward Bapaume. The Seventeenth Army was not to hold its front line, but to give battle in a position three to four kilometers in the rear; the front line was merely held by outposts, who were to fall back on to the main position before the attack. There was thus a possibility of bringing the enemy's first onslaught to naught and getting notice of his intentions in time.

Southeast of the battle front between the Somme and the Oise, the Ninth, like the Seventeenth Army, had made all preparations to put up a stout resistance. An attack between the Oise and the Aisne was anticipated and might be launched at any time about the middle of August. The reserves surrendered by this army to the Second had been fully replaced, and it was now well equipped in every way. Two counter-attack divisions were held in readiness near Cuts and Nouvron, where the enemy's main thrust was expected. The Army Headquarters Staff had thought out and organized everything with the greatest care.

There was less probability of an enemy offensive on the Vesle. There were no indications of an offensive on the sectors held by the German Crown Prince's, Von Gallwitz's, and Duke Albrecht's army groups. The situation might alter very quickly, however, in view of the advanced state of the enemy's preparations on all fronts.

General Headquarters had to be prepared for the extension of the enemy's offensive to Crown Prince

Rupprecht's army group (especially between Arras and the Ancre) and to the Ninth Army, without neglecting the other sectors. The divisions of the Seventh and First Armies, which had been withdrawn from the line as late as the end of July and beginning of August, could not be given a long rest. Some of them had already had to be put into support behind Rupprecht's army group, and this was, of course, very hard on them. An additional strain was thus thrown on the railway communications in the West.

On August 21 the English attacked south of Arras between Boisleux and the Ancre; this was the first of a series of attacks on Crown Prince Rupprecht's sector, which lasted almost uninterruptedly to the end of the war and made the heaviest demands on the Group Headquarters and their armies.

The Seventeenth Army had fallen back in time, and the English attack broke down in front of the new line. On the 22d the Seventeenth Army, by permission of General Headquarters, counter-attacked on its whole front. They were successful, but it would have been better not to attempt it. Immediately afterward the English offensive spread southward. On both banks of the Somme there was heavy fighting, the main weight of the attack being directed between Albert and Bray; the Australians had no success. The first two days had thus gone well for us. I began to hope that here, at least, luck was going to turn. During the following days, however, the English, who had but few fresh reserves at their disposal, gained ground toward Bapaume after very severe fighting. The characteristic of their tactics was narrow but deep penetration by tanks after short but extremely violent artillery preparation, combined with artificial fog. Mass attacks by tanks and artificial fog remained hereafter our most dangerous enemies. The danger increased in propor-

FIG. 42.  DEFENSIVE BATTLE BETWEEN THE SCARPE
AND THE SOMME, 1918

tion as the morale of our troops deteriorated and as our divisions grew weaker and more exhausted. The depth of penetration was soon known, but not the length of front to be attacked. Well-timed counter-attacks by reserves generally succeeded in restoring the situation. There remained the danger, however, of the local command throwing in its troops too hurriedly and piecemeal. As the offensive developed, the enemy succeeded on the north in pushing us back from the Ancre. At this point a Prussian division, known to be a poor one, it is true, and for that reason given a sector covered by the river, had refused to fight. This threw the whole line into confusion. The natural difficulties of fighting in the shell-hole area of the Somme battle-field, east of Albert, were increased by the fact that, owing to bad railway communications, it was very hard to get reserves up in this region. The situation there became extremely critical about August 25. It was certain that the enemy offensive would continue.

South of the Somme, on the Péronne road, only local attacks had been launched. The Eighteenth Army was constantly engaged, but put up a splendid fight. In view of the events east of the Oise, the left wing was swung back closer to Noyon; the handling of the Eighteenth Army by General von Hutier was particu-larly cool, and he was very ably assisted by his Chief of Staff, Lieutenant-Colonel Buerckner.

Between the Oise and the Aisne the great French attack had already succeeded on August 20. By the 17th the French had pushed back our advanced troops on to the main line of defense. I found out later that these had offered stronger resistance than they should have done. The fighting strength of several divisions was thereby diminished to an extent that had not entered into my calculations. The attack on August

20 developed exactly as had been anticipated. The counter-attack divisions stationed near Cuts, however, were not thrown into the fight. A deep salient was made here, rendering the position of the troops, with

EXPLANATION

▬▬▬ German line on the morning of Aug. 20.
➤ Direction of French attack on Aug. 20.
●●●● German line on the morning of Aug. 21.
▬ ▬ ▬ German line on the morning of Aug. 22.

1:300000

FIG. 43.  DEFENSIVE BATTLE BETWEEN THE OISE AND THE AISNE, AUGUST 1918

the Oise in their rear, exceedingly uncomfortable. In the direction of Nouvron, also, the enemy broke into our line, but was driven back, although not completely, by counter-attacks delivered by good German Jäger divisions. Even apart from the two points of penetration, we did not succeed in maintaining our main line of resistance intact. The position was now such that it seemed unwise to attempt to maintain our line in front of the Oise and the Ailette. General Headquarters decided to withdraw the right wing of the Ninth Army behind the Oise on the night of the 21st, and on the night of the 22d, while holding the ground to the northwest of Soissons, to withdraw the center of the army behind the Ailette. The battle had again taken an unfavorable course, in spite of all our precautions; the nerves of the army had suffered. In some places the men would no longer stand the tremendous artillery barrages and tank attacks, which had become still more severe. Again we had suffered heavy and irreplaceable losses. August 20 was another black day, literally compelling the enemy to continue the offensive.

I calculated on the continuation of the enemy's attack between the Oise and the Aisne toward Laon; an advance here would be fruitful of results, rendering untenable the positions of the Eighteenth Army to the north of the Oise, and of the Seventh to the north of the Vesle. The enemy was pressing the Soissons-Chauny line strongly. Fierce fighting ensued here, with varying success, and the end could not yet be foreseen.

The Eighteenth Army, which took over the command of the troops on the Oise, was at this point directly and seriously menaced from the south.

As a result of the course of events east of Albert and south of the Oise, the position of the German troops between the Somme and the Oise was by no means so secure as the general military situation demanded. It would have been fatal to run risks at this point.

The army groups of the Crown Prince Rupprecht and Von Boehn were therefore ordered to retire during the last days of August to the line already reconnoitered

ast of Bapaume—in front of Péronne—Somme—in
ront of Ham—the heights northeast of Noyon. As
heir reserve line, the Siegfried system was now to be
put in order. Von Boehn's army group had attached
importance to the retention of the left bank of the
Somme, in front of Péronne, because from there favorable flanking movements against the area north of
Péronne were possible. Between Ham and Noyon a
canal, which offered a good obstacle to tanks, determined the position of the line. These movements were
carried through about the night of August 26.

The Seventeenth Army, which had only a short
wheel to the rear to perform, and the Eighteenth
carried out the retirement without a hitch and in good
order, and held their new positions against enemy
attacks. The Second Army was less fortunate. Northwest of Péronne the new line failed to hold. The
division to the southwest of the town let the enemy
gain the left bank, thus rendering the situation very
difficult for the troops on the northern bank. Again
some divisions failed, putting a terrible strain on other
gallant troops.

During this time, Field-Marshal Haig had extended
his offensive northward as far as the Scarpe, in order
to get to the rear of the Siegfried position, north of
the Croisilles-Moeuvres line. To achieve this, he had
to take our Wotan position, which had been built in
1917, starting in the north, and running through
Biache St.-Vaast, and along the Scarpe to the east of
Monchy, in the direction of Bullecourt.

On August 26 the English offensive against the Arras-
Cambrai road opened.

Here again the troops at first fell back according to
plan, the early stages of the fighting developing favorably for us. Subsequently the English reached the
Wotan system. On September 2 a strong assault by

English tanks overran obstacles and trenches in thi
line and paved a way for their infantry.  Shortly afte
two o'clock in the afternoon General von Kuhl an
Lieutenant-Colonel von Pavelsz, the Chief of Staff o
the Seventeenth Army, reported that it would n
longer be wise to form a new line in front of the Arleux
Moeuvres canal.  They requested permission from
General Headquarters to withdraw the Seventeent
Army to that line, while holding the position north o
the Scarpe.  We had to admit the necessity for thi
measure.  In concert with Von Boehn's army grou
we had to take another important step on account o
the position of the Second Army, withdrawing its lin
and that of the Eighteenth Army to the Siegfried pos
tion.  It would no doubt have been possible to kee
the left wing of the Eighteenth Army in front of th
Siegfried line, on the Crozat canal, but that require
more men than the defense of the St.-Quentin-L
Fère line, with the broad valley of the Oise in front of i
General Headquarters rejected this idea and brough
the entire Eighteenth Army back into the Siegfrie
line.  The Ninth Army, and also the right wing of th
Seventh, had to conform to this movement, the latte
abandoning the Vesle and taking up a position behin
the Aisne, while the left wing of the same army con
tinued to hold the Vesle to the northeast of Fismes.

Meanwhile the Ninth Army had been heavily en
gaged, battles of tremendous violence developing o
several occasions.  Thanks to the unflagging skill an
foresight of General von Carlowitz and his Chief o
Staff, Lieutenant-Colonel Faupel, and to the gallantr
of several divisions, this army for the most part main
tained its positions.  The 1st Guard-Infantry Division
coolly and ably led by Prince Eitel Frederick, and th
well-tried dismounted Guard-Cavalry Division, fough
magnificently, quite undaunted by tanks.

It was no easy decision to withdraw the entire front from the Scarpe to the Vesle, but it shortened our line and economized men, which, considering our huge wastage, was an advantage worth some sacrifice, notwithstanding that it was shared by the enemy. Conditions were easier for the troops in and to the east of the Siegfried line, while the enemy was compelled to occupy ground rendered desolate by the withdrawal in the spring of 1917.

The center of the Seventeenth Army was to be withdrawn behind the Arleux-Moeuvres canal during the night of the 3d, while in general the retirement was to be undertaken as one movement, the detailed orders being prepared by the army groups.

In addition, the long-prepared evacuation of the Lys salient by the Fourth and Sixth Armies was now carried out in order to economize man-power.

At the same time General Headquarters gave orders, after consulting the commanders of the army groups, for the reconnoissance and strengthening of a new line, the Hermann line, behind the two northern army groups. The line was to start on the Dutch frontier east of Bruges, follow the Ecloo canal southward to the Lys, continue up-stream to the east of Courtrai, and then along the upper reaches of the Scheldt to southwest of Valenciennes. Further south it was to follow the Solesmes-Le Cateau-Guise line. Southwest of Marle, the Hermann line joined the Hunding-Brunhild position, which, constructed in 1917, passed by Sisonne to the Aisne and continued up-stream along that river. To the east of the Aisne the defensive position was continued by the rear lines of Von Gallwitz's army group, which terminated in the Michel line, which, flattening out the St.-Mihiel salient, ran across the Woevre plateau to a point west of the Moselle, near Pagny. The positions which already existed were to be strengthened as much as available labor permitted.

Further, we had a second reserve position reconnoitered, running to the west of the Antwerp-Brussels-Namur line, and then up-stream along the Meuse; this was called the Antwerp-Meuse line. The fortresses in Alsace-Lorraine were put into a state of defense. Lastly, orders were given that all military material not required for immediate use should be removed from the region west and south of the Hermann-Hunding-Brunhild line, while preparations were to be made for the thorough demolition of railways and roads and for putting the coal-mines out of working order. Villages were not to be interfered with unless for urgent tactical reasons. Large-scale evacuation to Germany was undertaken. Our railway communications were not favorable for this. In the north, they were hemmed in toward Liège by the strip of Dutch territory running south to Maastricht; the line we built near Visé had not proved sufficient to overcome this difficulty. Farther south, important railways converged on the Charleville-Montmédy line, and presented a particularly favorable target for enemy air-raids.

Supplies from Germany had already been cut down to absolute essentials.

The withdrawal of the front line to the Siegfried position made Avesnes no longer a suitable position for General Headquarters, and we accordingly returned to Spa, which we had left in March so full of hope and confidence.

The enemy's strength was heavily taxed, as well as ours, as he attacked again and again on various sectors with the same divisions. His losses, too, must have been heavy, but they were on the offensive, and we had to submit to his raining blows on us, just as we did in 1917. Our experiences in those battles

FIG. 44. EVACUATION OF THE LYS SECTOR, 1918

were repeated, our troops fighting better in attack than on the defensive. Our relative strength in divisions was more favorable at the beginning of September

than it had been in the previous year, but some of our
divisions were very weak; we had, while retaining the
machine-gun companies, to reduce our battalions from
four to three companies. The material ordinarily
needed by four companies was excessive in relation
to the actual strength; for example, we did not need
four field-cookers to a battalion, two or three being
amply sufficient. With the breaking up of a number
of our divisions, and the arrival of further Americans
in the fighting-line, the balance of numbers was bound
to be still more unfavorable to us.

Shirking at the front became more prevalent, especially among men returning from home leave. Over-
staying of leave increased, and the fighting-line
was more thinly manned. The Ministry of War
was at last prepared to call up exempted men in
greater numbers for the army, with what success
remained to be seen. What would be the morale
of these men? From the divisions in the East
we had long ago extracted every man who could be
employed in the fighting divisions of the West. Our
position in the East at the time was more satisfactory.
The Soviet Government had paid the first, quickly followed by the second, instalment of the Russian indemnity; relations had been established with the Don
Cossacks. We were thus able to dispose of a few
divisions of poor fighting quality, consisting of older
classes not up to the standard of the Western front.
Should the peace endeavors of the Government prove
unsuccessful, and the war continue over the winter and
into the following summer, export from the Ukraine
would become a vital matter both for ourselves and
for Austria. It was as important as ever to maintain
the blockade against Bolshevism, and to prevent the
Allies forming a new line in the East. For this reason
the three German dismounted cavalry regiments, and

the scanty artillery, under General Count von der Goltz, remained in Finland, faithfully watching the Murman Railway and the gates of Petrograd. Our plans against the English garrison in Baku were still being carried out.

The Dual Monarchy could still spare a division or two for the West.

All this, however, was not even numerically, let alone morally, adequate to compensate for the increasing strength and confidence of the enemy in the West. It was quite clear that the distressing manifestations in the German Army would not decrease, but rather multiply with the constant retreats and the disintegrating influences from home.

It was exceedingly difficult for General Headquarters to reinforce the army groups of Crown Prince Rupprecht and Von Boehn. My task would have been easier had General Headquarters insisted at the end of July on withdrawing the battle-worn or decimated divisions of the Seventh Army from the line, and had now taken the same course with all the armies in the line, especially the Second.

Our position was now so serious that General Headquarters could not hope that air-raids on London and Paris would force the enemy to make peace. Permission was therefore refused for the use of a particularly effective incendiary bomb, expressly designed for attacks on the two capitals, of which sufficient supplies were ready in August. The great amount of damage that they were expected to cause would no longer have affected the course of the war, and sheer destructiveness had never been permitted. Count von Hertling, too, had requested General Headquarters not to use these new incendiary bombs, on account of the reprisals on our own towns that would follow. My views of the general military situation, however, were the real ground for the decision.

I retained the policy of ordinary raids on London and Paris, in order to immobilize enemy anti-aircraft material, and to prevent the troops noticing the reduction in our strength, but I no longer pressed matters. Only one or two more small raids were made on Paris, while London could not at this time be reached, owing to adverse weather conditions.

I was constantly worried with regard to the morale of the army and the people at home. On the visit of the Minister of War to Avesnes in August, I had officers from the front introduced to him with a view to convincing him of the bad influence exercised by the home population on discipline. He and other leading men in the War Ministry had always refused to realize this, or, at least, its full significance. The visit bore no fruit, in spite of all my earnest representations to the minister.

In the interior our attempt to improve the morale of the people by means of propaganda never got beyond the initial stages. After my pressing the matter for two years, the Chancellor had at last, in August 1918, decided to create a Central Bureau for press and propaganda purposes, both at home and abroad, It did not rank above the departments of the Imperial Government, but was attached to the Foreign Office, an unhappy appendage devoid of real authority. I had to content myself with achieving this much, for I could get nothing else done. My constant proposals and suggestions, repeated time and time again, both verbally and in writing, for the appointment of an Imperial minister of propaganda, met with no response; nobody but a minister or Secretary of State, who could see in its proper perspective the entire military, political, and economical situation, could wield the mighty weapon of propaganda in the manner demanded by the war and the hour. He alone would have been able to decide when, where, and by what department a public official statement should be made. He would have to work on a carefully prepared system. Colonel von Haeften, who occupied a leading position in the newly created Central Bureau, took great pains to achieve something. Secretary of State Solf did indeed make one effective speech on his advice. The Chancellor's speech on his birthday, early in September, was very feeble. The Vice-Chancellor spoke, too, but his words were not telling, like those of Clemenceau, when German troops were within eighty kilometers of Paris. Later, Colonel von Haeften's suggestions to the new Chancellor, Prince Max of Baden, did not result in any more propaganda work being done, although it was particularly necessary in so serious a situation.

III

Tension was high on the Western front. It had increased since our first peace suggestions of the middle of August. We still had reason to hope that we would maintain our position; in Italy and Macedonia our flanks and rear were covered. There was, however, no longer any chance of a victorious issue. On September 3 we answered to this effect an inquiry from the Chancellor, which was prompted by his representative at General Headquarters, Count Limburg-Stirum, after he had been informed of our intention to withdraw to the Siegfried line. Count Limburg-Stirum was invariably kept informed of all events. The inquiry rather surprised me, because, ever since August 13, the Chancellor must have been fully acquainted with the situation; the explanation was, however, that

Count Limburg-Stirum knew nothing of the discussion of August 13 and 14.

General Headquarters had no news from Secretary von Hintze; all it knew was that he was to go to Vienna at the beginning of September to confer with Count Burian about peace. I considered that a further discussion with him and the Chancellor was urgently required. It would have to be held in the first days of September, immediately after our return to Spa. Secretary of State von Hintze arranged to attend as soon as he should return from Vienna, but his advanced age prohibited the Chancellor's attendance.

The discussion in Spa with Secretary von Hintze was held on September 8 or 9. He informed us that Count Burian intended to despatch a note to all the belligerents, inviting them to a peace discussion; he added that, according to accounts received in Vienna, the Austro-Hungarian Army could hold out only until the winter. The need for peace there was growing more urgent. As regards his own efforts, Von Hintze said that he confidently hoped for mediation through the Queen of Holland; I could not ascertain from his statements on what ground he based his hope. He had no expectation that the vague move to be taken by Count Burian would lead to any result, and feared that they would make the mediation of the Queen of Holland more difficult; he considered a definite step, such as he intended to take at The Hague, to be better. On that point I quite agreed with him; Count Burian's proposals, of which I had only recently heard, were much too shapeless.

It was probably on the Count's advice that the Emperor Charles had recently had certain questions put to the Field-Marshal through General von Cramon, concerning our strategic aims and our views as to the making of a peace proposal. General von Cramon asked me on the telephone to answer him as accurately as possible, as the Emperor Charles attached great importance to it. Of course my replies had to be cautiously worded, because there was a leakage from Vienna to France, as proved by the Emperor Charles's Parma letters. We replied that the German Army would hold its present line in the West, in particular the Siegfried line, but that we were in favor of immediate peace proposals; we did, however, advise against those of Count Burian. I drafted this reply, and it was discussed at our conversation with Secretary von Hintze before being despatched.

Secretary von Hintze was informed in detail of the military situation. As a result of the discussions of September 9, he wired from Spa to the Ministry of Foreign Affairs, stating that His Majesty and General Headquarters agreed to an immediate appeal to the Queen of the Netherlands, and requesting that our allies should be invited to approve this step and to join in it.

Austria-Hungary did not abandon Count Burian's plan in favor of ours, and his note was published on September 14. I do not know whether our proposal appeared to them too distant, or what other reasons guided the Dual Monarchy. The Emperor Charles explained in a letter to His Majesty that the telegram he had received from General Headquarters had induced him to take early steps for peace. I remarked to Colonel Heye that it was perhaps as well that Count Burian had taken the step he did, and it was thus with my approval that we did not assume an attitude of opposition to it.

I cannot agree with the diplomats that Count Burian's peace note rendered mediation by the Queen of the Netherlands impossible. It made it more difficult, but did not exclude it by any means. Above all, I cannot understand why Dutch mediation was not sought before the publication of Count Burian's note, for which there would have been time enough. I do not believe that Secretary von Hintze seriously discussed the matter with the Dutch ambassador in Berlin. In those days I no longer concerned myself to any extent with military-political questions. Secretary von Hintze discussed the Polish question with General Headquarters on lines laid down by the Chancellor. I replied, as my duty dictated, and gave him my views. In a communication dated August 28, after conferring with a Polish gentleman in Berlin, the Secretary of State placed definite proposals before us, as to how Poland might best be constituted and our relations with that state might be governed. He particularly wanted to give Vilna to Poland, as it would always constitute a foreign element in any Lithuanian state; Poland must certainly undertake to fulfil certain conditions, particularly the military convention, to our complete satisfaction.

General Headquarters replied on August 30, signifying its agreement with the Secretary, and calling attention to certain points which had been raised in the previous discussions of which he might be unaware. We laid stress, for example, in the interests of our economical and military policy, on the necessity of a railway alliance with Poland, and of insuring safe communication through Poland to Russia.

I considered it essential, too, that the fulfilment of Poland's obligations should be more closely secured in some way, for I could not overcome my mistrust of that country. Vilna had formerly been promised to the Lithuanians by the Chancellor. It was to be feared that they would very naturally regard the cession to Poland as a breach of faith. It was a matter for the Foreign Office to take steps to avoid the disadvantages resulting therefrom. With regard to Lithuania, even after this serious mutilation, I was still of the same opinion, and emphasized the necessity of attaching it as a self-governing state to Germany or Prussia through personal union. Torn from its context, this minute was used in the Reichstag to convict me of muddled political thought. The story of its origin is simple, but it is not clear how it came to be purloined from the Foreign Office. Plans should be followed as long as possible, provided damage in other directions does not result therefrom, which there was in this case no ground to fear. In this instance the policy of the Foreign Office was sound and my position quite correct.

From the same point of view we were at that time in favor of the formation of a Baltic state and the settlement of the question of the Finnish throne according to Finland's desires.

Conditions in Rumania were also discussed with Secretary von Hintze. The obvious military superiority of the Entente had strongly affected the Government in Jassy, which was entirely under the influence of the Entente ambassador. Its attitude to us became cooler and cooler; the weakness of the Bucharest Peace made itself felt now. In agreement with Secretary von Hintze, General Headquarters seriously considered the inauguration of a new campaign against Rumania with the troops that had been released from the East for the West. General von Arz promised his support, provided the Emperor Charles would agree, but, in spite of the military necessity for this step, the latter refused to sanction any special pressure on Rumania. We therefore renounced the idea of taking military measures, and the troops were ordered to their original destination in the West. In the end, however, they had to be sent to Siberia. Later on, Austria-Hungary herself suggested armed intervention in Rumania, but by that time it was too late.

Meanwhile Admiral von Holtzendorff, who had a severe attack of heart disease, had resigned, and Admiral Scheer became Chief of the Naval Staff. He was an unusually clear-thinking man, capable of swift decisions. I got into touch with him as soon as possible in Spa, and talked over with him the situation in the West and the submarine campaign. The evacuation of our submarine base at Bruges might soon become necessary. Admiral Scheer did not think that this would have a decisive influence on the submarine campaign, as the vessels already had to travel to Flanders round the north of Scotland, being no longer able to enter the Channel. Of course he did not welcome the necessity for massing submarines on our German coasts.

He thought, too, that submarine building could be speeded up and a better result obtained. He asked me to assist him in the matter, saying he needed more workmen to turn out more submarines. I explained that General Headquarters was not in a position to supply them, and could agree to release only a certain number of specially trained engineers and skilled hands. This involved only a few men. These discussions lasted into October; the situation had assumed an exceedingly grave aspect; nevertheless I gave instructions for the release of these men. This order also led to considerable public controversy. The Supreme Command could not give in until the sword should be wrested from its hand. There was no need to abandon any desirable political aims, or to forgo any useful supplies of material, until absolutely compelled by necessity. In spite of all the difficulties, of which I was only too well aware, I was not the man to throw up the sponge prematurely, and I held strongly to the

opinion that the stronger we were in the field the better
our position would be in any peace negotiations.

I had introduced a change on my staff; I found in
Colonel Heye an older assistant, and placed him in
control of several departments that previously had
been under my immediate supervision. Their reports
went to him, but I reserved to myself decisions of
moment. What I had gone through would leave no
man unmarked. I had been appointed to General
Headquarters, not to make peace, but to win the war,
and had thought of nothing else. Like Clemenceau and
Lloyd George, I had wanted to call up the entire nation,
but I was not, as has so often and so falsely been stated,
a dictator. Lloyd George and Clemenceau had the
control of the Parliaments which ruled their countries,
for they were "their" Parliaments. At the same time,
they stood as the heads of the entire administrative
and executive Governments; I, on the other hand, had
no constitutional power directly to influence the German Government in order to enforce my views as to
the steps necessary for the conduct of the war, and I
was frequently confronted with the lack of understanding and energy of the departments whose duty it was
to take these steps. Peace not being obtainable, I
had striven to carry the war to the successful issue
which alone could save us from the fate we now suffer.
I understood now that this successful issue was impossible, and I saw the approach of the disaster which
it had been my life's work to prevent.

## IV

While these events were proceeding in Spa, the army
groups of the Crown Prince Rupprecht, Von Boehn, and
of the German Crown Prince had carried out the withdrawals from Kemmel and the Lys plain behind the

Arleux-Moeuvres canal, into the Siegfried system, and on the Vesle. The movement went without a hitch and was completed by the Eighteenth Army, which had farthest to go, by about September 7. The armies had not fallen back everywhere to the German trenches; they manned, in some places, parts of the old enemy line. Everywhere the enemy followed close on our heels. He soon resumed the offensive, which developed in a particularly keen manner between Moeuvres and Holnon against the left wing of the Seventeenth, the whole of the Second, and the right wing of the Eighteenth Army, and between the Ailette and Aisne against the left wing of the Ninth and the extreme right of the Seventh Army. Fighting was very keen, but our line recovered itself, except that in the Second Army some weakness still remained. On September 18 and 19 particularly severe attacks were launched on the Moeuvres-Holnon sector; the left wing of the Second Army was pressed back several kilometers on to the Scheldt-Oise canal, north of St.-Quentin, the Eighteenth Army being forced to withdraw its extreme right to conform with this retirement. Otherwise the line was held, severe local fighting continuing up to September 25 and 26. The French extended their offensive farther toward St.-Quentin. It goes without saying that these days, too, took heavy toll of our entire army.

The German Crown Prince's army group had taken over command of the Ninth Army from Von Boehn about the middle of the month. This army and the right flank of the Seventh were constantly in action. The army group had to find its own reinforcements. Tension was particularly high on both sides of Rheims and, after the 22d, also on both sides of the Argonne, where on the 26th another great battle was to break out. The completion of the Hermann line behind the two northern army groups had begun, and similar work was actively proceeding in the rear of the Crown Prince's group.

Behind the line between the coast and the Meuse, the work of evacuation was often interrupted by successful enemy air-raids. Huge supplies of material had to be moved, which were essential for the further prosecution of the war. Many sectors had worked on bad supply systems and the result was now felt.

In front of Von Gallwitz's army group, between St.-Mihiel and the Moselle, much movement had been noticed as early as the end of August, and an American offensive seemed probable there. General Headquarters pushed up reserves. I discussed with the Chief of Staff of the army group and of Army Detachment "C," which was exposed to the attack, the evacuation of the salient, which had long ago been planned and prepared. Local commanders were confident in spite of my demurs. General Headquarters was reluctant to evacuate the salient, on account of the industrial centers lying behind it, and, unfortunately, did not order this step until September 8. At the same time the southern front of Army Detachment "C" was to increase its distance from the enemy, much as had been the case with the Seventeenth Army in the middle of August. Advanced guards only were to be left in the most forward trenches.

The work of evacuation had not been carried very far when, on September 12, the attack developed between the Rupt and the Moselle, accompanied by a secondary offensive movement against the northern end of the salient on the Combres heights. The enemy penetrated our line in both places. On the southern sector he broke through a Prussian division, and the reserves were not sufficiently close enough up to restore the position immediately. On the Combres heights there was an Austro-Hungarian division, which might have fought better. As early as noon the local army headquarters ordered the evacuation of the salient. I was dissatisfied with myself, but also with the local command. The earlier reports indicated that the evacuation was proceeding satisfactorily, this being facili-

FIG. 45.   BATTLES IN THE ST.-MIHIEL SECTOR, 1918

tated by the enemy not following up. I founded my official *communiqué*, which turned out later to be too favorable, on these reports.

It has been said that my *communiqués* were unreliable. They were indisputably true, and they were framed in accordance with our duty to the army, the people at home, and our allies. The evening *com-

*muniqué* merely described briefly the events of the day. That of midday was founded on the reports which reached General Headquarters up to the time of my signature—generally 10.30 A.M. I wrote them principally for the army; our soldiers had the right to have their achievements and sufferings reported. The unit, officer, or man mentioned in the *communiqué* was proud of it; was it not uplifting to have one's fame announced to the world? It provided a stimulus of no mean value to the conduct of the war, and an important psychological encouragement to achieve. The people at home, too, were rightly proud to have their sons' deeds recognized. Every word in the official *communiqué* was carefully weighed; great events were given in detail; only the most important of lesser engagements could be mentioned. In quiet times a frequent report read: "Nothing particular," or "No events of importance"; from this an intelligent reader gathered that on all parts of the wide front German men stood night and day doing their difficult duty to the Fatherland with loyal devotion. I should certainly have preferred, in times of stress, to have employed short phraseology rather than to give full reports, for the events of such times were appropriate to these phrases. But a report on the Flanders battle, "Langemarck is held," or lost, would have satisfied nobody.

Losses of ground were mentioned, if they affected the general situation, but not until no harm could be done to the troops engaged by doing so. Nobody could expect me to communicate our losses in guns and prisoners to the enemy, not even the German who thinks so objectively! We were not the iron people about which I was so often told in those very days. The habit of reading enemy *communiqués* had done damage enough already. Suspicion of the reports from General Headquarters went at times so far as to cause them to be compared with enemy reports. That was typically German!

Was it not, for example, a great strategic victory for us to have held the line in Flanders in 1917, although we suffered tactical reverses that cost us prisoners and materials of war. If I mentioned in my report that the enemy had reached our artillery lines, one could deduce the loss in prisoners and guns. Was that not sufficient? Did people wish to wallow in misery?

General Headquarters had allowed the enemy *communiqués* to be published, relying on the clear-sightedness of the German people. I had the impression later that it was a mistake. The enemy used his *communiqués* for propaganda, and lowered our morale. A belated order forbidding the publication of these reports seemed to me even more questionable. France knew what she was doing when she forbade the publishing of our *communiqués*, although ours were never used for propaganda.

I have mentioned that I had also to consider the effect of our official reports on our allies. This was important in our case because our allies relied entirely upon us.

One thing must be admitted, Wolff's commentaries on my reports, edited in Berlin and intended solely for the neutrals, were not happily worded. There was good reason for the tone of these telegrams, but I stopped them, although too late, as soon as I realized the harm they did.

On the Woevre plateau the evacuation of the salient was carried through, though with heavy losses, and the Michel position was occupied. The fighting was dying down by the 13th. According to the reports that reached me, the continuation of the offensive against the Michel position seemed probable. After the 22d the situation changed in front of Von Gallwitz's army group. The likelihood of an offensive here diminished and a battle on both sides of the Argonne appeared imminent.

Duke Albrecht's army group sector, too, was considered in danger, but that was based rather on the conjectures of my colleagues than on reports. I, on the other hand, clung to my opinion that the development of the offensive between Rheims and the Meuse was more likely than an attack in Lorraine.

Our troops had suffered severely; their numerical strength diminished, exhaustion increased. The situation grew steadily worse, but the line held, with the exception of a few weak places on the Second Army sector.

The Austro-Hungarian line held in Italy. There were no indications of an Italian offensive.

Thus matters stood when events in Bulgaria forced us to grave decisions.

On September 15 the armies of the Entente attacked in Macedonia, east of the Vardar, in the mountains between Vardar and Cerna, and also with weaker forces near Monastir. On both flanks the attacks broke down. In the center, where the attack was faced with the greatest obstacles, the Bulgarian 2d and 3d Divisions offered no resistance; they simply surrendered the position. No other explanation exists for the rapid advance of the Entente troops over broken country, eminently suited for defense, hilly, even mountainous. General von Scholtz sought to bring the Bulgarians to a stand on the second line by bringing reserves up in good time, but his hopes were not realized. The 2d and 3d Bulgarian Divisions retreated, as if on a definite plan, without any show of resistance, behind the Cerna in one direction and behind the Vardar in another. The Bulgarian reserves, equal in strength to three German divisions, did not fight at all.

The German troops, which had recently been re-inforced by battalions from Rumania, could not close the gap unaided. The northern descent to the valley

FIG. 46. THE COLLAPSE OF BULGARIA

of the Vardar in the neighborhood of Krivolac was open to the Entente. All further efforts to reorganize and make a stand failed. The Bulgarian Army went home. Only the Bulgarians incorporated in German forces between Lake Prespa and the Cerna behaved better for a time.

On the 16th, or at the latest the 17th, General Lukoff, in command of the troops on the Struma, wired to the King that he must conclude an armistice; he could not desert us publicly and throw himself into the arms of the Entente too soon.

A few days after the 15th a secret report of the French General Staff fell into my hands which made it evident that the French no longer expected any resistance from the Bulgarian Army. Entente propaganda and money, and the United States representative, who had remained in Sofia, had done their work. In this instance again the Entente had made a thoroughly good job of it. Possibly, too, Bolshevist influences from Russia had crept in. Neither the King nor our representative in Sofia knew anything of this. General Jekoff knew all about it; a few days before the battle, which was known to be imminent, he developed ear trouble, I understand, and went to a clinic in Vienna.

General von Scholtz and all the Germans had done their utmost. Where Germans were in command the Bulgarian Army held out. On the mountain sector the Bulgarians refused to have a German command. They even went so far as to leave a divisional general there whom General von Scholtz wished to have removed because he did not trust him, and they made numerous alterations in personnel in that sector.

The suggestion, put forward by the Bulgars to cloak their defection, that I was informed that soldiers' councils had been formed among their troops, is untrue. It is equally untrue to say that we had broken a treaty obligation to leave six divisions on the Bulgarian front, for this obligation was confined to the Serbian campaign of 1915. When I came to General Headquarters in August 1916, there was about one division in Macedonia. The obligation must also have lapsed on the formation of the German Supreme Military Command for the Quadruple Alliance in September 1916. This Supreme Command did not in any way neglect Bulgaria. The forces opposed to each other there were of about equal strength. The Greek troops with the Entente had had no military experience, and their choice of sides was not based on conviction. The Bulgarian Army had had a long rest. It had had the opportunity to strengthen its forces, and ought rather to have helped us in the West than to have sought aid from us. We knew well that the Bulgarian Army was, in fact, in a bad state; but there was ground for the hope that it would be able to withstand the attack which we expected, as, indeed, was the case wherever the men were still willing to fight. We anticipated, now as previously, as did the German chiefs in Bulgaria, partial failure, but we did not expect the complete collapse of their army. The rumor which had circulated in Sofia, to the effect that the army would not continue fighting after September 15, found only too terrible confirmation. We could not answer every single cry for help. We had to insist that Bulgaria must do something for herself, for otherwise we, too, were lost. It made no difference whether our defeat came in Macedonia or in the West. We were not strong enough to hold our line in the West and at the same time to establish in the Balkans a German front to replace the Bulgarian, as we should have had to do if we were to hold that front in the long run.

The Bulgarian Government did nothing whatever to keep up the morale of the troops and the population or to maintain discipline. It gave free rein to enemy influence, and took no steps against any of the anti-German agitations. Entente bribery was the finishing-stroke, even the troops that streamed back to Sofia being well supplied with enemy money. These were true causes of the defection of Bulgaria from the Quadruple Alliance.

There were no illusions about the seriousness of the situation created by the collapse of Bulgaria.

Turkey, too, was now in great difficulties. Her Palestine front was broken beyond repair. Here, again, the German officers and men had done their duty and had fought like heroes on the Jordan. There were, however, limits to our strength, and we could keep the Turkish Army together only for a time.

The English were gaining ground rapidly northward along the coast and along the railway to Damascus. This, it is true, did not amount to a threat to Constantinople, but it had grave effects on the Turks' power to resist. Having regard to the loyalty of Enver and Talaat, this would not have had any decisive effect by itself on the attitude of Turkey; but the Entente had now substantial free forces in Syria, and was also, as a result of the Bulgarian collapse, able at any time to march on Constantinople across the Maritza. There were only very weak Turkish forces here, the task of protecting this line having been hitherto left to the Bulgarian Army on the Struma. It was, of course, possible to bring reinforcements from the Caucasus, and perhaps also from the Ukraine, but we had never succeeded in arranging transportation of troops on any large scale across the Black Sea, the available shipping being insufficient. Reinforcements were, however, moved at once, some battalions from the Ukraine being sent to Constantinople. It was not possible, however, to achieve any permanent result. Constantinople was bound to fall, and whether it fell in November or December made very little difference to the situation as a whole. Once the town fell, it was to be expected that the Entente fleets would establish communication with Rumania through the Black Sea, and send troops through Bulgaria to the Danube. We could not hope to keep Rumania neutral. Sooner or later, the arrival of enemy troops in that country was certain.

It was obvious that the Entente would attempt to recover Serbia, and to make an attack from there on Hungary and Austria, thus giving the *coup de grâce* to the Double Monarchy. Our Balkan front was unstable, and it was quite uncertain whether we would be able to reconstruct it in Serbia and Bulgaria, or even on the Danube. The position in Sofia at first was far from clear. We could not even tell whether the whole Bulgar Army was really demoralized. The Serbian Army had fought for years outside its own country, and had shown a fine example of true patriotism. The Bulgars could well have done the same. Of Old Bulgaria, too, not a foot was in enemy occupation.

If the Bulgar Army fell out altogether, then it would certainly be the time for Germany and Austria-Hungary to send substantial forces to the Balkans.

In the then situation it was vital to do everything to secure our position in the Balkan peninsula, in order to prevent the Entente moving into Hungary and making a flank attack on Germany and Austria. We sent a German division from Sebastopol through Bulgaria and Rumania to Sofia. General von Arz also despatched an Austro-Hungarian division from the Ukraine through Rumania to Serbia. Three German divisions from the East, which had been released for service in the West, and had, in part, already set out on their journey thither, were diverted to Serbia. Lastly, two divisions from the Italian front, which had been handed over to us by General von Arz for service in the West, were also sent. Finally, even from the hard-pressed Western front, General Headquarters sent the Alpine Corps to Serbia; this corps had just been withdrawn from the line, and still had its mountain equipment, which was urgently needed for Serbia. The West thus lost six or seven divisions.

While the German division was to be assembled at Sofia, to support the Government, the others were intended to be grouped at Nish. Transportation was so bad that this could not be completed before the middle of October.

It very soon became clear that nothing more was to be expected from Bulgaria. The division from Sofia was sent to Nish. The King abdicated and left the country. The Government threw itself into the arms of the Entente. The army scattered or allowed itself to be disarmed. The conclusion of the armistice, which would hand the country over completely to the Entente, was to be expected at any moment.

The German troops that had been fighting in the Bulgar Army maintained their order fully. While the Entente troops advanced without ceasing up the Vardar toward Uskub, they withdrew in perfect order westward to Mitrovitza and eastward to Sofia. The establishment of our new front in Serbia depended very largely on the resistance of the Austro-Hungarian troops.

The position in Rumania remained in the highest degree obscure and anxious. We could bring but few troops thither, even including those from the Caucasus.

In the East the Bolshevists were still hostile. Our policy in Great Russia had won us no friends who could now help us.

There was the utmost doubt as to whether we could succeed in establishing in Serbia and Rumania a new flank protection for Austria-Hungary and our Western

front, and in keeping up communications with the
Rumanian oil-fields.

In Italy an attack was sure to come, and it was quite
uncertain how the Austro-Hungarian troops there
would fight.

The general military position could become only
worse; whether it would move slowly or with terrifying
speed could not be foreseen. It was probable that
matters would come to a definite conclusion in a
relatively short time, as actually happened in the
Balkans and on the Austro-Hungarian front in Italy.

In these circumstances I felt compelled to undertake
the responsible task of hastening the end of the war,
and for this purpose to move the Government to
decisive action. Since September 9 General Headquarters had heard nothing of the peace proposals
placed before the Queen of Holland. Since the middle
of August time had passed without anything being
achieved. Count Burian's note had had no success.
Our diplomacy, in the face of the enemy's determination
to destroy us, had a hopeless task. With all this in
mind, I came, not suddenly, but bit by bit, from the
beginning of August onward, and through many hard
inward struggles, to the conclusion that I must act, and
I called Secretary von Hintze to Spa on September 26.

v

Meanwhile the position in Berlin had become most
discouraging, the struggle for power coming ever more
prominently into the foreground. The outward and
visible sign of this struggle was Erzberger's attack on
Count von Hertling, which had raised passions to a
very high pitch. The Emperor's appeal of August 14
for a united and resolute Government had remained
unanswered. I have never fully understood the events

of those days. I did not regard the position of the Chancellor as seriously shaken, his great parliamentary experience having hitherto enabled him to ride every storm. Events in Berlin caused Von Hintze to fix his arrival as late as Sunday, September 29. The Chancellor was also invited to attend by Count Limburg-Stirum. On this occasion I had not asked for his attendance, as early in September his advanced age had been put forward as a reason for not causing him to travel; but I was very glad indeed that he was coming, especially as I was growing clearer and clearer in my own mind as to the steps that ought to be taken.

In the mean time tremendous fighting had broken out again in the West. East of Ypres the Entente attacked, and over all the old Flanders battle-field drove us out of our foremost positions, and, in part, also back over the artillery protective line. We were compelled to withdraw the army to a rearward position.

In the direction of Cambrai, on the 27th, a strong enemy attack gained ground beyond the canal, although every possible step had been taken to resist them. Farther south, up to the Vesle, the front held.

In Champagne and on the western bank of the Meuse a big battle had begun on September 26, French and American troops attacking with far-reaching objectives. Westward of the Argonne we remained masters of the situation and fought a fine defensive battle. Between the Argonne and the Meuse the Americans had broken into our positions. They had assembled a powerful army in this region, and their part in the campaign became more and more important. We held their push, however, the 27th being in the main a day of success for us, while on the 28th, too, we held our lines, apart from certain modifications of our front which were carried out in accordance with our plans.

The whole Western front was thus again the scene of tremendous fighting.

On the 29th of September and following days there was further fighting, bringing the usual difficulties, but not compelling us to sudden, momentous decisions. I wish to insist on this fact in what follows, as earnestly as I do upon the fact that since the middle of August the Government had done nothing whatever to secure peace. This did not surprise me. Was it for General Headquarters to wait until Turkey or Austria-Hungary, who were more urgently affected than we were, moved in the matter? That would have been easy, but did not seem to me to accord with my duty.

Were we to hope, after all our pressure, that the Government would at this stage spur the people to further efforts, or would really take a step toward peace through the medium of Holland? Were there any real prospects of this? Duty compelled us at last to substitute action for idle time-wasting and empty words. The enemy had to be asked for peace and armistice. The military position, which could only get worse, demanded this. We were not yet bound to surrender unconditionally. The enemy would have to speak. Would he talk of conciliation or of violence? In my judgment of Clemenceau and Lloyd George, I feared the worse. Wilson, however, had often stated his terms in the most solemn form imaginable. He, and the great country he represented, must feel themselves bound in honor by these declarations. Besides, the decisive help given in France by the United States, without which the Entente would long before have suffered a military defeat, made it highly likely that Wilson would be able to maintain his views, which he had expressed in the most binding manner, against England and France. We had to secure a clear vision on this matter. If our views of Wilson were right, then we could accept as the basis of negotiations his fourteen points, hard enough, but, at any rate, clear and definite. If, on the other hand, we were disappointed in him, if the enemy imposed too severe conditions, if even their military chiefs refused us the respect to which our brave struggles entitled us, then the fight would have to continue, however hard it might be, and then at last the Government and the people might be brought to heroic measures, when at last they saw clearly what was at stake for Germany in this war.

It was in this respect that I simply could not give up hope of a new moral reinforcement at home. If the enemy gave the same answer as he did in January 1917, then, with any proper leadership, a new spirit of determination and unity would surely appear among the people, which could not be without a favorable effect on our morale. I cannot doubt that this would have had a powerful effect in encouraging the army and the whole war industry, and the sooner it came the more powerful would be the effect. We would thus have the strength to speak once more with no uncertain voice, if the enemy would not listen to reason. There was nothing unduly optimistic in this view. France, Serbia, and Belgium had suffered far more than we had, and had held out. If the war should approach our own territory, if the feeling that he was protecting home and all that the word meant, entered into the heart of each man at the front, who knew full well the meaning of such terms as "theater of war," "battle-field," "lines of communication," if the war with all its destruction threatened German soil, then I felt that our seventy millions of Germans would stand like one man, determined and ready to sacrifice for their country all the mighty strength that still remained to them. Whether France herself, bled

white and suffering worse than we were, would remain
in the field for long after her territory was evacuated,
also was doubtful. In any case, our position was not
so bad that we could have justified a capitulation to
our people or our descendants; on the other hand, we
plainly must sue for peace if peace could be had.

I had slowly come to this fateful conclusion, and now
felt bound and eager to act upon it, whatever others
might say who were not so well informed as to the
military situation as I was. In all the great decisions
of this war, I have followed my own views with a full
sense of my own responsibility. That I should be all
the more abused and held responsible for every misfortune I knew well, but personal considerations could
not weigh with me in the matter.

At six o'clock on the afternoon of September 28, I
went down to the Field-Marshal's room, which was
one floor below mine. I explained to him my views
as to a peace offer and a request for an armistice. The
position could grow only worse, on account of the
Balkan position, even if we held our ground in the
West. Our one task now was to act clearly and firmly,
without delay. The Field-Marshal listened to me with
emotion. He answered that he had intended to say
the same to me in the evening, that he had considered
the whole situation carefully and thought the step
necessary. We were also at one in the view that the
armistice conditions would have to provide for controlled and orderly evacuation of the occupied territory
and the possible resumption of hostilities on our own
borders. From the military point of view, the first
was a tremendous admission. We did not consider
any abandonment of territory in the East, thinking
that the Entente would be fully conscious of the dangers threatening them as well as ourselves from Bolshevism.

The Field-Marshal and I parted with a strong hand-shake, like men who have buried their dearest hopes and who are resolved to hold together in their hardest trials as they have held together in success. Our names were associated with the greatest victories of the World War, and we now shared the conviction that it was our duty to sacrifice our names to insure the step being taken that we had done everything humanly possible to avoid.

## VI

The lines of the discussion to be held with Secretary von Hintze had been settled even in detail at my conversation with the Field-Marshal on September 28. The discussion took place at ten o'clock in the morning of the 29th, at the Hôtel Britannique, Colonel Heye being present.

After the usual courtesies, the Secretary began at once to explain the political situation at home without referring to international matters. He described the position of Count von Hertling as so shaken that he could not remain any longer in office, and even his own position, he stated, was by no means secure. The domestic position was such that a complete change of system, and the formation of a Parliamentary Ministry in Berlin, was essential. He even spoke of the possibility of a revolution. Up to this moment I had assumed that General Headquarters would have to discuss the further steps that it thought necessary with the existing Chancellor and Secretary of Foreign Affairs. A change in these offices at this moment would of necessity bring delay, confusion, and disadvantage. With such deep changes a Government is bound to lose continuity and the grip of business for a time. To whatever conclusion His Majesty might come, of course, the Government would remain to General Headquarters the Government, however changed it might be in form or personnel. The incoming ministers would be fully conscious of the responsibility they would bear if they took office in the existing situation. General Headquarters would have to urge its views upon the new Government just as it would have done on the old, and would have to insure, if an honorable armistice were really obtainable, that the army did not suffer by reason of the change of Government.

In spite of my objections, Von Hintze regarded a change of our whole system of government as essential. He did not think it would be difficult to carry out. I was unable to form any view as to this, as I was not *au courant* of affairs in Berlin.

The Secretary further informed us that the proposal to approach the Queen of Holland had not been carried out, and that no other steps had been taken toward securing peace. Nothing positive, thus, had been done.

After this explanation, the Field-Marshal and I explained the military position and our views as to the armistice conditions. Von Hintze thought the best course was to approach President Wilson with a proposal for an armistice and peace. The Swiss ambassador in Washington had again spoken to our Government of Wilson's high ideals. It was clear, of course, that communications with Paris and London *via* Washington were bound to work slowly, and that an armistice could not be secured by such means at a moment's notice, but only after a lapse of time. The Field-Marshal and I were quite in agreement with what Von Hintze said, and we fully agreed with his proposal, although we suggested that a note identical with that to Wilson should be sent, for information, to the English and French.

After the discussion we went at once to His Majesty, who had come from Cassel to Spa. Von Hintze gave the same explanation of the internal situation, adding his proposals as to the offer to President Wilson for an armistice and peace. The Field-Marshal then described the military situation, which I shortly confirmed. His Majesty was unusually calm. He expressed his concurrence with the proposal to approach President Wilson. In the afternoon, at Von Hintze's suggestion, an order of His Majesty was sent to the Chancellor, who had arrived in the mean time, for the introduction of the parliamentary system into Germany. General Headquarters did not know of this order until after its publication. Count von Hertling thought himself unable to carry it out, and resigned. The search now began in Berlin for the new Parliamentary Chancellor. It was a curious proceeding, in which the Sovereign abandoned all initiative.

To my inquiry, when the new Government would be formed and in a position to come to decisions, and when the note would be agreed upon with our allies and ready for despatch, Von Hintze answered with the date of Tuesday, October 1.

For the time I held fast to this limit.

At the request of Secretary Count von Rödern, who had also come to Spa, and who was to carry on with the Vice-Chancellor the negotiations with the parliamentary leaders, General Headquarters sent Major Baron von dem Busche to Berlin on the evening of the 29th. He was to give explanations in the Reichstag of the military position, if the Government thought it advisable.

Later, at my request, the Field-Marshal decided to accompany His Majesty to Berlin on the evening of the 30th, in order to represent General Headquarters in Berlin. I was, unfortunately, indispensable at Spa, owing to the position in the field.

Already, on the evening of the 30th, Major Baron

von dem Busche had had a short conversation, in the presence of Vice-Chancellor von Payer, with Prince Max, who had meanwhile come to Berlin, and had expressed himself to the Prince in the same sense as he was to address the party leaders of the Reichstag on the following morning. He also gave explanations privately to Von Payer to the same effect.

We thought it better to refuse a suggestion of Count von Rödern, that Von dem Busche should also address the Prussian House of Lords, as I suspected that some influence was intended thereby to be brought to bear on Prussian home politics, the House of Lords being compelled by this direct pressure to abandon the attitude hitherto taken by it to the question of the Prussian Constitution.

At nine o'clock in the morning of October 2, Vice-Chancellor von Payer introduced Major Baron von dem Busche to the assembled Reichstag party leaders, and remained present while the Major spoke. The Major knew my views and intentions, and had committed them to writing before making his speech. His speech was quite to the point. He described the position in the Balkans, as resulting from the defection of Bulgaria, perhaps a little too favorably, and the position on the Western front with full confidence, praising the troops. As was his duty, he stated that the question of reinforcements was very serious, and that we were no longer able to cover wastage. Battalion strength had been reduced to five hundred and forty men, and even this could be maintained only by breaking up twenty-two divisions—i.e., sixty-six regiments of infantry. The morale of our reinforcements was bad.

Major Baron von dem Busche concluded thus:

"We can carry on the war for a substantial further period, we can cause the enemy further heavy losses, we can lay waste his country as we retire, but we cannot win the war.

"Realizing this fact, and in view of the course of events in general, the Field-Marshal and General Ludendorff have resolved to propose to His Majesty that we bring the fighting to a close, in order to avoid further sacrifices on the part of the German people and their allies.

"Just as our great offensive was brought to a stop on July 15, immediately it was seen that its continuation would involve undue sacrifice of life, so now we must make up our minds to abandon the further prosecution of the war as hopeless. There is still time for this. The German Army has still the strength to keep the enemy at bay for months, to achieve local successes, and to cause further losses to the Entente. But each new day brings the enemy nearer to his aim and makes him the less ready to conclude a reasonable peace with us.

"We must, accordingly, lose no time. Every twenty-four hours that pass may make our position worse and give the enemy a clearer view of our present weakness.

"That might have the most disastrous consequences both for the prospects of peace and for the military position.

"Neither the army nor the people should do anything that might betray weakness. While the peace offer is made, you at home must show a firm front, to prove that you have the unbreakable will to continue the fight if the enemy refuses us peace or offers only humiliating conditions.

"If this should prove to be the case, the army's power to resist will depend on a firm spirit being maintained at home, and on the good morale that will permeate from home to the front."

In this speech Major Baron von dem Busche expressed both my program and my views, and this not only for the members of the Reichstag, but also for the new Government that was to be formed from their ranks. The soldier who has had to fight heavy battles for four years with insufficient weapons becomes hardened to dangers, but the man is in a very different position who suddenly has such difficulties, of immeasurable greatness, placed vividly before him.

I had been writing to the Government for two years on end with reference to the shortage of reinforcements. The Auxiliary-Service law, my efforts to have it amended and to bring women more and more into service, my suggestions for rounding up shirkers and deserters at home, were all fully justified, not only by the Hindenburg program, but also by the need of man-power at the front. All my suggestions for raising morale at home constituted questions of infinite importance in the conduct of the war, for the solution of which the Chancellor was responsible to the whole people. All these problems were interdependent. If morale was good, the shirkers and deserters would be kept at the front, the exempted men at home would be more readily released for service; there would be less shortage of reinforcements, and the moral effects of the fighting would be better overcome. The Chancellor never put these considerations before the representative of the people, the Reichstag, although he was expressly requested by General Headquarters so to do. Indeed, all this must have been actually withheld from the Reichstag, just as was my view as to the military situation and the need for peace since August 8. Only thus can one understand the misconception of the whole position that existed in Berlin.

I was so surprised by the effect of Major Baron von dem Busche's speech that I questioned him on his return as to whether he had said anything different from what we had discussed. He gave me the draft of his speech, to which he had kept word for word. This draft lies before me now as I write. I do not know whether the manner in which the Major spoke, or the seriousness of his personality, heightened the effect of his words on his hearers, but such an explanation is humanly possible. The Major himself noticed the great shock his words produced.

His rightly earnest peroration as to what was needed of the people met with no response. I think that, in their great excitement, his hearers did not really understand them. It is inexcusable that the speech was immediately published, and that, too, in a manner calculated to do us the very greatest harm. There was no better means of informing the enemy of our weakness.

It was highly regretable that the outgoing Government did not inform the Major that there was a Pole among his hearers. It must have known that this individual would immediately publish at home and abroad everything that he heard.

On the assumption that the new Government would be informed by October 1, and in my views as to my duty to the army, I held conversations in Spa on September 30 and October 1 with representatives of the Chancellor and of the Foreign Office, and also instructed Major Baron von dem Busche to co-operate with the Field-Marshal in pressing urgently for the despatch of the note on October 1 or at the latest at noon on the 2d.

My principal motive was to avoid further loss of life, but I also attached great weight to the view that the earlier we began the more favorable would our position be at the commencement of the negotiations. If it could not at this time be described as threatening, it might within two or three weeks become of the greatest importance whether the army was to have an armistice, or (if it had to fight on) the moral encouragement from home, twenty-four hours sooner or later. In this position, any delay in the formation of the new Government beyond the time regarded by Von Hintze as essential was inexcusable. I spoke often with my staff to this effect and always acted on this view. In general, I took my stand on what Von Hintze had said and on the speech of Major Baron von dem Busche. These present a complete picture. I am unable to understand how the idea ever arose that I had said that the front would break if we did not have an armistice within twenty-four hours. Between my discussion of September 29 and the Major's speech on October 2, which are wholly consistent with each other, there was no particular military event that could have led to any modification of my views.

I had repeatedly begged Von Hintze to retain his secretaryship, if the new Chancellor would be willing, in order to secure a certain degree of continuity. This was in vain, however. In the night of October 1 the General Staff had simplified communications between His Majesty and the Grand Duke of Baden by laying down a trunk telephone line in order to hasten the appointment of Prince Max. I acted all the time in the same point of view, that, once the decision was taken, we should act at once. We should not let days be wasted, let alone, as so often before, the whole thing come to nothing. I repeat that it was no question of obtaining an armistice in twenty-four hours, but simply of initiating communications with the enemy in some way or another. That this was not equivalent to getting an armistice no one knew better than I, who had a better judgment of the enemy's views than the new Government. In my quiet but anxious thought I was completely mystified by the events in Berlin and could find no explanation thereof, save this, that the members of the Reichstag, not having been properly informed of anything at the right time, had now, in their anxiety and excitement, greatly increased by surprise, misunderstood what Major Baron von dem Busche had said, and that even Prince Max and the new Government were not sufficiently well informed to understand the position properly.

Late in the night of October 1 and in the course of the 2d Colonel von Haeften rang me up repeatedly and described to me the difficulties which were delaying the formation of the new Government and also the despatch of the note. I had informed him on September 30 of the events at Spa and had instructed him to urge the Government to act quickly and energetically; he was not to "jostle" it, but to make clear the grave disadvantages that would follow every day of hesitation and inactivity. To Colonel von Haeften also Von Hintze had explained on the afternoon of September 30 that the new Government would be formed at the latest on the afternoon of October 1, so that the peace offer could be despatched on the evening of the same day.

After the discussion with Colonel von Haeften on the evening of the 1st I understood the situation and realized that Von Hintze's expectation would not be realized. I instructed Von Haeften to see that no unnecessary delay occurred, but in view of the position in Berlin I resigned myself to a postponement of the despatch of the note.

On October 3 the new Cabinet had a meeting, the Field-Marshal being present to represent General Headquarters; he spoke in the same sense as we had done to Von Hintze on September 29, and he set out again, for the benefit of the Chancellor, in my view with absolute accuracy, the views of General Headquarters in a statement running as follows:

General Headquarters holds to the demand made by it on Monday, September 29 of this year, for an immediate offer of peace to the enemy.

As a result of the collapse of the Macedonian front, and of the weakening of our reserves in the West, which this has necessitated, and in view of the impossibility of making good the very heavy losses of the last few days, there appears to be now no possibility, to the best of human judgment, of winning peace from our enemies by force of arms.

The enemy, on the other hand, is continually throwing new and fresh reserves into the fight.

The German Army still holds firmly together, and beats off victoriously all the enemy's attacks, but the position grows more acute day by day, and may at any time compel us to take desperate measures.

In these circumstances the only right course is to give up the fight, in order to spare useless sacrifices for the German people and their allies.   Every day wasted costs the lives of thousands of brave German soldiers.

[Signed]   VON HINDENBURG.


The Field-Marshal had added in his own handwriting that the sole motive of the above-mentioned demand for peace of September 29 was to pave the way to the achievement of an honorable peace.

On October 4 the Field-Marshal returned to Spa, and on the 5th the first note to Wilson was despatched.

General Headquarters had no further influence in the drafting of the note or on the course of the political negotiation.   I regarded the note as somewhat weak in tone, and proposed a more manly wording, but no attention was paid to my demands.   It was, unfortunately, inevitable that we should stand on Wilson's fourteen points.   They were not dissimilar in their general line to the Social Democratic views that had come forward in Germany, and so far as number goes they corresponded with the Austro-Hungarian note to Serbia of the end of July 1914.

In a telegram on October 2 I emphasized "that the

fourteen points of the Wilson note were to serve as the basis for the discussion of peace terms, but were not to be regarded as conditions imposed on us by the enemy." The Field-Marshal had taken the same standpoint in Berlin, but had met with no support from the Secretaries of State, Vice-Chancellor von Payer alone agreeing with him. I was later given the following explanation that all the Secretaries of State were of the opinion that, although the Alsace-Lorraine and Polish questions had now become international, that did not necessarily involve the abandonment of Alsace-Lorraine and of large territories in the East.

A commission was assembled at Spa to work out the armistice conditions. General von Gündell presided, and the Chancellor was represented by Von Hintze. The other members were General von Winterfeldt, Major Brinckmann, and Naval Captain Vanselow.

Efforts were made, by explanations to the army, to eliminate any weakening effects of the request for armistice and peace.

Subsequent to September 29, I discussed the offer with many of the commanders. Those who knew the whole situation agreed that it was the right step, while those who were not so well informed could not see the necessity for it. I had the satisfaction that their confidence in me was not impaired at that time.

## VII

In his first important Reichstag speech, on October 5, dealing with the necessity for continuing the struggle in the event of the conditions being unacceptable, Prince Max took the same point of view as the Field-Marshal and myself.

The Prince said:

"With stout hearts and full of confidence in our

strength, we are resolved, if it be inevitable, to make still further sacrifices for our honor, our freedom, and the happiness of our descendants."

And again:

"Whatever the result of our offer of peace, I know that it will find the country firm and united in its readiness either for an honorable peace or for a life-and-death struggle to the last, on which our people are determined, if it be unavoidable. I am not afraid when I contemplate the possibility of this second alternative, for I know the great strength that still resides among our people, and I know, too, that the clear conviction that each man is fighting for his life will redouble this strength."

The president of the Reichstag spoke to the same effect:

"Every German at home is ready, like every soldier at the front, to sacrifice everything for his country, if need be."

These were fine and stimulating words, which convinced me that the Chancellor, the Reichstag, and General Headquarters were fully agreed as to continuing the fight if the worst came to the worst. But it seemed that the Chancellor and the Reichstag failed to realize that every German had been engaged since 1914 in a fight for his life, and that this fight demanded every sacrifice from us all. The clear consciousness of this had been lost among the thousands of catchwords with which both from inside and outside the soul of the German people was poisoned. It was not until May 1919, when the incredible peace terms were published, that this fact really penetrated the minds of the people and of the National Assembly. Again the selfsame president spoke, using noble and moving words, which seemed like a call to instant action; but the official report did not dare to repeat them. This time also, however, the words remained, simply words. But the situation was there in which the country should have answered their call.

In those days I went quietly forward on my difficult way. When it became quite clear to me, later, after the receipt of the second Wilson note, that Wilson could not or did not wish to prevail, but that Clemenceau and Lloyd George would have their way, and that we were to be enslaved, then I certainly thought it was time to translate words into deeds and not to rest content with empty speeches. I expected from Prince Max and his Government a fulfilment of their professions once they and the country realized that they stood at the grave of all their hopes of a peace by understanding.

It may be that I should have acted more wisely and cleverly if I had definitely put to the Government at the beginning of October the question which it would have ultimately to decide: Will the people fight on for honor's sake and will the Government call up the last man and stir the people again to a real and sacred enthusiasm? I still believe to-day that an appeal to the people at that time would not have met with sufficient success. After four years of war, as appeared from the speeches of October 5, there was still no perception of what the war meant, and neither Government nor people had realized the terrible seriousness of the position. The enemy had not then clearly disclosed his determination to destroy Germany which he made plain for all to read in the second Wilson note.

Prince Max was of the opinion that it would have been more advantageous to have sent the note off about a week later, after first publishing a detailed program of our war aims, making clear to the world our agreement with the principles of President Wilson and our readiness to make heavy sacrifices of our national interests to these principles.

We had already, on October 5, declared ourselves in favor of Wilson's principles. What else was to be done later?

The fact that I, without coming into the public eye, succeeded in moving the Chancellor to swift and energetic action, after all the time since the middle of August had elapsed without anything being done, did nothing to injure the general position. On the other hand, the open mention of the fact that General Headquarters had desired the armistice, and had pressed for it, did as much damage, if not more, than the distorted reports of Major Baron von dem Busche's speech.

Do Prince Max and his supporters really believe that if the step had been taken in the middle of October it would have been regarded as due solely to motives of noble humanity, and as such would have received a friendly welcome from the Entente? The enemy's point of view was altogether too material and self interested for this. Our enemies were also much too clever. They had as good a view of the military position as our General Headquarters. They knew the conditions in the German Army and in Germany as well as they knew the weakness of the Austro-Hungarian Army in Italy and the position in Austria-Hungary itself. From the statements of the numerous German prisoners they took, who often said far too much, they must have had a clear indication of the weak strength of our battalions and of the number of battalions that we had had to break up. Not less can they have been ignorant of the poor morale of the troops and people. From Berlin they heard everything. They anticipated our collapse with the same certainty as they had anticipated that of Bulgaria. No doubt they saw more clearly than we did ourselves that the manner in which the Emperor's order to Count von Hertling, of September

29, was carried out was paving the way to the revolution of November 9.

Any offer of peace without an offer of armistice would also have had no effect whatever on the enemy determination to destroy us. That is made plain by the fate of our earlier offers, which were treated by the Entente as insincere and dishonorable, and by the result of Count Burian's step. In view of the attitude of the enemy, an offer of armistice alone could convince him of our real desire for peace. An offer of peace alone presupposed an enemy ready to meet us half-way and the possibility of concluding negotiations within a reasonable time. Had people forgotten the length of the negotiations in Brest and Bucharest? Now everything was more complicated. The negotiations were bound to last for an indefinite time. Was the army to suffer and bleed all this time, perhaps to no purpose, and without support from home? And if during all these long negotiations our military position became worse, would not that in its turn have a serious effect on the terms of peace?

Only an offer of armistice would enable us to see at once whether those were right who maintained that we could obtain an honorable peace, which I would have heartily welcomed, or whether we should be faced by the offer of a peace of violence, which would have spurred us to new action. There was no time to be lost, for the army was in urgent need of reinforcement from home.

The Entente had to show its colors, and we had to act accordingly. At the present day no more doubt is possible as to the intentions of the enemy. Will those who have been talking continually of reconciliation and of the peace by understanding now at last confess frankly that they have misjudged the enemy, and, after the events of the revolution, that they have misjudged mankind in general, and that the world is not yet ripe for such lessons.

Are we still to believe that labor in the Entente countries is at one with the holders of the theory of the reconciliation of mankind in a peace of understanding?

The German people have gradually realized the futility of this idealism. On February 5, 1919, after the victory of the Government troops in Bremen, *Vorwärts* wrote:

"As Social Democrats we regret deeply that the application of force was necessary. It goes without saying that we are opponents of the use of force. But opposition to force does not mean that we must suffer without resistance every act of violence on the part of our opponents. The love of peace can be maintained only when it is met by similar sentiments. Whoever, from a revulsion in principle to the use of force, cannot make up his mind to oppose force to force is, in the long run, strengthening the rule of violence—that is, the rule of his opponents."

*Vorwärts* thus recovered the position it held in 1914. It upheld the view that I have upheld all my life. The use of force, abroad or at home, brings joy to no man. In 1914 we had to have recourse to arms, to oppose the rule of violence under which we now suffer.

Theory and practice are not the same.

### VIII

President Wilson's answer to our offer of October 5 reached Berlin by wireless on the 9th. From the military standpoint it demanded as a condition precedent to the conclusion of any armistice the evacuation of the occupied territory in the West. We were quite prepared for this. The note left the way open for further discussion.

At the request of Prince Max I went to Berlin and had a long conversation in private with him. I knew the Prince already, he having visited General Headquarters twice, and we had conversed for a considerable time and heard each other's views with interest. We had not much in common. Vice-Chancellor von Payer had now pointed to him as the only possible Chancellor. I was not disposed to differ. I regarded Prince Max, as Prince and officer, as fitted to introduce the new régime. I thought that he would yield, but act as a brake at the same time. After all, he came of an old princely stock that had a real feeling for the greatness of Germany, and there was hope that he might be of use to the country in its anxious hours. The hope was not, however, fulfilled.

With a view to this discussion, the Prince had had a questionnaire placed before me, which was so detailed that it was impossible to answer, but was quite characteristic as showing how little the gentlemen in Berlin knew about the war. I answered it as best I could, in accordance with my views of the situation. I had no reason to be evasive. Wilson's note still allowed us to hope that we should obtain a peace that would not amount to destruction.

Prince Max begged me in confidence to cut myself off from General von Bartenwerffer, Colonel Bauer, and Lieutenant-Colonel Nicolai. I asked what was the accusation against these men. He replied that he did not clearly know and was merely repeating what had been said to him. I thereupon begged him to let me have definite reports, and I would have them carefully examined in the interests of the parties concerned. Nothing was ever received. If any definite complaint had been made I would have investigated it, as was my duty, but I could not get rid of conscientious and loyal men on malicious gossip or unsupported suggestions. The request made a very painful impression on me. That was the sort of work a German Government in Berlin found time to do in such an anxious time.

The Prince also wanted to hear the views of other high officers on the situation. Only General Headquarters, however, had a view of the whole position. The conditions were different with each army. A *posteriori* reasoning from one army to the entire front was impossible. I refused his request. The Field-Marshal and I had alone to bear the responsibility. His Majesty could demand explanations at any moment, but not the Chancellor. The army was still subject to the Emperor as War Lord. At the beginning of November, after I had left office, two army chiefs expressed their views to the War Cabinet, and in essentials they agreed with me. Their differences were all explicable by the limited view which is all that an army chief can have of the whole position.

As is always the case after the defeat of an army, criticisms have been expressed or published, which may be correct so long as they avoid all conclusions that the critic is not himself in a position to check. Conditions in the whole army, and on our extended front, were too varied to admit of generalizations, which personal experiences at one point are apt to tempt men to make. Such generalizations are as dangerous as the empty catchwords which have poisoned the whole of our political life. In science they rank as the most pronounced symptom of the half informed.

Officers who think that they foresaw everything would have done better to go honestly to General Headquarters, in which they had confidence, and there to explain what was in their minds. I received but few letters from such men, and if there was anything new in their letters I summoned them to discuss th matter. For example, I saw in this manner Colonel Bakhaus, of the 78th Field Artillery, who gave me information of considerable value.

It was now time, at last, to ascertain definitely whether the German people would fight on, if the negotiations with the enemy did not lead to an acceptable peace. Preparations had to be made. The press had given us a favorable view of the possibility of continuing the fight. Prince Max had so far done nothing since his speech on October 5 to carry out the intentions he then stated. I therefore put the necessary question. I had also to ascertain the attitude of the new Government to the Eastern question, in order to make the necessary military preparations at General Headquarters.

The sequence of affairs in Russia was quite unknown to the new Cabinet, Vice-Chancellor von Payer being alone acquainted with it. I did not know whether the problem was still the same as it had been in February. In view of the extraordinary importance of the question, I thought a discussion necessary. I questioned the Prince on the Government's views as to the Bolshevist danger, and as to whether the Ukraine was a necessity to us in the future from the point of view of supply. For the settlement of the last question considerable inquiry, and also discussions with Austria-Hungary, were necessary.

On the same day I was present at a meeting of the War Cabinet.

The questionnaire was discussed. I, too, put my questions. Everything was gone over, as above described. No particular resolutions were come to. Walter Rathenau's article in the *Vossiche Zeitung* on the Levée en Masse was also discussed. Such catchwords mean little to me. The position was quite different from that of 1870–71. Strength and energy, however, were in truth available among our people, and had to be thrown into the fight. There were thus some who agreed with my view that the German people, in spite of all they had done, could still do more. The pity of it was that they had not come forward before. It seemed to be particularly characteristic, and filled me with new hope, that men who in other respects held the same views as myself should be arguing for the continuation of the struggle.

At the end of the Cabinet meeting Prince Max thanked me for coming. With the approval of the Field-Marshal, I stated expressly in a short answering speech that we would loyally support the new Government.

The Cabinet was too large. It was called a War Cabinet, but had no resemblance to the War Cabinets of our enemies.

In the evening various leading men in public life came to see me for short moments, and asked me whether General Headquarters had really brought about the offer of peace and armistice. I answered most emphatically that this was correct, as I had already communicated to the public by the press interview of October 9, when there was no longer any military damage to be feared from the disclosure. I owed such a declaration to Prince Max's Government. It was not my function to explain to these gentlemen any further what I thought and how I felt about the matter.

The Government and General Headquarters were quite in agreement over the answer to Wilson's first note. I managed to have inserted in this answer a question as to whether France and England also took their stand on the fourteen points. General Headquarters had nothing to do with the matters of internal politics discussed, nor could we approve the tone of the note. It seemed to show an undignified haste to jettison everything which had hitherto been sacred to us. Our enemies must have marked with satisfaction the way in which we brought ourselves ever nearer to our own ruin.

All over the world the talk of a peace of reconciliation, with its idealistic catchwords, died down suddenly. That was, after all, not surprising, for the press of the world was following the hints of the enemy propaganda, which was itself abandoning the use of the phrase. The Entente had achieved its object by the use of the word, and could now throw off the mask and work for a peace of force. In Germany, too, the word took a more modest place. The men who had hitherto preached the doctrine, and had represented a peace of justice and conciliation as perfectly possible and easy of achievement, had not now the moral courage to confess that they were mistaken as to the enemy's intentions, that they had led the people astray and brought them to their ruin. They were, or some of them were, ready to speak in thoroughly un-German language of Wilson's fourteen points as a peace of justice. So far had we trodden the path of disgrace already. They began a strong agitation against me, alleging that I had now, by undue haste in the armistice offer, brought the people to new misfortunes, after previously making all peace impossible by the extravagance of my demands. Thus did they direct the anger of the people and the army against me. If all those who had previously talked of the peace of reconciliation had spoken of the war and the terrors of defeat, had they seconded my efforts to bring out the last strength of the people and keep them morally equal to the fight, then I should never have needed to ask for an armistice. The time will come when this will be clearly seen.

On October 12 the second note to America was despatched.

## IX

The battle which had broken out on the Western front at the end of September had meanwhile continued to rage. It took the form of a powerful attempt on the part of the enemy to break through the army groups of the Crown Prince Rupprecht and Von Boehn in the direction of Ghent and Maubeuge, and through those of the German Crown Prince and Von Gallwitz on their inner flanks on either side of the Argonne in the direction of Charleville-Sedan. The same idea had been at the root of every offensive operation of the Entente since the autumn of 1915. Up to the present the Entente armies had failed through their own exhaustion and our power of resistance. Now we were weaker, and first one and then another division failed to fight. The number of shirkers behind the front increased alarmingly. The information stations, established to direct stragglers to their positions, were no longer equal to their tasks. The men who fought in the front line were heroes, but there was not enough of them for the long line. They felt themselves isolated. The men looked to their officers, who bore the brunt of the fighting. These officers, with their loyal men, achieved miracles of bravery. Regimental, brigade, and even divisional commanders, with officers and a few soldiers, often with their clerks and servants, personally restored the position, and prevented from breaking through the vastly superior but no longer enthusiastic enemy troops. We may be proud of the men who fought these heroic fights. Our losses, however, were heavy. Our best men lay on the bloody battle-field. Many of our battalions could muster only two companies. Leave was stopped. On account of difficulties of transportation, men on leave at home had to remain there for a time. They stayed longer than was good for them. In the critical November days there should have been very few men on leave in Germany, but, in fact, there were only too many.

The periods allowed to divisions for rest and repair of their equipment and clothing became even shorter. Good divisions had more work thrown on them than the less reliable ones. That, too, had undesirable consequences. The men could not understand why they were so often thrown into the gaps, and in consequence their morale failed. The strain became greater and greater, and strength was exhausted. It was uncommonly difficult to find the true medium and at the same time to reinforce the weak spots. Cases increased where second-line divisions had to be thrown hurriedly into line, and in which formations broke up altogether.

The strain on the nerves of the leaders at the front increased steadily, and they had a heavy task; but they never lost their proud courage or their clear perception of their country's needs. Nothing could break them.

While its right wing held firm on the Yser, below Dixmude, and its left wing held round Armentières, the main body of the Fourth Army was forced back on Roulers and Menin in continual fighting in the early part of October. It developed into a series of local engagements which passed off without important events. On October 14 the enemy renewed his attack. In the direction of Roulers he gained ground beyond the town. Kortemarck, too, we lost. On the other hand, he could not advance much toward Menin. Near Wervicq we beat him off. Local successes also attended the enemy on the 15th, causing our army to fall back to the line Dixmude-Thourout-Ingelmunster-Courtrai. The divisions of the Fourth Army were numerically weak, and the only explanation of the enemy not obtaining successes greater against them, apart from the admirable leader-

ship of the army, lies in the fact that the enemy had
no longer much stomach for the fight. The Fourth
Army was still under the command of General Sixt
von Arnim, whose Chief of Staff was now Major
Humser, a gifted soldier.

The Fourth Army was by this time in such a difficult position that General Headquarters had to withdraw it temporarily from the fight and shorten its line.
The army was ordered to retire on the Hermann line,
behind the canal at Ecloo and the Lys. This involved
the abandonment of the Flanders coast. The submarine station had meanwhile been removed. These
movements of the Fourth Army were undertaken on
October 17, on which day I traveled to Berlin again,
to attend a discussion of the second Wilson note, which
had by this time arrived.

At the same time the Seventeenth Army had to
undergo a difficult time since the enemy break-through
at Cambrai on September 27. Up to October 8 there
were violent battles with varying fortunes on both
sides of Cambrai, and we succeeded in holding the town.
The Second Army was not so successful, being pressed
farther and farther back toward Le Catelet in the early
days of October. Toward Bohain the enemy gained
ground. The right wing of the Eighteenth Army, which
was also engaged in heavy fighting, was affected by
this loss. On the 8th it met another heavy blow in
the neighborhood of Le Catelet and southward therefrom, which it repulsed. In the night of October 9
we were compelled to withdraw the Second Army into
the Hermann line, as there were no reserves to aid it.
To conform with this movement the Seventeenth Army
had to move its left wing and its center back to a line
half-way from Cambrai to Valenciennes, the right wing
for the present being stationed immediately to the
west of Douai. The Eighteenth Army had, like the

Second, to fall back to the Hermann line. Its left wing remained at La Fère.

The decision that the Second and Eighteenth Armies should occupy the Hermann line, whose construction was but little advanced, was a great disappointment to us. I had hoped that the Siegfried line would have held for much longer. Already in the fighting at the beginning of October to the north of St.-Quentin we had been gradually forced out of the position at many spots, but we had, generally speaking, kept the line. We had not even completed the evacuation of the ground in front of the Hermann line.

The retirements were carried out smoothly. On the 10th the enemy had already attacked the new positions and was beaten off. On the 11th, to the northeast of Cambrai, he had a local success against the Seventeenth Army, which was prevented from extending. During the days following up to the 17th there was new fighting on the front of the Second and Eighteenth Armies, which, on the whole, were successful for us.

As a result of the withdrawal of the Fourth Army behind the Lys, we were now compelled to withdraw the Sixth and Seventeenth Armies behind the Scheldt into the Hermann line. On the 17th, the Sixth Army still stood to the west of Lille, and was to evacuate the town on the night of the 18th. Farther to the south the right wing of the Seventeenth and later the whole of that army had to conform to this movement.

It had been decided that in the event of the occupation of the Hermann line the Boehn army group was to be withdrawn. It had now become too narrow, and did not contain sufficient reserve strength. The Second Army now fell under the Rupprecht army group, and the Eighteenth under that of the German Crown Prince. In this group, the Ninth Army was taken over by the Seventh. Here, too, especially having regard to the arrangement of rear communications, there was no longer room for a separate army. General von Carlowitz took the command of the Second Army, and General von Marwitz received that of the Fifth Army near Verdun. His Chief of Staff was Lieutenant-Colonel Wetzell, who had hitherto acted as my assistant. A special Group Headquarters was established for General von Gallwitz. In this case, too, it had proved undesirable to burden a Group Headquarters with the command of an army.

The necessity for economizing forces had led, at the end of September, to the German Crown Prince's army group abandoning the Laffaux salient, which has caused so many losses, and withdrawing to the position behind the Oise-Aisne canal, which we had occupied after the disastrous engagement of October 22, 1917.

On October 2, as had been arranged, the left wing of the Seventh and the right wing of the First Army fell back to the position from which the attack of May 27, 1918, had started. Unfortunately, before this movement was carried out, one division was, in a wholly unexpected manner, crushed on the heights northeast of Fismes. The center of the Seventh Army held the Chemin des Dames firmly, in the face of many enemy attacks.

The defensive battle in Champagne and on the Meuse, on either side of the Argonne, had followed a favorable course, in spite of the absolutely overwhelming superiority of the enemy, which was considerably greater here than on the fronts of the two northern army groups. Our leadership was distinguished for exceptional calm and judgment, and the enemy gained ground but slowly.

The continued and violent assaults on the left wing of the First and on the Third Army caused the army group of the German Crown Prince to decide in the early days of October to break off the fight and to withdraw all the troops to the Hunding-Brunhild line —*i.e.*, half-way to Laon-Marle-Sissone-Aisne from Rethel upward to Grand Pré. General Headquarters was unable to give this group, which husbanded its men carefully, any new forces. It approved the proposal, which was carried out as arranged in the days ending with October 13.

The army group of the German Crown Prince began in the early days of October to withdraw the troops before Rheims behind the Suippes. In the night of the 10th the whole front from the Chemin des Dames to the Argonne was given up, after strong attacks had been beaten off by the Third Army. By the morning of October 13, the Seventh, Third, and First Armies stood ready for defensive fighting in their new and well-constructed line, and the evacuation of the ground in front thereof had been almost completed. The engagements of the last two armies mentioned at the end of September and beginning of October present a fine example of completely successful defensive fighting, of which the leaders and the men may well be proud. The army commanders, Von Einem and Von Mudra, and their chiefs of staff, Von Klewitz and Hasse, once more rendered their country exemplary service.

The enemy followed up the retirement of the German Crown Prince's army group energetically between the Oise and the Aisne, and heavy fighting soon developed round our new positions. In the sweep of the Aisne toward Rethel, the enemy advanced more cautiously. On the other hand, he soon attempted, at first without success, to capture the Vouziers-Grand Pré bend of the Aisne. In the Aire valley, west of the Meuse, the American pressure against our Fifth Army was unusually severe. The battle extended to the east bank of the

Meuse also. In spite of their enormous numerical
superiority, the attacks of the youthful American
troops broke down with the heaviest losses. Their
success on September 26 was merely due to the failure
of a German Reserve Division, and to the fact that at
another point their attack was met not only by a
division, which, though a brave one, was very battle-
worn and had an extended front to hold.

For the present, an attack on the Michel line and the
army group of Duke Albrecht seemed unlikely.

On the 17th the position was thus, that we had fallen
back on the whole of the front west of the Meuse. On
the right wing the retrograde movement was still in
progress. A serious loss was the fact that, in falling
back to the Hermann Hunding Brunhild position, we
had to sacrifice a number of installations that served
the convenience of the troops. For example, we lost a
number of disinfection stations, which were a serious
loss. General Headquarters anticipated a continuance
of the attacks in the direction of Ghent and Maubeuge
between the Oise and the Aisne, and between the upper
Aisne and the Meuse, the latter extending to the right
bank of the Meuse. I also expected considerable wastage
in strength and nerves. At many points we had actually fought with success, and at others the enormous
superiority of the enemy had brought him only small
gains. The result of the further fighting depended
mainly on the maintenance of the men's morale. Every
man required to be kept at the front, and to be inspired
with the utmost determination. The armistice offer
had had an unfavorable effect on the men's spirits, and
war weariness had increased. No stirring call from
home came as a counterblast, and the work of explain-
ing the situation seemed to have been abandoned there.
On this point there were many complaints from the
army. In the end the army and the people would have

to show their colors and let it be seen whether they were really determined to fight, for only thus could we hope to improve the morale of the army. The commands and explanations issued to the troops from Spa were not in themselves sufficient. The intimate connection between feeling in the army and feeling at home could never be more clearly perceived than it was in these critical days. The army wanted to know definitely what was to be expected from the people at home.

The evacuation of the ground behind the new positions was carried on with all speed. The railways were continually worked to the utmost limit of their capacity. Enormous masses of war material had to be dealt with, involving weeks and months of work. I laid great stress on the importance of thorough preparation for the destruction of lines and bridges, which could not but have its effect on operations, and upon the removal to Germany of our own material. I continually discussed with the chiefs of staff the problems of evacuation and destruction. We dealt with the people with the greatest leniency, as we always had done. We have statements to this effect from the inhabitants themselves. It is true that they begged not to be forced to give evidence publicly for us, as they feared opinion in Paris. A neutral commission also came from Brussels to the front, and reported on the care we took of the inhabitants as well as of the damage done to them by the enemy artillery and airmen. What the population had to suffer were the results of the state of war, and not of the manner in which we carried on the war. This is quite plainly established. The Entente, however, brought accusations against us in order to influence Wilson further in its direction.

Farther in the rear we were working hard on the

Antwerp-Meuse line, and I had a new line surveyed along the German frontier.

The Italian front was quiet, but there was talk of an imminent Entente attack. This could be looked forward to only with increasing anxiety, in view of the poor fight the Austro-Hungarian troops had given in Serbia.

In the Balkan peninsula the situation had developed still further to our disadvantage, Bulgaria having surrendered to the Entente.

The submarine station at Cattaro was abandoned and moved to Pola.

In Serbia, General von Kövesc had taken over the command, with a view to the defense of Hungary. Under his command were the troops that had retired under General von Pflanzer-Baltin from Albania to Montenegro, and the allied troops on the Morava under the Eleventh German Army Headquarters—General von Steuben. General von Kövesc had a difficult task. The Austro-Hungarian troops were of little value, the Germans were of an old class and were not up to complement, and the Alpine corps was battle-weary.

Austro-Hungarian troops were supposed to cover the deployment of the German and Austro-Hungarian troops in the Morava valley south of Nish.

The formations which retired by way of Sofia had gone farther back to Lom-Palanka, to be transported across the Danube. French divisions were in pursuit. They reached the Danube on the 17th. Unrest was increasing in Rumania.

The Headquarters Staff of Von Scholtz had been removed to Rumania. Here, under instructions from Field-Marshal von Mackensen. it undertook the defense of the Danube.

The position in Serbia and on the Danube was thus not safe, but it was also not yet in collapse.

At Adrianople and from the Maritza downward there were already English troops. The Turkish frontier guard was unusually weak there. The German troops and officials in Constantinople were preparing, in the event of an Entente attack on the town, to leave by sea and proceed to Odessa.

This was the military situation that I had to consider in deciding my attitude to the second Wilson note.

## x

In his answer to our second note Wilson gave us nothing; he did not even tell us whether the Entente took its stand on the fourteen points. He demanded, however, the suspension of the submarine war campaign, stigmatized our conduct of the war in the West as a violation of international law, and once again sought in obscure phrases to meddle with intimate questions of our domestic politics. No doubt was any longer possible as to the intentions of our enemies, or as to the predominating influence of Clemenceau and Lloyd George. Wilson was not prepared to stand against the comprehensive claims of France and England. We had weighty decisions to make. We now faced the question whether we were to surrender unconditionally to the Entente or whether the Government was to call on the people to fight a last fight of despair. We had to return a firm and dignified reply to the note, and to emphasize once more our honorable anxiety for an armistice, but at the same time to maintain warmly the honor of our brave army. We could not allow ourselves to be deprived of our submarine weapon, for this would amount to capitulation.

The note was discussed on October 17 at a meeting of the War Cabinet in Berlin. Colonel Heye and I were present. I had also requested General Hoffmann to attend. On this very day the Eighteenth Army was fighting a desperate battle at the front.

The Chancellor again asked a number of questions, and, turning to me, made a statement to the following effect: that a new note had arrived from Wilson, containing an increase in his demands; that Wilson had plainly been placed in a difficult position through pressure from external influences; that he apparently hoped that we would give him the opportunity to continue negotiating with us and to overcome the opposition of the "never-endians." In order to reply to the note, it was necessary to understand quite clearly the military position.

I had a different view as to the sentiments of the enemy, and could see nothing but his intention to destroy us.

To the many questions that were put to me, I took up in general the following position:

"Already on a previous occasion I have been asked a number of questions to which it is impossible to give precise answers. War is not a sum in arithmetic. There are in war many probabilities and improbabilities. What will actually happen no man knows. When we went to East Prussia in August 1914, and the orders were given for the battle of Tannenberg, even then none knew how things would go, or whether Rennenkampf would or would not move. He did not move, and we won the battle. Part of war is luck, and luck may come Germany's way again.

"I can only tell you my convictions. For what I tell you the responsibility is mine, and has been mine for four long, weary years."

In particular the question was discussed whether by transferring from East to West all our divisions, or even a part of them, the front could be so strengthened that we could hold out a for a long time. To deal with this, one had to know how much General Headquarters could withdraw from the East. To know this, I had to have an answer from the Government to my two earlier questions as to the danger of Bolshevism and the importance of the Ukraine to us. If the Government had a different attitude from that which it took up in February, then it must tell me so. At this time we had in the East, in Russia, and Rumania, twenty-six divisions composed only of men over thirty-five, and weak in strength. In Lithuania there was one soldier to every eighteen square kilometers (seven square miles). In the West there were 185 divisions; many had had to be broken up. Divisions recently removed from East to West had not done well under their new conditions, and I had had very unfavorable reports of them. In spite of the shortage of men, drafts from the East were received with the greatest reluctance. They brought a bad morale and had an unfavorable effect on their fellows. According to the explanations of General Hoffmann, the temptations to which the men were exposed from the corruption of Jewish traders in the East and from Bolshevist propaganda, and, indeed, also by propaganda from home, had broken their fighting spirit. How far this had gone was not known until the beginning of November. The views of the General as to the possibility of employing these divisions in the West were quite in accord with my own experience. Nothing that they could do could produce any such alteration in the military situation as would bring the enemy to negotiate with us. They lacked the necessary strength to fight in the West. For any work that might fall to them in the East, even for an attack on the Soviet troops, they seemed still fully capable.

Our blockade against the Bolshevists was now everywhere very thin and only barely effective. General

Hoffmann and I explained that the danger from Bolshevism was very serious, and that the maintenance
of this frontier guard was essential.

The Government as such did not appear to take any
definite stand on principle against Bolshevism. It did not
speak clearly or decisively.  In spite of the objection of
General von Lynder, the president of the Imperial court
martial, the Government had released Liebknecht from
prison, and it stood idly by while Herr Joffe distributed
money and pamphlets and prepared for the revolution.
Our warnings, as well as those of the Headquarters Staff
in the Mark of Brandenburg, received no attention.
It appears that about this time General Hoffmann,
through his relations with Herr Solf, at last succeeded
in opening the eyes of some members of the Government.  As a party, the Majority Socialists recognized
the great danger of Bolshevism.  But while *Vorwärts*
on the one hand issued warnings against this force,
on the other it gave it the greatest help by its attacks
on constituted authority and its advocacy of class
hatred.  At last, at the end of October, Joffe was dismissed.  We were thus once again at war with Russia,
and the need to take precautions against Bolshevism
became all the greater.

At this meeting I emphasized once more the infinite
economic importance of the territory under the control
of the Commander-in-chief in the East.

No decision could be made as to evacuating the
Ukraine, the necessary preliminary discussions not having yet taken place, and the question being one quite
impossible to settle out of hand.  Count von Rödern
wanted to abandon the Ukraine, as the civil population
got little benefit from it.

Secretary Solf mentioned the great wealth of the
Ukraine, and desired also that it should be retained on
humanitarian grounds.  I could not look at the ques-

tion from any other point of view than that of Germany's advantage.

Secretary von Waldow brought no enlightenment, but enlightenment was essential, and I begged the Chancellor to have the question exhaustively examined. General Headquarters had occupied the Ukraine in February in agreement with the Government, the latter being then fully convinced of the absolute necessity for the step, not merely to avert the danger of Bolshevism, but also to secure the supply of the Quadruple Alliance. In the summer, Austria-Hungary had been kept alive only with the help of the Ukraine. We in Germany had obtained from the country cattle and horses, and much raw material, even if we had not the corn we expected. The war was not over. Rumania's harvest was a complete failure. By early threshing we had again had to mortgage our future. We and our allies had to look somewhere for additional foodstuffs, and the Ukraine was the only possible source. Without this aid, there would be a severe crisis in the early summer of 1919. The Government never cleared up this question of the value of the Ukraine in the autumn of 1918. Had we evacuated at this stage, which would have taken us a considerable period of time, we should have gradually released ten divisions which were not really fit for the line. The advantages would not have been equal to the disadvantages that we should have brought upon ourselves by evacuation.

I am confident that not a man too many was kept in the East.

We now turned to discuss the vital question of how much the people could and would still give to the army. Everything else depended on this. I had hoped that the Government would have been clear on this point. The new Minister of War gave me a more optimistic account of the prospects for reinforcements than I had hitherto received. He estimated a figure of 600,000 men. I could not check his figures. I was very greatly impressed by the statement that 60,000 to 70,000 men were immediately available to be sent into the army. Why had they not been sent sooner? I said, "If I have these reinforcements now, I can face the future with confidence, but I must have them immediately." The Minister promised not to lose a day.

I now turned to the question of morale at home and in the army. I expressed myself as I have so often done in this book. I emphasized that the army, at this moment above all, was in need of support.

The Chancellor requested the three Parliamentary Secretaries of State to give their views.

Secretary Grœber did not speak quite to the point on the matter.

Secretary Scheidemann spoke very seriously. He was glad to believe that we could still release hundreds of thousands of men for the army, but it would be quite wrong to suppose that these men would improve the spirit in the army. Everywhere working-men were beginning to say, "Better a terrible end than terrors without end." Scheidemann stated that the cause of this regretable attitude was the lack of food, which he attributed partly to the shortage of wagons. I agreed instantly to adopt, so far as lay in my power, every measure that could relieve the shortage. In general his statement constituted a serious indictment of our Government, which had allowed the splendid spirit of 1914 to be so terribly changed. Secretary Scheidemann's speech amounted to a declaration of bankruptcy of the domestic policy of the Chancellor and the Majority parties.

Secretary Haussmann thought that an appeal to the people would have considerable effect.

Secretary Erzberger was not present. He had recently lost his son in the service of his country.

Vice-Chancellor von Payer did not take so serious a view as Scheidemann. He spoke in agreement with me, more or less to the following effect:

"The arrival of the second Wilson note consolidated public opinion, as people saw that it was a question of life and death, but the mood has changed again. Men realized that the nation is, speaking economically, to be destroyed. If we say to people: 'There is just a chance, if you hold out. But if you cannot hold out for another fortnight, then you must expect Germany to be more or less wiped out from among the nations. You must expect an absolutely crushing burden of indemnities'—then you will never rouse them again.

"If you succeed in having the note so regarded that the people gain the certainty, 'We are, true, in an anxious situation, but we are not throwing up the sponge,' then we are not lost."

Secretary Friedberg spoke to the same effect, adding the view that in any case we must act quickly.

In addition to the question of reinforcements, there was always the question of nerve strain, on which everything depended. Why had not these gentlemen, who knew of these available men, called them up sooner? This is to me an insoluble and disastrous riddle.

Of the general military situation I had nothing new to say. Of the Western front I repeated what I had said on October 10: "I regard a break-through as possible, but not probable. If you ask me on my conscience, I can only answer that I do not expect it."

I stated, however, that the position might grow worse at any moment. The recent fighting had brought no surprises. The front had held neither better nor worse than before. Our troops had done what we expected of them. The enemy's strength in attack seemed to be falling off.

The negotiations with Wilson had so far led to no result. We were in every respect masters of our own actions and could break off or continue the negotiations. We had a free hand to do either. Is it a crime to fight on when one honestly wants peace and cannot get it? Is it a crime to abandon the hope of a compromise for which one has honestly striven when the opponent demands more than one can give? Did any one accuse Trotzky of dishonesty when at the beginning of February he did not sign the peace treaty? None could doubt that we honestly desired peace. On the other hand, we had every right to protect our life and our honor to the last. The Government owed a duty to the people to use every possible means, at any rate, not to break off too abruptly the negotiations for the compromise that it had so honestly sought. It was a principle of elementary common sense; the stronger we were in the field the better we could negotiate.

Moreover, it was no more than our duty to continue the fight, unless we were prepared to surrender unconditionally to an enemy from whom we had nothing to hope. Negotiations might improve our position, but, in any case, could not make it worse. The best elements of the army, and a large part of the people, expected us to negotiate.

The majority of the German people were ready and willing to sacrifice the last of their strength to the army, and it was the duty of the Government to carry out this sacrifice. I spoke to this effect, using the same tone as that of the Chancellor in his speech of October 5, and I also suggested that Ebert, as leader of the Social Democrats, should be given some leading post, in order by his help to strengthen the resistance of the people and bring new strength into the fight. I agreed with Admiral Scheer in holding it impossible to abandon submarine warfare, which was continually reducing England's strength. To throw down a weapon at the enemy's bidding would be the grossest confession of weakness imaginable, and would immeasurably increase the enemy's demands.

Secretary Solf accused me of a change of front. I replied, in astonishment, that the Government had also been willing to continue the fight if the worst came to the worst. Even if I had now spoken with more confidence than before, the Secretary could and should be glad to hear any more favorable judgment of the situation, since the negotiations must thereby be rendered more easy for him. Besides, I was not thinking of breaking off at the moment, but was only pressing for clearness in our thought and final aims. I summed up my views once again in the following phrases:

"Now, as before, I hold that if it be in any way possible, we must initiate armistice negotiations. We cannot, however, accept any conditions that do not provide for an orderly evacuation of the territory. This involves a time limit of not less than two or three months. Nor must we accept anything that makes it impossible for us to renew hostilities. The note forces one to assume that this is the object of the enemy. The conditions are designed to put us out of the field. Before we go into details, the enemy must tell us clearly what his terms are. We do not wish to break off with Wilson out of hand. On the contrary, we must say: 'Do tell us clearly what we are to do! But, if you ask anything inconsistent with our national honor, or desire to render us incapable of fighting further, then our answer must be "No!"'

"In saying this, I am not departing from my previous position in the least."

I then dealt with the destruction which the Entente alleged that we had carried out on the retreat.

"We have, in accordance with our duty, done everything to limit the destruction as far as is consistent with military needs. It would be absolutely inexcusable to leave houses undestroyed, for billets are of great help to the enemy. The enemy himself destroyed the houses afterward. In Lille we left unhurt the electric light, the water-supply, and the trolley line, but destroyed the telegraphs, telephones, and railways. The worst damage was done by the English cannon and airmen.

"The army is not responsible for isolated cases of brutality. I have done my best to stop any such abuses. I request that this be emphasized in the note to Wilson, for the army has a right to that."

The meeting then closed. Secretaries Grœber and Haussmann, near whom I was sitting, expressed to me their pleasure that I had so improved their spirits. I traveled back to Spa in confident mood.

There was some discussion at this meeting about a catastrophe which General Headquarters was said to have reported at the end of September or the beginning of October. This, taken together with Secretary Solf's idea that I had changed my views, led me to discuss once again with Major Baron von dem Busche his speech of the beginning of October. He could again only refer to his notes. Colonel von Haeften, too, had never spoken of any such catastrophe.

The improvement in spirits in Berlin lasted until noon on October 19, when optimism disappeared. I have no better knowledge of events there. Why did not the Secretaries of State, who had expressed themselves so confidently on the 17th, move to action? They knew well what was at stake. It is to me wholly incomprehensible that, on May 12, 1919, Secretary Konrad

Haussmann should say, amid great applause, "If our army, if our workers, had known on November 5 and 9 that the peace would take this terrible form, the army would not have laid down its arms, but would have fought on." Everything that has come about was plainly to be expected on October 17. That is a historical fact that cannot be denied. We warned them against capitulation. All that was required was to look the facts in the face, to cease deceiving themselves and the people, and endow themselves with resolution in action, such as was to be found at General Headquarters.

On the 20th we received the new draft answer at Spa. The submarine campaign was abandoned, the way to capitulation, with all its disastrous consequences, was undertaken. The Field-Marshal and I drew attention to this point of view once again, and again warned them of the consequences. We proposed a rallying-cry to the people. We refused to take any part in drafting such an answer. The War Cabinet became very excited at this; why, I do not know. We were men with views of our own, and we followed the course which we regarded as the right one, and which we had always pursued.

The answer to Wilson was despatched on the 20th. The submarine campaign was abandoned. This concession to Wilson was the deepest blow to the army, and especially to the navy. The injury to the morale of the fleet must have been immeasurable. The Cabinet had thrown up the sponge.

The Chancellor did not alter the situation by his speech on October 22: "The man who takes his stand honorably on the peace of justice takes also upon himself the duty not to bow unresisting to a peace of violence. A Government which had no sense of this would deserve and earn the contempt of the fighters and workers." This speech, too, was unaccompanied by action. Nothing was done to raise morale at home or in the field. Prince Max had pronounced judgment on himself and his colleagues.

The Minister of War alone did any work striving to provide the reinforcements. Here, too, nothing was achieved, for part of the men refused to go to the front, and the Government yielded!

XI

On October 23 or 24 Wilson's answer arrived. It was a strong answer to our cowardly note. This time he made it quite clear that the armistice conditions must be such as to make it impossible for Germany to resume hostilities, and to give the Powers allied against her unlimited power to settle themselves the details of the peace accepted by Germany. In my view there could no longer be doubt in any mind that we must continue the fight. From the impressions I gained at the meeting of October 17 I felt quite confident that the people, even after the loss of all these valuable days, were still to be won over to this course.

In the West events, from this date on, took the following course: the Fourth Army completed its rearward movement into the Hermann line, in the closest contact and in constant fighting with the pursuing enemy. Bruges, Thielt, and Courtrai were evacuated on the 19th. On the 20th there was fighting on the Lys, the enemy taking the eastern bank around Deinze. He attempted to force us to leave the Lys by strong pressure between the Lys and the Scheldt. On the 25th the fighting again took the form of a battle, in which the enemy, attacking the Scheldt, slowly gained ground toward Ghent-Oudenarde. Between the Lys and the Scheldt the fighting also implicated the Sixth Army.

The Sixth and Seventh Armies had abandoned Lille and Douai on the 17th, and had fallen back, in touch with the Fourth, behind the Deule canal, in the direction of Avelghem, Tournai, and Valenciennes. On the 20th the enemy was approaching these towns. The civil population again took part in the fighting.

The southern wing of the Seventeenth Army and the Second and Eighteenth were in heavy fighting, the enemy attacking heavily on the 17th and 18th between Le Cateau and the Oise. We were forced to withdraw the front behind the Sambre-Oise canal, from the district to the southwest of Landrecies as far as the Oise. After a pause on the 19th, the enemy attacks extended from the 20th onward toward the north. The enemy pressed on past Solesmes and Le Cateau, in the direction of Landrecies. Our losses were heavy, and the troops did not fight well at all points. Other troops, however, conducted themselves magnificently. It was the same as ever.

At first the army group of the German Crown Prince had left the wing of the Eighteenth Army in its position down the Oise as far as La Fère. The enemy's efforts to cross the Oise were defeated. On the 20th the Hermann line, between the Oise and the Serre, was occupied. The enemy attacked this line in force, and violent battles developed.

The Seventh and First Armies were attacked between the Serre and the Aisne. In the main they maintained their positions, and on the 25th they threw back a powerful enemy attack with heavy losses.

Again, on the Aisne, as far as Vouziers-Grand Pré, in the Aire valley, and toward the heights to the left of the Meuse, the enemy was applying strong pressure. The fighting was heavy and costly, but did not lead to any important changes in our line. As before, the battle extended to the eastern bank, without producing any essential alterations here, either. Farther southeastward, as far as the Swiss frontier, the line was quiet.

On the evening of the 25th the Western front was under the greatest strain. There was fighting from the Dutch frontier to Verdun. No help was coming from home. Every encouragement was absent. It was miraculous that the troops should fight so heroically.

The work of evacuation went on, in spite of the terrible condition of the railways.

The construction of the Antwerp-Meuse line progressed slowly. Its fortification was beginning. General Headquarters had to reckon with the possibility of withdrawing the front back to that line at the beginning of November in order still further to shorten it. Of course, this would be of advantage to the enemy also. On account of the railway destruction, the enemy attacks in the north would be bound to lose strength. It was to be expected that the enemy would now attack in Lorraine.

In Italy, on the 24th, the Italian attack began. At first it was directed to the mountain front, but from the 26th onward it was raging with full force on the Piave. By the evening of the 25th there had been no important developments. The Austro-Hungarian front was still holding. Nevertheless, I expected a quick conclusion of peace with Austria-Hungary. In cooperation with the Bavarian Ministry of War, the first protective measures on the Tyrolese frontier were arrranged.

In Serbia, General von Kövesc found it necessary to order the retirement behind the Danube. There was no change on the Danube frontier of Rumania, and on the line of the Rumanian Army beyond the Sereth. Matters there still hung in the balance.

A rallying of the German people would in any case

have improved matters. It is impossible to say for how long we might have continued the struggle. The enemy morale was not too clearly known to us. If only it had a firm will, a great nation was not to be defeated easily. France in 1870–71 had proved that, as had the Boers in their war with England. Winston Churchill's estimate of the military position is given in The *Sunday Pictorial* of January 12, 1919, in the following words:

"A very little more, and the submarine warfare, instead of bringing America to our aid, might have starved us all into absolute surrender. . . .

"It was neck and neck to the very end. But because the whole nation worked without flinching . . . we have at last come safely through.

"The more one knows about the struggle the more one realizes on what small, narrow, perilous margins our success turned."

On October 25 the Field-Marshal and I placed our views before His Majesty in Berlin, whither we had again traveled. We expressed the view that we must fight on. The new head of the Civil Cabinet, Excellency von Delbrück, was present. While keeping most opinions of his own in the background, he took the same point of view as Prince Max. We were surprised to learn that he was ignorant of the fact that we had discussed the question of peace with the Chancellor as early as the middle of August. His Majesty came to no decision, but he showed full confidence in me. He referred us to the Chancellor. The latter was ill, and Von Payer received us and Admiral Scheer at nine o'clock in the evening. He seemed personally ill disposed toward us, in contrast with his previous attitude. He knew well that the Cabinet wanted me to go, as I was for fighting on. The Minister of War was also called in. He had not stood up in the Reichstag and in the Government for the Emperor and the army, for had he done so he would have had to resign. It was a very sad hour, it being clear that the Government did not intend to fight any more. It thought it was necessary to sacrifice everything. Could it already hear the murmurs of the revolution of November 9? Did it hope to save the country from the revolution by capitulating to foreign enemies? I spoke seriously and deeply moved. I uttered a warning against the enemy's desire to destroy us, and against any hope being placed in Wilson.

I also spoke warningly of the spread of Bolshevism in Germany and of the agitation against officers which was then assuming large proportions. That has been the decisive turning-point in Russia, too.

I warned them not to do anything to shake the position of the Emperor. I reminded them that His Majesty was the chief of the army, which looked up to him as its head, and that we had sworn loyalty to him. These immaterial points were not to be underestimated, for they were part of our flesh and blood and held us fast to the Emperor. Whatever affected the Emperor affected the cohesion of the army.

The weakening of the position of the Corps of Officers and of the Supreme War Lord at a moment when the army was submitted to the severest test was the most short-sighted act imaginable. It constituted the heaviest blow against order in the army and the State at a time when the army was called to be the guardian of civil order. At a later stage it did more to undermine the discipline of the army than the hasty evacuation of the territory on the left of the Rhine, to which we allowed ourselves to submit.

I spoke in the same sense at the beginning of November to certain of the Social Democratic leaders. They, too, could not grasp what the Emperor meant to the army, not only to us regular officers, but also to the rank and file. My view has been confirmed by many incidents happening since November 9.

I did not discuss with Von Payer the incidents which had taken place in the Reichstag in the morning and were directed against General Headquarters. I had received but one report, and that an incomprehensible one, on the matter. On the evening of the 24th, shortly before leaving Spa, there was brought to me the following proclamation, already signed by the Field-Marshal, which expressed the views prevailing at General Headquarters on the third Wilson note. It appeared essential that General Headquarters, in its dealings with Berlin, should assume a definite attitude toward the note, in order to eliminate its ill effect on the army. The telegram to the army ran thus:

*For the information of all troops:*

Wilson says in his answer that he is ready to propose to his allies that they should enter into armistice negotiations, but that the armistice must render Germany so defenseless that she cannot take up her arms again. He will negotiate with Germany for peace only if she concedes all the demands of America's allies as to the internal constitutional arrangements of Germany; otherwise. there is no choice but unconditional surrender.

Wilson's answer is a demand for unconditional surrender. It is thus unacceptable for us soldiers. It proves that our enemy's desire for our destruction, which let loose the war in 1914, still exists undiminished. It proves, further, that our enemies use the phrase "Peace of Justice" merely to deceive us and break our resistance. Wilson's answer can thus be nothing for us soldiers but a challenge to continue our resistance with all our strength. When our enemies know that no sacrifices will achieve the rupture of the German front, then they will be ready for a peace which will make the future of our country safe for the broad masses of our people.

At the front, October 24, 10 P.M.

[Signed]  VON HINDENBURG.

I had been so busy that the major who had to draft the telegram, having regard for the imminent railway journey, had taken it first to the Field-Marshal and then to me. Usually all documents for signature by the Field-Marshal were submitted to me first to be countersigned. This order was not consistent with the answer sent to Wilson on the 20th. I was surprised, and asked the Major whether the tone of the order was really in harmony with the views of the Government. He said that it was, and that the order was wholly consistent with the explanations given to the representatives of the press in the Foreign Office by Colonel von Haeften and Privy Councilor von Stumm. I became hopeful again, and added my signature. It appeared later that the view that the wording of the telegram corresponded with the views of the Government was incorrect, and Colonel Heye stopped the publication of the order. From Kovno, where revolutionary organizations already controlled the telephones, it came to the knowledge of the Independent Socialists, and thus to that of the Reichstag. It was further, in the usual course, given out confidentially in the press discussion. At the Reichstag meeting on the 25th at noon a storm of indignation burst over General Headquarters. The Government did not move a finger to protect us, although we were still the head of a mighty army. It was not until late on the evening of the 25th that I heard of this incident or I would have discussed it with Von Payer. Later the history of the creation of this order was explained in all its context to the Government. Meanwhile, however, the distortion of the facts had achieved its end and I was dismissed.

The discussion on the 25th in the Ministry of the Interior lasted about an hour and a half or two hours. General von Winterfeldt and Colonel von Haeften waited for me below. I was deeply moved and could say no more than: "There is no hope. Germany is lost." These two were greatly touched.

In the German note of October 27 we capitulated.

At eight o'clock on the morning of the 26th, still in the mood of the previous evening, I wrote, tendering my resignation. In this I adopted the point of view that, in the discussion of the previous day with Vice-Chancellor von Payer, I had gained the impression that the Government would not act in the crisis, that His Majesty, the country, and the army were thus placed in an untenable position, that I was counted as anxious to prolong the war, and that, in view of the attitude taken by the Government to Wilson, my departure might ease their position. I therefore begged His Majesty graciously to accept my resignation.

In accordance with his usual practice, the Field-Marshal came to see me at nine o'clock on the morning of the 26th. I had placed my letter on one side, as I had made up my mind not to speak to him of it until the letter was before His Majesty. The Field-Marshal was master of his own destiny and I did not want to influence him. The form of the letter attracted his attention, and he begged me not to despatch it, but to retain office. I ought not to desert the Emperor and the army at this time. After an inward struggle I consented. I became convinced that I ought to retain my post, and proposed to the Field-Marshal that we should make another effort to see Prince Max. He did not receive us, still being ill. While I was waiting for news on this point, Colonel von Haeften reported to me that the Government had succeeded in persuading His Majesty to dismiss me, the ostensible reason put forward being the order above mentioned. His Majesty would shortly send for me to the Bellevue Castle. I was no longer capable of astonishment, and had no anxiety about myself per-

sonally. Before this conversation ended we were
suddenly called, at this unusual hour, to attend His
Majesty.

On the way from the General Staff Office to the
Bellevue Castle I told the Field-Marshal what I had
just heard. Later I heard it stated that Prince Max
had put the question of my dismissal forward to His
Majesty as a Cabinet question.

The Emperor seemed wholly changed. Speaking to
me alone, he spoke especially against the army order of
the evening of the 24th. There followed some of the
bitterest moments of my life. I said respectfully to His
Majesty that I had gained the painful impression that
I no longer had his confidence and that I accordingly
begged most humbly to be relieved of my office. His
Majesty accepted my resignation.

I went back alone. I did not see His Majesty again.
After my return to the General Staff Office, I said in
bitterest grief to my officers there, among whom was
Colonel von Haeften, that in a fortnight there would
be no longer an Emperor in Germany. They held
clearly the same view. On November 9 Germany and
Prussia were republics.

A moment later the Field-Marshal came to me in
my room. I could only show him the tender of resignation which three hours before he had prevented me
from despatching. We then separated.

I gave up my post at once. I sent off the letter
which I had written in the morning; I should have now
worded it differently.

On the evening of the 26th I went back to Spa, to say
farewell to my officers, with whom I had shared joys
and sorrows through so many years, and to put my
personal affairs in order.

On the morning of the 27th I was at General Headquarters. In the afternoon I said good-by. I was much

moved. It was very hard for me to leave my officers and the army at this anxious time, but, however hard it was, I could do nothing else, in my view of my position as an officer over against the supreme head of the army.

In my life as a soldier I have trodden but one path, the straight path of duty. One and only one great thought has moved me, the love of my country, of the army, and of the hereditary ruling house. For them had I lived, even in these last four years. My one aim was to break the enemy's desire for our destruction and to secure Germany's future against new hostile attacks.

On October 27 I stood in Spa, in the prime of my life, at the end of a military career which had brought me infinite work to do, and at the same time a responsibility such as falls to the lot of few men.

In the evening I left Spa. In Aachen I sought out my first war billet. I thought of Liège. There I had found my manhood, and had not altered since. My muscles stiffened. I went back home.

# CONCLUSION

FROM the end of October events followed one another at an increasing pace. In the West, on November 4, the German Army was withdrawn in good order to the Antwerp-Meuse line under the pressure of the enemy from Verdun upward. The Alsace-Lorraine front, well organized, awaited an enemy attack.

The Austro-Hungarian Army was completely dissolved as a result of the fighting in Upper Italy from October 24 to November 4.

Hostile troops were moving on Innsbruck. General Headquarters took comprehensive measures for the protection of the southern frontier of Bavaria. In the Balkan theater we held the Danube.

We stood alone in the world.

At the beginning of November the revolution, brought about by the Independent Socialists, broke out, starting in the navy. The Government of Prince Max had not the strength to nip in the bud the outbreaks which, at first, on the Russian pattern, were only local. It was incapable of leadership, and let things run their course.

At noon on November 9 Prince Max, of his own initiative, announced the abdication of the Emperor. The old Government gave orders to the troops which amounted to a prohibition of the use of weapons, and immediately afterward it disappeared.

The Emperor was confronted with a *fait accompli*. On the advice given to him in General Headquarters at Spa, he went to Holland. The Crown Prince followed him, after Berlin had refused his unconditional offer of further service. The princes of the states abdicated.

On November 9 Germany, lacking any firm hand, bereft of all will, robbed of her princes, collapsed like a house of cards. All that we had lived for, all that we had bled four long years to maintain, was gone. We no longer had a native land of which we might be proud. Order in State and society vanished. All authority disappeared. Chaos, Bolshevism, terror, un-German in name and nature, made their entry into the German Fatherland. Soldiers' and workmen's councils, prepared in long, systematic underground work, were now established. Men had occupied themselves with these matters who, if they had served at the front, might have insured victory. Many of them were classified as fit only for garrison duty; others were deserters, but all were indispensable.

The bulk of the troops in depots, in whom the idea of revolt had long been gaining ground, went over to the side of the revolutionaries.

The lines-of-communication troops, including those stationed in the occupied territories, both in East and West, among whom also preparations had no doubt been made for the revolution, lost all discipline and order and streamed home in wild confusion, plundering as they went. The troops in Rumania and on the Danube front marched off into Hungary, there to be detained.

On the fighting front in the West, soldiers' councils, with approval from high quarters, could not be formed fast enough.

The new rulers and their camp-followers abandoned all resistance, and without any authority signed our unconditional capitulation to a merciless enemy.

In the West the army crossed the frontier in an orderly

manner and passed beyond the Rhine, there in its turn to dissolve through too hurried demobilization and through contact with the revolutionary hordes at home.

Men who had fought magnificently against the enemy lost their nerve and abandoned the army and the country, thinking of nothing but themselves. Officers even were among them, forgetting the duties of their class and their historical mission. We passed through scenes that no Prussian had thought possible since 1806. All the more highly must we value the loyalty of the officers, non-commissioned officers, and men who, even in the new circumstances, held themselves at the service of their country in accordance with their old sentiments.

Army property was wasted in all directions, and the defensive power of the country completely undermined. Goods of incalculable value were lost.

The proud German Army, after resisting victoriously its superior enemies for four years, achieving feats of unprecedented greatness, and keeping our enemies clear away from our frontiers, disappeared in a moment. Our victorious fleet was handed over to the enemy. The authorities at home, who had not fought against the enemy, could not hurry fast enough to pardon deserters and other military criminals, including in part among these themselves and their nearest friends.

They and the soldiers' councils worked with zeal, determination, and purpose to destroy everything military. This was the gratitude of the newly formed homeland to the German soldiers who had bled and died for it in millions. The destruction of the German power, achieved by these Germans, was the most tragic crime the world has witnessed. A tidal wave had broken over Germany, not by the force of nature, but through the weakness of the Government represented by the Chancellor and the crippling of a leaderless people.

Those who for decades had confused the people and made them false promises, who have all the time agitated against authority in State and army, and have now destroyed it, soon found themselves forced to abandon the principles they had hitherto propagated. A new authority had now to be created, a new army formed, in order at home to oppose force to force, in a manner never theretofore necessary. It is not the troops formed by the revolution, but the voluntary formations with the spirit and discipline of the army of 1914, that are rescuing Germany, an enlightening glimpse into this fateful time; mankind was, after all, not ready for the alleged blessings of the revolution. What the revolution thinks that it has achieved might have been won on constitutional lines without self-destruction. It was a terribly criminal game that they played with Germany in her hardest hour, and Germany is paying for it with her life and her ideals.

Before all these events the world has stood astonished; it could not believe its eyes when it saw the collapse of this proud and mighty Germany, the terror of her foes. The Entente feared us even in our destruction, and could not do enough in using the opportunity to weaken us still further internally by propaganda and to force a helots' peace upon us.

Germany, by her own fault, has been brought low. She is no longer a great Power; she is not even an independent state. Her very existence is in danger.

Out of this world struggle she comes weakened and diminished in every respect, and robbed of districts and people which have been hers for generations.

She loses her colonies.

Her right to defend herself is taken away. The German has lost the right to serve his country in the army.

Germany's merchant fleet disappears from the high

seas. Her industrial strength is broken, and the fragments that remain are placed under enemy supervision. The livelihood of 70,000,000 Germans stands on insecure soil. They cannot live at home, and what is to become of the surplus population no man knows.

The indemnities we have to pay are beyond our power.

The debt which the revolution has laid on itself does not end merely with this terrible peace. It makes the heavy yoke, under which it has sent the German people into bondage, into an absolutely crushing one.

She places a premium on idleness and destroys the feeling that work is greater than money reward. She hinders the employment of creative energy and obliterates personality, replacing it by mob rule and mediocrity. All motive for reconstruction in government and political economy in reconstruction is lost for years to come or, at any rate, incalculably weakened.

In Germany there is civil war. German property is being destroyed. The public moneys are wasted and put to selfish uses; the finances of the Empire, the states, and the towns become rottener day by day. The fallen morale of the population rushes unrestrained into the "freedom" of the revolution; the lowest instincts of mankind develop unrestrained and regardless of consequences. Everywhere are disorders, shirkings, deceit, and overreaching, accompanied often by the most disgusting frenzies of luxury, and this at the graveside of the millions who have died for the country and in the sight of the many cripples on whom our eyes rest. Germany offers a hideous and contemptible spectacle, filling every true German heart with indescribable grief, but awakening among our enemies and neutrals nothing but contempt.

German men came forward and accused their country of crimes to the enemy, to please the foe and achieve leniency for themselves. Germans who fought loyally for their country were delivered up by their Government to the enemy, to serve for his triumph. That is the depth of our humiliation, which fills one with shame and disgust at the German people.

By the revolution the Germans have made themselves outcasts among the peoples, incapable of making allies, helots in the service of foreigners and foreign capital, and deprived of all self-respect.

"In twenty years' time the German people will curse the parties who boast of having made the revolution." A true word and a terribly grave, spoken at the second Congress of Councils in Berlin, in April 1919, by a Social Democrat to his fellows.

The present fate of the German people is concluded by the peace. The future lies dark before us, the only bright spot being the acts of the men of Scapa Flow.

All delusions have vanished, mob suggestion begins to fail. We look into nothingness. Self-deception, empty words, hope from others or hope in phantoms, lip courage, bringing vain promises for the future and weakness in the present; all these will never help us, as they have never helped us in the past.

Something different is needed.

Fearless thinking and manly action from each one of us, and at the same time unselfish submission and the sinking of the ego in national discipline, are what we require. That alone can restore our national dignity, whose recovery is a condition precedent of the renaissance of Germany. That is the first commandment.

Love of home, love of the daily task, devotion to work, and tireless energy in creation, industrious labor, free activity for our economic life, coupled with consideration for one's neighbor, the co-operation in full confidence of rich and poor, of hand and head, in the same duty to work, and freedom for honorable work, are the basis of German wealth and the condition of our revival. That is our second commandment.

Devoted to duty, honest and sincere, and in full courage must the German work once more, and moral earnest must be his guide; that is the third commandment. The saying of Fichte, that to be a German and to have character are synonyms beyond controversy, must again become the truth. Only so can we recover our self-respect, which alone can win us that of others.

In national character and education, in German work, in hard labor, and in human dignity, looking clearly into the hard reality of our bare and disconsolate future, so and so alone will the Germans find themselves again. Such action will help us once again to win ourselves a country and to fill ourselves with the old selfless patriotism which gives us strength to live (and, if fate demands, to die as the heroes of this great struggle have died) for our ideals, for all that is Germany, for the prosperity and security of our German home, and for her restoration to strength.

In the four war years our people did mighty deeds, an eloquent testimony to their indwelling strength, that to-day has been destroyed by the revolution. A nation of such achievements has the right to live. May it now have the strength to throw off the fetters that it has laid upon itself; may it now find men, rejoicing in their responsibility like the generals at the front, to lead it, firm of will and tenacious of their aim, and to restore the sunken national life and inspire it with fresh and powerful enthusiasm, men who, followed by all that is best in the nation, will unite all our creative forces in great creative action.

After our great fall, let us, in memory of the heroes who have fallen in their trust in Germany's greatness, the heroes whom the country now so needs, learn once again to be Germans, and to be proud that we are Germans.

God grant it!

# INDEX

Marcard, Major von, i, 39, 43.

March-battalions, i, 268, 272, 279.

Marienburg, i, 55.

Marine Corps, formed, i, 254.

Markau, Captain, i, 235.

Marmalade factories established, i, 232.

Marne, German retreat from, i, 83; crossing, ii, 309, 310, 314.

Marquard, Colonel, Chief of Staff, i, 117, 186.

Masonic lodges, in, Anglo-Saxon service, i, 435.

Massow, Colonel von, Chief of Staff, i, 127, 305.

Masuria, winter campaign, i, 134–162; plan of operations, 136–150; Russian counter-attacks, 153–159; East Prussia free, 161–162.

Masurian Lakes, battle of, i, 74–80, 140, 193.

Material, raw, demand for, i, 99; shortage, 362, 391; from neutral and allied countries, 406, 413; distribution, 406; from occupied territory, 412, 413.

Max, Chancellor, Prince, of Baden, ii, 353, 380, 384, 385, 387,

**THE END**